Restless Valley

Restless Valley

Revolution, Murder, and Intrigue in the Heart of Central Asia

Philip Shishkin

Yale UNIVERSITY PRESS

New Haven & London

Yale University Press books may be purchased in quantity for
educational, business, or promotional use. For information, please e-mail
sales.press@yale.edu (U.S. office) or sales@yaleup.co.uk (U.K. office).

Designed by James J. Johnson.
Set in Stempel Garamond, Garamond MT, and Meta types
by Integrated Publishing Solutions.
Printed in the United States of America.

Library of Congress Cataloging-in-Publication Data

Shishkin, Philip, 1977–
Restless valley : revolution, murder, and intrigue in the heart
of Central Asia / Philip Shishkin.
pages cm
Includes bibliographical references and index.
ISBN 978-0-300-18436-5 (cloth : alkaline paper) 1. Kyrgyzstan—
Politics and government—1991- 2. Uzbekistan—Politics and
government—1991- 3. Revolutions—Kyrgyzstan—History—21st
century. 4. Revolutions—Uzbekistan—History—21st century. 5. Violence—
Kyrgyzstan—History—21st century. 6. Violence—Uzbekistan—History—
21st century. 7. Intrigue—Political aspects—Kyrgyzstan—History—21st
century. 8. Intrigue—Political aspects—Uzbekistan—History—21st
century. 9. Kyrgyzstan—History—1991- 10. Uzbekistan—
History—1991- I. Title.
DK918.8757.S55 2013
958.43086—dc23
2012047741

A catalogue record for this book is available from the British Library.

This paper meets the requirements of
ANSI/NISO Z39.48–1992 (Permanence of Paper).

10 9 8 7 6 5 4 3 2 1

To Silvia, Julian, and Vera

Contents

Introduction

Imagine a region so rife with tensions and intrigue that in less than a decade it managed to produce two revolutions in the same country, murders straight out of a thriller, a massacre of unarmed civilians, a civil war, a drug-smuggling superhighway, and corruption schemes so brazen and lucrative they would be hard to invent. On top of all that, the region has served as a staging ground for the American war in Afghanistan.

The subject of this book is the wild recent history of post-Soviet Central Asia, mostly of two countries sitting above Afghanistan's northern border: Kyrgyzstan and Uzbekistan. In 2001, merely a decade out of Moscow's rule, the two nations were thrust into America's Afghan campaign. Washington installed military bases in both places, a decision that rattled Russia and China and pushed America into uncomfortable alliances with local dictators. Meanwhile, clandestine drug labs across Afghanistan turned booming poppy harvests into heroin, a ruinous drug that has spread misery, disease, and corruption throughout Central Asia. The region emerged as a key smuggling hub for heroin heading to the growing markets in Russia and Western Europe.

Through it all, Kyrgyzstan and Uzbekistan struggled with enormous challenges of nation building and governance. The collapse of the Soviet Union left them adrift and searching for a new economic footing, their mostly rural societies in a state of flux. Authoritarian governments emerged in both places, visiting all sorts of abuse on their citizens while drawing support, and cash, from their alliances with Washington. With two revolutions in the space of five years, and many calamities before, after, and in between, Kyrgyzstan charted a highly unusual path of national development. In neighboring Uzbekistan, the regime proved far more durable and inoculated itself against challenges by retreating deeper and deeper into repression. Central Asia's rich and difficult history, including Stalin's ethnic gerrymandering, casts a shadow over the present, igniting yet more conflicts. The restless valley of the title refers to Ferghana Valley, where Kyrgyzstan, Uzbekistan, and Tajikistan come together in a jagged mess of borders, and where several of the book's narratives converge.

This is not a history textbook, nor is it an exhaustive policy analysis. Rather, it is an attempt to reconstruct Central Asia's most dramatic recent episodes and let you experience them through the eyes of their participants, both powerful and powerless. Our story begins in 2005 in Kyrgyzstan, the land whose roller coaster of political unrest is the principal focus of this book. From there, the story stretches chronologically to the present day, exploring the neo-Stalinist landscape of Uzbekistan and the heroin-smuggling route that begins in Afghanistan, traverses Tajikistan, and wends its way toward Europe. There will be revolts, contract hits, and larger-than-life characters, including an enigmatic witch doctor and a banker who cut his teeth assisting the Italian mafia. There will be a few brave souls trying to stand up to the adversity around them; there will be villains and heroes, and people somewhere in between. There will be money laundering and international intrigue involving fuel for the American warplanes. There will even be a motorized parachute flying bags of heroin across a mountain river.

I began writing about Central Asia in the pages of the *Wall Street Journal* soon after the American invasion of Afghanistan. For years, I kept returning to the region, addicted to its fascinating history, not to mention the cuisine, and unable to let go for too long. I was born and raised in Russia, and as a side benefit of writing this book, I rediscovered parts of my own family that had landed on the Asian periphery of the old Soviet empire and made it their home.

A note on sources: This book is a work of nonfiction. I either directly witnessed the events recounted here or reconstructed them through interviews with participants and eyewitnesses, and through documents and published accounts. Material that comes from direct observation and from my own interviews appears in the body of the book without notes, except for those rare occasions when context requires elaboration. Information drawn from other sources, such as newspapers, other books, and original documents, is identified as such. To avoid distracting the reader with excessive annotation, I usually describe the source in the body of the book itself. But when doing so would clutter the narrative, or when the information is so important that its origins need to be carefully explained, I use notes.

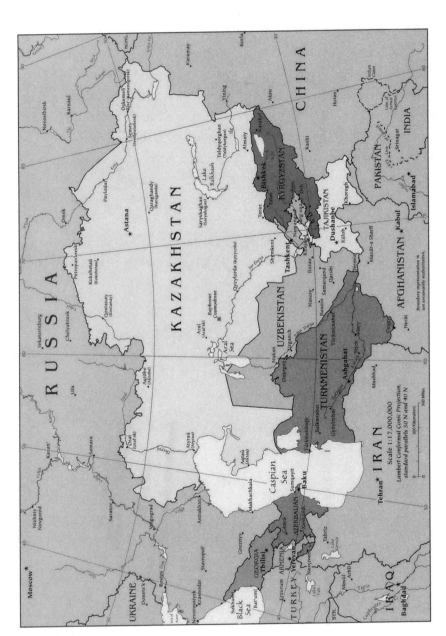

Map of Central Asia. (Courtesy of University of Texas Libraries)

CHAPTER 1 *The Tulip Revolution*

*W*hen the end came, all that was left to do was swig the president's wine straight from the bottle and plunder his collection of neckties.

The president, soon to be former, was already gone, and his spacious wood-paneled office on the seventh floor of a labyrinthine slab of government headquarters was now a scene of chaotic celebration. The foot soldiers of the revolution, many of them young and covered with grime and a little banged up but delirious with joy and adrenaline, swarmed around the president's desk and took turns sitting in his chair. Until a few hours earlier, this had been nothing less than a king's throne, but now it was just a fancy office chair where a commoner could recline, kick up his feet, grin into the camera, and pretend for a brief moment to be president. Until he was shoved aside by another protester eager to do the same.

"Who wants some wine?" a young man said to no one in particular. In each hand, he held a bottle of French wine that he'd just pulled from the president's cabinet.

"Look, this is Askar's tie!" said another man, a kid, really, pointing at his own chest, where a silky piece of presidential neckwear dangled haphazardly over a T-shirt. "Holy shit!"

Askar was Askar Akayev, the president of Kyrgyzstan, a small Central

Asian nation that had never been an independent state until the collapse of the Soviet Union fifteen years earlier. The empire's fall released the Kyrgyz from centuries of foreign dominion and made them masters of their own destiny. And what a ride it had been.

Independence began, as if often does, with a surge of euphoria and pride. An optical physicist by training, Akayev cruised to the presidency amid popular demonstrations cheering the historic moment. With the curved, bald rise of his bowling ball of a head fringed by a wreath of black curls, Akayev projected a measured, professorial, soft demeanor. His early governing style earned Kyrgyzstan the unlikely distinction of being a display window of Central Asian democracy, a Switzerland of the East. The Alpine comparison ended with the mountains that both countries possess in abundance. Kyrgyzstan was poor and rural, and Akayev's good intentions got bulldozed by nepotism and corruption.

Despite its small size, Kyrgyzstan started playing a big role in international affairs. To manage and resupply the military campaign in nearby Afghanistan after the 9/11 attacks, the United States needed an air base in the region, and Akayev jumped at the chance to raise his country's profile and earn some cash in the process. Ignoring grumbles from Russia and neighboring China, both leery of American soldiers camped in their backyard, Akayev allowed the United States to set up a sprawling military base on the edge of Bishkek's international airport. The base became the main transit point for troops bound for Afghanistan. And it added yet another layer to Kyrgyzstan's fat onion of corruption, intrigue, and geopolitical games that would dog the country for years.

And now, on the afternoon of March 24, 2005, Akayev was on the run toward Moscow, fleeing an uprising whose danger to his rule he so blithely underestimated. Meanwhile, things were getting a little tense in his old office. Some employees of the presidential administration hung back on the seventh floor, watching in shock as protesters surged into the president's old digs and made themselves comfortable.

"You are wearing a fancy jacket, but your president is nothing!" one protester shouted to a woman who stood in the anteroom in a huddle of junior government officials. She wore a light leather jacket of no discernible luxury.

The government employees stuck around partly out of curiosity and partly out of a vague sense of duty. They hadn't expected events to unfold at such a rapid clip. And neither did the revolutionaries. That morning, protest leaders had still planned to pitch tents in front of the presidential palace for an indefinite sit-in. Instead, they were now wandering, a little dazed, through the dark hallways of the trashed palace.

"But he is my president!" the woman in the allegedly fancy jacket was saying.

"Let's take her out of the room," someone suggested. Then everyone forgot about her; too many other exciting things were going on.

Someone knocked over a statue of a camel, and it lay broken into several pieces on the intricately inlaid parquet floor. On the president's bookshelf, next to works by Gogol and Proust, I saw one of Akayev's own rambling opuses. It was called *The Greatness of My People*.

"This is such a mess!" said Evgenii Razinkin, who introduced himself as a member of the presidential honor guard. He wore a military uniform and appeared to be in his midtwenties. He was unarmed. "We had enough bullets here to kill thousands," Razinkin said. "But we gave our oath to the people, to the constitution, not to the president."

Before fleeing the palace, Akayev told his underlings not to open fire on the protesters. Though his flight was later cast as a final act of cowardice, there's no denying that Akayev helped avoid bloodshed by removing his much-despised physical self from the scene and obviating the need for his guards to defend him.

"Had he stayed, his guards would have had to shoot to kill," said Chingiz, a man in a dark suit who claimed to work for the government's economic department but whose calm, watchful presence suggested he had some security connections to the old order. As years went by and much more violent things happened in Kyrgyzstan, the president's order not to shoot would become his biggest achievement. Slinking away quietly and not killing his compatriots, Akayev became a hero by dint of not being a villain.

Back in his old office, the ragtag group of revolutionary foot soldiers swelled to include some protest leaders. Among them I saw Tursunbek Akun, a slight, perpetually animated man who'd participated in so many anti-Akayev rallies that he maintained a large collection of ripped pants as mementos of tussles with riot police. In the months before the revolution, he shot to fame by claiming to have been kidnapped in circumstances and by people he could not describe because of the onset of temporary amnesia. Even fellow opposition activists didn't know what to make of his story. Akun acknowledged that many people thought "I kidnapped myself," which, he said, wasn't true. Akun would eventually become Kyrgyzstan's perennial human-rights ombudsman. But for now, he jostled with others for a chance to sit briefly in the president's chair, his head topped with a tall felt hat.

Chingiz the economist watched all of this in quiet bemusement from a few feet away. "You see how many new leaders have piled in here?" he finally said. "Tomorrow they'll rip one another's throats out."

According to legend, the Kyrgyz were asleep when God was distributing lands to the peoples of the Earth. When the Kyrgyz woke up landless, they pleaded with God to give them at least something. God took pity on the hapless Kyrgyz and gave them a patch of land that he had initially planned to keep for himself. And you can see why. It is a beautiful piece of real estate crisscrossed by mountain ranges. Landlocked on China's western flank, the territory of modern-day Kyrgyzstan zigzags in the midst of three other post-Soviet Central Asian republics, swerving around a large blue dot that appears on maps in the shape of a tear. The dot is Lake Issyk-Kul, a sea-sized freshwater oasis sitting in a basin ringed by mountains.

Sometime in the seventh or eighth century—the exact dates are obscure in the foggy confluence of history and myth—a warrior named Manas united the Kyrgyz in a rebellion against the tribes of modern-day China. Kyrgyzstan hasn't been the same since.

The endless battles and skirmishes, embroidered with monsters, magic, and, of course, fair maidens, are chronicled in the *Heroic Epic Manas*. Part history, part foundation myth, part rumination on good and evil, and part national liberation tract, the epic defines Kyrgyzstan in a way that no single work of literature dominates the collective psyche of any other country.

Befitting its stature, the epic is long, about five hundred thousand lines of verse. *Manas* is longer than other famously voluminous historical epics: Greece's *Iliad* and *Odyssey*, and India's *Mahabharata*. For centuries, *Manas* wasn't written down, existing only in the oral recitations performed by traditional bards. These Manaschi speak the lines in a singsong rapping style, and the best are reputed to have committed the whole thing to memory. The bards often trace the origins of their talent to mystical dreams in which Manas himself or his associates offered encouragement.

In one scene in the epic, Manas exhorts his followers to reclaim lands that once belonged to their ancestors but were now in the hands of the Kitai tribes from modern-day China:

> Letting Kitai control them now,
> We have besmirched our honor, I vow!
> Can a chopper in rock make a dent?
> Break a huge stone where blows are spent?

A few lines down, Manas tells his people not to be intimidated by the stronger enemy and not to fear death: "There's birth, and there's death." He says nothing of taxes.

> Trusting in their numbers alone,
> How those Kitais make others groan!
> You have seen this with your own eyes.
> Free your feet from fetters, and rise!

Though the epic is more than a thousand years old, Manas weaves a web of immediacy over modern-day Kyrgyzstan, lending his name to countless places, and his mystical grandeur to political ambitions. In 2002, President Akayev wrote a book titled *Kyrgyz Statehood and the People's Epic Manas.* In it, the professorial president teased out "seven lessons of Manas" key to modern governance. In Lesson 7, he declared Kyrgyzstan to be "a country of human rights."

After Akayev fled the country, his successor was cast as the nation's great democratic hope. He clung to the job for five bad years—until he too was overthrown and chased out of Kyrgyzstan. Shortly before his own downfall, the successor tried to wrap himself in Manas's cloak in a strange episode that pitted the Kyrgyz against China again.

In 2009, the United Nations' cultural arm inscribed the epic *Manas* into something called the Representative List of the Intangible Cultural Heritage of Humanity. That would be fine—except *Manas* was nominated by the Chinese, the same hated Kitais whom Manas had spent his life fighting. China said it acted on behalf of a small Kyrgyz minority living within its borders. But in Kyrgyzstan the news was interpreted as theft of a national treasure by a giant neighbor. A discussion on who dropped the ball ensued on the front pages of Kyrgyz newspapers.

One afternoon in Bishkek, I went to see Sadyk Sher-Niyaz in his lime green, Mac-studded office at Kyrgyz Film, the state movie studio. A former currency trader turned director, Sher-Niyaz launched a foundation to support the art of the bards who recite the *Manas* opus. Sher-Niyaz was working on a cartoon version of the epic, large chunks of which he said he knew by heart. He wore a red shirt, and his cascading hair and doughy face evoked an older Elvis. Sher-Niyaz was furious about China's move on *Manas.* "Imagine if we took ethnic Germans in Kyrgyzstan and declared the works of Goethe to be a Kyrgyz masterpiece? Or if we found some Jews here and presented Torah as the masterpiece of Kyrgyzstan?"

Equally incensed on behalf of his compatriots, the Kyrgyz president tried to claw *Manas* back from the Kitais. He submitted to Parliament a bill "concerning the Epic Manas." Ominously, the bill obligated Kyrgyzstan to "defend its interests in connection with the *Epic Manas,* both at home and abroad." A week later, the president was overthrown. Sher-Niyaz saw a connection. After the UN fiasco, "everything went haywire," he told me. "The spirit of Manas was disturbed, and there you go, this is what happens."

More recently, the Kyrgyz took Manas worship to new extremes. The epic hero was dragooned into the service of Kyrgyz nationalism as a new crop of leaders sought to fortify the country's wobbly statehood and identity shaken by a succession of uprisings and violent clashes.

In 2011, in a curious move bordering on absurdity, the government ordered the demolition of Kyrgyzstan's statue of liberty, a winged woman erected on Bishkek's central square to celebrate the country's independence. Workmen cut down this symbol of freedom and replaced it with an equestrian bronze statue of Manas in a helmet, his robe fluttering behind him. Never mind that another Manas on a horse had been sitting on a nearby street for years.

Not to be outdone, local authorities plunked down their own Manas statue in Osh, the country's southern hub where the Kyrgyz had only recently fought with the Uzbek ethnic minority, for whom Manas either means nothing at all or stands as a symbol of Kyrgyz militancy. Osh leaders bragged that their Manas is the tallest equestrian statue anywhere in the former Soviet Union.

It doesn't stop there. In 2012, yet another Kyrgyz president visited Moscow and unveiled yet another Manas statue in the Russian capital's Friendship Park, the first Manas monument on foreign soil. As dignitaries pulled a ceremonial orange veil from the monument, the horseman that emerged featured grotesquely short legs. The steep price tag of the statue prompted wags to wonder whether the poor Central Asian nation was really in a position to spend hundreds of thousands of dollars on a bowlegged horseman abroad.

At the unveiling of the monument, the new Kyrgyz president stunned his compatriots further by announcing that Manas had been an ethnic Russian, an unorthodox interpretation of Manas's genes considering his centrality to the Kyrgyz national identity. Having mobilized to wrest Manas from China a few years earlier, the Kyrgyz now watched their new leader voluntarily hand him over to Russia.

In a meeting with the Russian president, the Kyrgyz head of state said he hoped to build yet another Manas statue in Siberia, to further "bind our two peoples together." The Russian said, "Let's do it!" One wonders if the Americans could jump into the Manas free-for-all and claim him as their own, based on his connection to the Manas Transit Center, as the U.S. military base in Kyrgyzstan is officially known. Since Manas is a figure of myth as much as of history, he can be whatever you want him to be. And of course there can never be too much Manas.

A small nomadic people, the Kyrgyz have always lived in the shadow of bigger powers. They wandered into their new Central Asian homeland

The statue of Manas in downtown Bishkek. (© Philip Shishkin)

sometime in the ninth century from the banks of the Yenisei River in southern Siberia. At the time, Central Asia was a chaotic agglomeration of rival Turkic, Mongol, and Persian tribes, shifting alliances, and campaigns of territorial expansion. In their new environment, the Kyrgyz didn't hesitate to make their presence known. They briefly conquered and laid waste to a nearby Uighur kingdom, but eventually fell under the sway of the rising Mongol empire that blazed its way through much of Eurasia.

Other suzerains followed, until it was Russia's turn to invade and rule Central Asia in an unbroken stretch that began in the second half of the nineteenth century, survived the Communist revolution in Russia, and lasted until 1991. It was a classic colonial land grab. The Russian empire needed access to natural resources and to new markets. The plains of Central Asia, especially modern-day Uzbekistan, were ideally suited to growing cotton, and Russian colonial administrators increased production dramatically. Russian settlers began to arrive in the region in droves. They included imperial engineers, construction workers, teachers, clergymen, farmers, and soldiers. The conquest of Central Asia coincided in time with a momentous social shift within Russia itself. By imperial decree of 1861, the czar abolished agricultural slavery, better known as serfdom, which had been the bedrock of Russia's economy for centuries. Some of the newly freed serfs headed to Central Asia in search of a new life and new land.

In Bishkek one day, I met an elderly Russian man whose great-grandparents had been Russian serfs. Free but landless, his ancestors and their neighbors received parcels of land on the shores of Lake Issyk-Kul. They moved from the Russian heartland to the outer edge of the empire, building a new village that resembled the old one down to the street names. Such resettlement created tensions with the Kyrgyz, who saw their historical pastureland being transformed into farmland for Russian peasants. Unlike the British, Spanish, and Portuguese empires, which sought colonies across continents and oceans, the Russian empire expanded contiguously overland, like an ink stain on blotting paper.

In his waning years on the throne, the Russian czar scrambled for warm bodies to dispatch to the trenches of World War I, and imperial enforcers pressed newly subjugated Kyrgyz nomads into military service. Kyrgyz men saw no reason why they should leave their families to fight a remote, brutal, and irrelevant war and quite possibly die—all because some Russian guy on a throne said they must. They rebelled. They objected again when the Soviets, who inherited the czarist empire, herded them onto collective farms, a concept nearly as alien to them as trench warfare in Europe. Many died of starvation and disease.

Some Soviet officials showed remarkable disdain for the Kyrgyz. One functionary had this to say about their reluctance to get on with the program: "From the Marxists' point of view, the Kyrgyz are weak. They have to die out anyway, so it is more important that the Revolution spend its resources on fighting its enemies on the front than on fighting the famine."[1]

In the late 1920s, the Soviets broke up what was once the single czarist province of Turkestan into five ethnic republics, including Kyrgyzstan and Uzbekistan. The divisions saddled the region with an erratic set of borders that sliced up ethnic groups, particularly in the Ferghana Valley, and sowed the seeds of future ethnic unrest.

Why did Moscow break up Turkestan? One theory is that the Soviets feared the rise of a unified pan-Turkic state, an idea championed by some Central Asian intellectuals at the time. Following the divide-and-conquer principle, Moscow decided it would be much easier to deal with five small ethnic republics than with a single Turkic entity that might find sustenance through Islam, a religion brought here by Arab invaders centuries ago. That is how Kyrgyzstan and the other Central Asian states acquired their present-day boundaries. Within the broader construct of the Soviet Union, they remained little more than theoretical lines on the map, but they turned into real borders once the republics became independent.

Tucked away in the back pocket of the Soviet empire, Kyrgyzstan gave the world few reasons to know of its existence, except one: Chingiz Aitmatov, one of the Soviet Union's foremost writers whose complicated life both mirrored and shaped Kyrgyzstan's modern history. He came of age during World War II, or the Great Patriotic War, as it was known in the Soviet Union. Facing annihilation, Moscow conscripted all able-bodied men to fight the Germans. The draft swept through towns and villages across the country, sucking away men old enough to fire a rifle and leaving behind only women, kids, and old men. In his Kyrgyz village, Chingiz was fourteen at the time, too young to go to war. When all the men left, Chingiz was appointed secretary of the village council because of his rare ability to read and write in Russian.

He was in that first generation of Kyrgyz who would grow up fully integrated into the Soviet system. The council's elderly chairman, for instance, knew how to write only the first five letters of his last name. As his village's registrar and postman, Aitmatov had a particularly difficult task. "The most frightening experience and the greatest lesson for me were letters from the front, the so-called black letters, saying 'so-and-so' died a heroic death," he told me one afternoon in Brussels, where he served as the Kyrgyz ambassador to a big chunk of Europe. "I had to go to the relatives to console, to explain."

War would provide a backdrop to many of Aitmatov's writings, though never as a fighting-and-bombing spectacle but as a lens amplifying human emotions and moral choices. "Face to Face," the first short story that established him as a serious writer, describes the furtive existence of a deserter who jumps off a war-bound train and lurks in the woods near his home village, sustained on the lam by his wife and mother. When his mother dies, the fugitive can only watch the funeral from a spot on a nearby hill. Once everyone leaves, he crawls toward the grave, his hands shaking: "And here he fell on the fresh mound, and he cried hugging the clay, his sobs suffocating and hoarse."

And one of his latest short stories, "To Kill or Not to Kill," takes us back to World War II. An idealistic youth, still struggling to overcome the pain of his first unrequited love, is on the train to the front, tormented by a choice he may soon have to make. His mother has pleaded with him not to kill anyone, while his father, himself a former soldier, says that's what war is all about, kill or be killed. Aitmatov leaves us guessing as to what will happen to the boy.

Even before the war, Aitmatov's childhood was anything but normal. His father, one of Kyrgyzstan's leading Communist Party officials, was executed in 1937 during one of Joseph Stalin's regular purges. Many years later, Aitmatov remembered how his father, then living in Moscow, had put his family on the train back to Kyrgyzstan shortly before his death. "And there he bid us farewell, and I will never forget it," he said. "I understood from the words and facial expressions of my parents that there was something final to this meeting." Shortly afterward, his father was shot by a firing squad. Aitmatov found his grave only in 1993.

In his best novel, *The Day Lasts More than a Hundred Years,* there's a scene of a young woman receiving news of her husband's death during a KGB witch hunt, and the torment of a man who has to break this news to her. Aitmatov wrote the novel in one stroke of inspiration, spending three months on the shores of Kyrgyzstan's spectacular Lake Issyk-Kul. Set in a hamlet lost along the railway in the most inhospitable corner of the Central Asian steppe, the novel begins with the death of an old man and quickly develops into a mosaic of intertwined narratives and mini-novellas. They include a parable about Genghis Khan, a contact with an alien civilization, the brutality of Stalin's repressions, and the mating rituals of a particularly horny camel. Yet the novel never loses focus, with all the parallel narratives somehow reinforcing one another.

In college, Aitmatov studied animal husbandry, in keeping with Kyrgyzstan's agrarian, nomadic roots. In a May Day parade once, the young agronomist marched together with his cows, who were visibly uncomfortable in the crowd of celebrating workers. We'll never know whether animal husbandry lost a worthy practitioner, for Aitmatov was soon on his way to Moscow to study literature. Living in a dorm room downtown, Aitmatov wrote *Jamilla,* a classic love story. When he finished the last sentence, it was already past midnight, but he was so excited that he went for a stroll in a deserted park and sat on a bench. Later in life, whenever he passed by his old Moscow dorm, he would often look up at the window of the room where he wrote *Jamilla.*

Upon completing his studies, Aitmatov moved back to Kyrgyzstan and landed a job as roving Central Asia correspondent for *Pravda.* Though he doesn't remember most stories he wrote, he does recall covering an earthquake in Uzbekistan. A mountain collapsed into a river, blocking it and threatening to wash the towns downstream off the face of the Earth once the water broke through. His reportorial instincts helped him in his fiction. Some of his characters were informed by the chats he had with random passengers during long and boring train journeys.

To read Aitmatov is to step into a world where ancient myths of the Asian steppes share the pages with futuristic space stations; where animals—horses, camels, hawks, wolves, and an owl—get nearly as much ink as the human beings; where love, courage, and decency manage to thrive even when war, treachery, and repression conspire against them; and where a lapsed seminarian becomes a marijuana dealer. Rooted deeply in the region's history, customs, and folklore, Aitmatov's work has had a lasting impact on Kyrgyzstan.

"His works gave us a great push to talk about national identity, about sovereignty," said Zamyra Sydykova, a political activist who named her son after the writer. Natalia Ablova, a human-rights campaigner in Bishkek, saw a more universal appeal in his writings. "Every family reads him and then rereads him; his books taught us to be braver. He proved to us that even a single man can change things." Aitmatov is often referred to as the father of the nation.

One reason Aitmatov's talent was allowed to reveal itself so fully across the Soviet Union and beyond is that he cultivated the Soviet system that ground up and ejected equally gifted but more prickly authors. Aitmatov was no dissident in the tradition of Aleksandr Solzhenitsyn or Joseph Brodsky, both writers of his generation. Aitmatov's relationship with the Soviet power was cordial. He was among thirty-one Soviet writers who signed a public letter condemning Solzhenitsyn and Andrey Sakharov, the Soviet nuclear physicist and human-rights activist who became the symbol of the dissident movement. "The behavior of people like Sakharov and Solzhenitsyn—who slander our state and social system, who try to breed mistrust toward the amicable policies of the Soviet State, and who call on the West to carry on with the Cold War—cannot inspire any other feelings except deep resentment and condemnation," reads the letter, published in *Pravda* in 1973.[2]

Soviet authorities cherished the Kyrgyz author, publishing his books in large print runs, turning them into movies, and giving him access to the full spectrum of perks available to the Soviet literary elite. He was a remarkable Soviet success story: born in distant Kyrgyzstan and nurtured through Soviet education. He wrote in both Russian and Kyrgyz.

Having established himself as a good Soviet citizen, Aitmatov never allowed ideology to pollute his work. He was far from a hack, a whitewasher, or an apologist, plenty of whom populated the Soviet literary landscape. And he tackled head-on politically tricky subjects like Stalin's purges, in which he had lost his own father. It was as if, having proven his loyalty, Aitmatov was allowed to take liberties in his work that may have otherwise invited wrath.

In *The Day Lasts More than a Hundred Years*, Aitmatov described a medieval technique of enslaving captives by tying them up and placing them out in the desert sun with a piece of camel hide stretched over their shaved heads. As the hide shrank in the sun, the captives' brains were squeezed and baked in a kind of a medieval lobotomy. The captives either died or forgot who they were, lost their will to fight or even to think for themselves, and became ideal slaves—or citizens of a totalitarian state. Aitmatov called this specimen a Mankurt, and the word became a metaphor for thoughtless, groveling devotion to authority.

> He was equal to a silent beast and was therefore fully obedient and safe. He never dreamed of fleeing. For any slave-owner, the scariest thing is the uprising of the slaves. Every slave is potentially a rebel. Mankurt was the only exception—the notions of a rebellion, of disobedience were completely alien to him. He knew no such passions. And that's why there was no need to guard him, and even less need to suspect him of harboring secret plots. Mankurt, like a dog, acknowledged only his masters. He didn't engage anyone else. All his dreams boiled down to filling his belly. He knew no other concerns. But he followed orders blindly, diligently and without wavering.

Alongside his writing, Aitmatov launched a political career. In the 1980s, Aitmatov was elected to the Soviet Parliament, and that is how he met the last Soviet leader, Mikhail Gorbachev. Those were the heady days of perestroika when the country had its first nibbles of freedom. "Perestroika for me is the brightest, the highest point of my life," Aitmatov told me. He soon became a cultural advisor to Gorbachev, whom he considered a close friend. But political work began to consume most of his time, leaving no space for literature.

Gorbachev advised him to return to writing, and the two hatched a plan: Aitmatov would become an ambassador, maintaining a perch high up in the Soviet hierarchy while gaining more time to write. "They offered me one big European country and then Luxembourg," Aitmatov said. "And I concluded that it's better for me to be in a small, compact country so that I would have more time to work." Nothing of significance happens in Luxembourg, and the move paid off. While there, Aitmatov wrote *Cassandra's Brand,* a difficult novel featuring a philosopher-monk traveling in outer space and pondering lofty issues such as human cloning.

Aitmatov's departure from his usual literary landscape of the Central Asian steppes, and indeed from Earth, invited some ridicule. "I was branded a cosmopolitan for it," he said when we met in early 2005. He appeared tired of the petty, the small, and the earthly. He had just suffered a heart attack and was cutting back on travel and public speaking.

His quiet writing retreat in Luxembourg was jolted in the late 1980s by developments in Moscow. The Soviet Union started ripping at the seams. In 1989, Aitmatov flew home to help mediate a brewing conflict between Kyrgyzstan and Uzbekistan. In the messy dissolution of the Soviet Union, the citizens of the two ethnic republics clashed over land in the border areas. The conflict quickly escalated, foreshadowing similar violence many years later. Aitmatov reached out to Uzbek writers and intellectuals in a desperate appeal to stop the slaughter. His involvement helped cool down the passions.

And then Kyrgyzstan became an independent country. Aitmatov's influence helped Akayev, the respected former physicist, secure support for the presidency. In 1991, when a clique of Soviet officials attempted a coup against Gorbachev and a restoration of Soviet rule, Akayev ignored the plotters' orders. When coup leaders sent a local KGB general to bring the disobedient Kyrgyz leader to heel, Akayev simply fired him. History was on Akayev's side, of course, and the coup eventually failed.

In independent Kyrgyzstan, Aitmatov fell back into a familiar routine: being a writer disguised as an ambassador. When I met him in 2005 three months before Akayev's overthrow, Aitmatov professed disinterest in politics, preferring to focus on his books instead. His work has been published in the United States, Europe, China, and as far afield as Bolivia and Kuwait. He was sometimes mentioned as a long-shot candidate for a Nobel.

When we spoke, Aitmatov had just started a new novel, rooted firmly on Earth this time. He had already written the introduction: it was about a mountain leopard. He never became friendly with computers, so he wrote everything in longhand. "I'm becoming a little ashamed to talk about it now," Aitmatov said. "I'm sitting there and scratching the paper with a quill like two hundred years ago." He finished that novel, and died in 2008. A statue of a very young Aitmatov, a jacket flung over his shoulder, now stands in downtown Bishkek, right across the square from that other literary hero of Kyrgyzstan, the horse-bound Manas.

Aitmatov's daughter, named Shirin, got elected to Parliament and became an irreverent voice in Kyrgyz politics. A mother to a toddler girl, Shirin inherited her dad's facility with words, and once wrote this: "Outside the window, visible through the trees that look like pencil sketches, the old Manas monument is racing in the snowy air of Bishkek's twilight. Suddenly, I hear, 'Mom, is Manas our Superman?' I laugh and answer, 'Almost.'"

It is hard to pinpoint precisely when Akayev the visionary builder of a new Switzerland turned into Akayev the bumbling professor of corruption. These things don't happen overnight, of course, and Akayev's slide into misrule took a few years to complete, culminating in the revolution. Among the milestones on that slide were the president's family dealings with the U.S. military base on the outskirts of the Kyrgyz capital.

In late 2001, three months after the September 11 terrorist attacks, the Americans planted an air force base next to Kyrgyzstan's Manas International Airport. The Pentagon needed a logistical staging ground for rotating troops into and out of the battlefield, and for maintaining tanker aircraft that would refuel U.S. warplanes in the air over Afghanistan. The Americans named their Kyrgyz base after Peter J. Ganci Jr., a firefighter who died in the collapse of the North Tower of the World Trade Center on September 11.

When I visited the base in the winter of 2005, green military tents stretched over the snow, while local contractors were building new "semipermanent" dorms, a military oxymoron suggesting that the base was here to stay. On the edge of the airfield, next to rows of parked U.S. aircraft, soldiers set up a fuel farm, a collection of bags resembling giant water mattresses bulging with jet fuel. As the Afghan war meandered along, the base became one of the world's largest buyers of aviation fuel. With hundreds of millions of dollars in rent at stake, the base presented an attractive deal to the cash-strapped Kyrgyz government. But there was more than just rent payments. Someone needed to fill those bags with fuel, and the Akayev family made sure it took a cut.

To supply the fuel, the Pentagon contracted with a heretofore unknown firm half owned by a secretive American, one of whose previous business ventures was a popular expat bar in Bishkek. The firm, in turn, dealt with two local companies that had a government-sanctioned stranglehold on handling all fuel deliveries to the airport. One of those two companies was controlled by Akayev's son and the other by his son-in-law, according to a subsequent investigation by a U.S. congressional committee. The fuel-supply chain directly benefited the president's family, and it was typical of other business arrangements in the country.

Word quickly spread that if you wanted to do business in Kyrgyzstan on any meaningful scale, you had to play ball with the first family. On the political front, the president's wife, Mairam, developed a reputation as an iron lady ruling behind the scenes. Officially, her role was limited to running a charitable foundation. Unofficially, she was much more than that. She could stop cold any political career, as evidenced by the fall from grace of the president's powerful chief of staff.

The chief of staff, Medet Sadyrkulov, is a tragic and important figure in modern Kyrgyz history, one whose name will surface time and time again, often in connection with murky schemes. An exquisite practitioner of palace intrigue, Sadyrkulov first attained notoriety in the so-called financiers' case, a riddle about the disappearance of half a million dollars from the state coffers.

In August 1999, four Japanese geologists were prospecting for gold in the remote mountains near the border with Tajikistan. As one of the country's few natural resources, Kyrgyz gold was just starting to attract attention from international mining companies eager to develop the potentially large deposits that had remained untapped in the Soviet days. The Japanese geologists made their way toward the Abramov glacier, a stark expanse of ice, rock, and frozen earth in the Batken province near the jagged confluence of borders with Tajikistan and Uzbekistan.

The geologists waded deep into a festering international conflict. In the early 1990s, a vicious power struggle in the newly independent Tajikistan pitted the fledgling government against a coalition of Islamist and nationalist groups. Nearly fifty thousand people were killed, and many more displaced. The war drew in neighboring states too. The Taliban-led Afghanistan supported the opposition, while Uzbekistan—fearful of the Islamist stirrings within its own borders—backed the government. By the late 1990s, a tenuous ceasefire had been reached in Tajikistan. But the hardcore Islamist factions never bought into the deal and continued to nurture dreams of a regional holy war as they roamed the mountains in the tri-state no-man's-land.

In 1999, one such faction, consisting mostly of ethnic Uzbek guerillas, crossed into Kyrgyzstan's Batken province and swept through the research camp at the foot of the Abramov glacier. En route to stir up trouble in Uzbekistan, the Islamists grabbed the four Japanese geologists and several Kyrgyz as hostages. The incursion by a few hundred grizzled Islamist fighters presented a huge challenge to Kyrgyzstan's weak conscript military. One Kyrgyz soldier later recalled that his battalion had been so poorly supplied that the soldiers had to scavenge for their own food as they supposedly pursued the Islamist guerillas. We "spent half a day chasing after mountain goats, and finally we bagged three of them. We ate them immediately." He also mused that the only reason his hungry comrades stayed alive is because the guerillas couldn't be bothered to kill them.[3] As a final humiliation to the Kyrgyz government, the Islamists snatched one of the country's highest-ranking generals as a hostage.

As the president's chief of staff, Sadyrkulov was thrust into the middle of the conflict. "The events in Batken demonstrated the need to re-shape the armed forces of Kyrgyzstan," he said publicly. Behind the scenes, the events also demonstrated the need for cash, lots of it. Sadyrkulov had to come up with half a million dollars quickly to fund a covert operation in Batken, possibly a ransom for the hostages. The secret order, Sadyrkulov said later, came directly from President Akayev. True to form, the chief of staff deployed his organizational talents to hunt for the cash in the nooks and crannies of the Kyrgyz state. There were many phone calls, trips to bank vaults, and currency-conversion operations. Sadyrkulov scrounged up $420,000 in cash, which he stuffed into a briefcase. That very evening, "he walked into the president's office with the briefcase and walked out without the briefcase," said Galina Kulikova, a close friend of Sadyrkulov.

The guerillas soon freed the Japanese geologists, the Kyrgyz general, and a few other hostages, though no public acknowledgment of a ransom was ever made. The matter would remain hidden for another six years, and then it would almost land Sadyrkulov in jail.

Just as Sadyrkulov was reaching the height of his influence in the presidential palace, his relationship with President Akayev began to fray. Sadyrkulov sent Akayev a memo called "The Lion's March" in which he argued a point that was quickly becoming obvious to anyone who paid attention: the presidential relatives' overreach into business and politics was hurting the president's reputation. The family's influence, Sadyrkulov wrote, should be reduced. It goes without saying that an unwritten corollary to all this was that Sadyrkulov's own influence should be increased. But in the contest for the president's favor, Sadyrkulov couldn't defeat the powerful wife. He was asked to resign. His final fall from grace happened to come on the same day as the funeral of his father-in-law. "They could have waited a couple of days to fire me," a gloomy Sadyrkulov told a close friend over drinks in a hotel bar. Terminator-like, Sadyrkulov added something else: "I'll be back." And he would eventually enter the scene again, serving as a consigliere to the man who would overthrow Akayev.

For now, in the time-honored tradition of sending inconvenient viziers to cushy assignments far away from the throne, Sadyrkulov was appointed ambassador to Iran. "There was one simple reason for it; the president's wife wanted to control everything," Aijan, Sadyrkulov's oldest daughter, recalled. Perhaps fittingly, since he knew a thing or two about the subject, Sadyrkulov used his Iranian exile to earn a PhD on the "peculiarities of the Kyrgyz democracy."

Meanwhile, back home, the government was lurching from crisis to crisis. In 2002, President Akayev ceded a piece of Kyrgyz territory to China, settling an old territorial dispute from the Soviet days. The sliver of uninhabited land in question lies in the remote mountains on Kyrgyzstan's eastern border. Its transfer to Beijing was just a matter of time, but the deal rekindled historical fears of China gradually swallowing up its tiny neighbor—the same fears that drove Manas to urge his compatriots to fight back. Some opposition activists seized on the apparent secrecy in which the transfer was negotiated and criticized the already vulnerable and out-of-touch president.

A member of Parliament named Azimbek Beknazarov introduced a motion to impeach him. The government overreacted and arrested the maverick deputy, dusting off an old case dating back to his time as a police investigator. Back then, Beknazarov had decided not to press murder charges against a student attacked by three drug addicts. In the ensuing scuffle, one of the junkies got stabbed to death. For seven years, the case remained closed, but in 2002 the government reopened it and accused Beknazarov of dereliction of duty.

He was thrown into a basement and told he would be jailed unless he toned down his criticism of the regime. Thousands of his supporters took to the streets, blocking the country's main highway and demanding his release. Though the matter began with the Chinese land transfer, it quickly outgrew its original cause and was now focused on the heavy-handed nature of the regime itself. The Aksy district where the riots took place was among the poorest in the country, and the poverty helped stir antigovernment passions. Faced with the increasingly vocal protesters, some of whom were demanding Akayev's resignation, the police panicked and opened fire, killing five people. The bloodshed tarnished the regime even further and energized the scattered opposition.

The authorities relented and released Beknazarov from detention. The dispute elevated him from an obscure regional populist to a national figure with a sizable following. "The government turned him into a big hero," Muratbek Imanaliyev, a former foreign minister, told me. The former cop would go on to play a key role in the events soon to come. His direct, plain-spoken style, a boxer's doughy face, a jaunty buzz cut, and a stocky build would eventually combine to earn him the strikingly fitting nickname "bulldozer of the revolution."

I first came to Kyrgyzstan in the winter of 2005 as the country was gearing up for parliamentary elections. The opposition was convinced the government would rig the process, stack the assembly with rubber-stampers, and get them to change the constitution, allowing Akayev to seek—and surely win—yet another presidential term in a ballot later that year. With the tin ear typical of aloof regimes, Akayev's handlers didn't bother to rule out this scenario. "If the new Parliament wants it, if it votes for it, then we'll have to swallow it," Osmonakun Ibraimov, a senior presidential advisor, told me at the time. Making pronouncements like this, Ibraimov became a deeply vilified figure. During the storming of the presidential palace a few months later, protesters found him in his office and beat him up.

When I spoke to Ibraimov, the placid post-Soviet political landscape was reeling from revolutions in Georgia and the Ukraine, which brought to a sudden end the seemingly perennial reign of local autocrats. Both of those revolts were triggered by fraudulent elections. Inspired by those uprisings, opposition activists in Kyrgyzstan were hoping to emulate the experience and nudge their own man in the palace from the throne.

Beknazarov, the bulldozer of the revolution, was out campaigning for a Parliament seat in a remote string of villages of his home district in southern Kyrgyzstan. In Bishkek, I hired a mildly crazy duo of Tatar brothers who agreed to drive me over a slippery mountain pass and look for Beknazarov on the other side. Ten hours later, we found him standing ankle deep in a snowdrift, addressing a huddle of villagers.

"What will happen to us if Akayev leaves?" someone asked him.

"Did people in Georgia or Ukraine suffer after their leaders left?" Beknazarov answered through a loudspeaker to drown out the donkeys braying all around us. "Do you deserve less than them? Rise up!"

Beknazarov was running against a dozen candidates, and his staff received constant reports of campaign fraud, such as handouts of cash and fresh meat to buy votes. Beknazarov told his constituents to take the money and eat the food and then vote whichever way they wanted. "Just look at the bribes as government investments that I can secure for you!" Beknazarov joked into his loudspeaker. The villagers laughed.

Then he invited me to a lunch in his honor to be held in the drafty shack of a local village elder, a stern man wrapped in many layers of clothing. My Tatar drivers were eager to get back to Bishkek and warned me that this "quick lunch" would last most of the day. I started to believe them on the seventh or eighth course when various soups, rice dishes, and many servings of meat gave way to *manti*, Kyrgyz steamed dumplings stuffed with mutton, onions, and chunks of fat. You eat them with your hands, and it is said that the true measure of a good dumpling comes from the sensation of fat trickling down to your elbow as you raise the dumpling from plate to mouth. In that regard, these dumplings didn't disappoint.

By the time I felt I could manage an escape from the lunch and crawl back to the car—since walking no longer seemed possible, given the gluttony—a man sitting next to me handed me a boiled head of some animal and a sharp long knife. Tradition demanded that a guest of honor cut strips of meat from the head and pass them around. Since I had traveled the farthest to be at this feast, it was decided that I should scalp the head, my neighbor explained. I protested that Beknazarov was the true guest of honor—I was just a pesky lunch crasher and therefore should be disqualified from the task. I didn't want to steal another man's boiled head.

Seeing my confusion, my neighbor laughed and passed the head to a Beknazarov aide, who proceeded to slice and dice it with an authority born of many such feasts. Sensing our lunch was starting to morph into dinner, I quietly slipped away. Beknazarov stayed behind, sitting crosslegged on the floor, chatting with the elders and enjoying being the man of the moment again. Within a month he would be leading crowds of protesters yet again.

Bishkek is a pleasant town located in the fertile Chu valley, in the foothills of the Ala-Too mountain range. The place used to be a frontier outpost and a fortress manned by the warriors of the Khokand Khanate, an Uzbek kingdom that ruled much of Central Asia until it was routed by the Russians in the nineteenth century. How Bishkek got its name is something of a mystery. The most colorful theory suggests the name derives from a Kyrgyz word for a wooden stick used to churn *kumys*, a mildly alcoholic fermented mare's milk, a traditional Kyrgyz beverage that is guaranteed to make a nonnative retch. Scholars have questioned this theory, but it persists in many guidebooks, perhaps because it's a tale that's too cute not to be true. Other, more plausible, theories link the name to various linguistic variations on the theme of mountains and foothills.

The Soviets ended the uncertainty by rebranding the city Frunze, a name of whose origins there is no doubt. Mikhail Frunze was born here back when it was a Russian garrison town and grew up to be a fearsome revolutionary, narrowly avoiding execution by the imperial authorities. In the Soviet days, he became a prominent military commander, helping defeat Central Asia's Basmachi revolt against Soviet rule. When Kyrgyzstan became independent, authorities scrubbed the militant Communist—and a non-Kyrgyz to boot—from the capital's name, and it reverted to Bishkek again. The scrubbing wasn't entirely complete: half of Frunze survives as FRU, Bishkek's international airport code.

Snow lay in a thick blanket and sparkled in the sun across Bishkek when I went to see Mike Stone, a jovial Illinois native and a college dropout whose base of operations was a frigid, cavernous shed. From there, Stone ran a printing press, a big yellow contraption on loan from the U.S. government. As the regime cracked down on dissent, the press became the only game in town for publishing criticism of President Akayev. Stone was a former newspaperman who'd worked in Virginia, Hungary, and Belarus, among other places. Now he was employed by Freedom House, one of several influential Washington nonprofits engaged in the business of democracy promotion. In other words, Stone was sitting in the trenches of a war between the opposition and the regime, a development he didn't quite expect.

Caricatured in a pro-government newspaper as Uncle Sam with a sledgehammer, the printing press published about sixty titles, most of them nonpolitical. "We'd print anything that comes through the door," Stone told me over black coffee and cigarettes. An armed guard stood in front of that door. Precisely because it would print anything, the impact of the press on Kyrgyz politics was hard to overestimate.

"Oh, it's our only savior," said Rina Prizhivoit, political editor of the opposition *MSN* newspaper. The government always looked for reasons to harass the paper and had recently accused it of predatory pricing. The paper was struggling financially, and the U.S. embassy gave it some old computers. The Kyrgyz government, in turn, cut off the paper's access to the state-owned printing press. So *MSN*'s only path to its readers lay through Stone's shed. A few days before I visited, Stone had served up a typical *MSN* offering: front-page photos of a palatial mansion above a photo of a boy in a decrepit alleyway. "Here's a house built by Akayev," screamed the headline. "And here's a boy deprived of a roof over his head." Using Stone's press, the paper also published information on purported business dealings of the presidential family. Akayev accused the paper of "systematic information terror" and vowed to sue it for libel.

Stone stirred the pot further, publishing a manual on how to defeat dictators, which included tips on hunger strikes and civil disobedience. Called *From Dictatorship to Democracy,* the manual was written by Gene Sharp, an octogenarian American scholar who loves tending orchids on the roof of his Boston row house in his spare time. Over the years, Sharp became a guru of nonviolent resistance, and his manual, originally written for Burmese guerillas, had already proved useful to protesters in Serbia, Georgia, and the Ukraine. (It would later become required reading for activists in Russia and across the Middle East.)

For now, Sharp's work was known to a relatively small circle of international activists. In Kyrgyzstan, a veteran human-rights campaigner commissioned the translation of Sharp's manual into Kyrgyz and then paid Stone to print it. She then distributed it to young activists mobilizing across the capital.

Energized by his Kyrgyz experience, Stone had big plans to expand his operation beyond Kyrgyzstan and into the entire authoritarian neighborhood. With money from George Soros's Open Society Institute, Stone had just bought modern computer-to-plate equipment. From the outset, Stone decided the press had to be run as a business, not as a political charity, and it was making money. "If we walked in the door saying our job is to flood this country with subsidized opposition papers, we'd probably fail," he told me. Opposition activists in Kazakhstan, Uzbekistan, and Tajikistan had already expressed interest in using the press to print their own newspapers. Stone had recently printed fifteen thousand copies of a Tajik opposition paper, but the entire print run was immediately seized once it entered Tajikistan. The official reason: the authorities needed to test the papers for hazardous chemicals in the ink. "And hey, we didn't get paid," Stone told me. In Kyrgyzstan, Stone was engaged in an information war, pure and simple. And the government fought back: it cut off the electricity to Stone's press, citing a "commercial dispute." The shed went dark. The U.S. embassy stepped in with emergency generators, and the press whirred back to life.

Stone's operation was part of a vast network of nongovernmental organizations that descended on Kyrgyzstan to promote democracy. Some of these NGOs received funding and support from the U.S. government, pitting Washington against the incumbent regime in a contest that would replay itself in other countries where homegrown opposition movements benefited from a little foreign help and were immediately—and unfairly—tarred as foreign stooges. Stephen Young, the U.S. ambassador to Kyrgyzstan at the time, told me Washington viewed the grassroots political stirrings in Kyrgyzstan as an important regional precedent, a way to bust open the entire autocratic neighborhood. "Kyrgyzstan could offer a signal of hope to the societies in Central Asia," Young said in the bunkerlike American embassy sitting out in the open field on the edge of Bishkek. In the meantime, Akayev was railing against an unspecified "international revolutionary organization" plotting his overthrow. His daughter Bermet told me the American envoy's conduct was causing "irritation" because of its "one-sidedness."

What exactly was Washington's game plan in Kyrgyzstan? The United States pursued several agendas. A significant part of the U.S. foreign-policy establishment was genuinely drawn to the idea of democracy promotion. When he ran out of other justifications, President George W. Bush even tried to cast the war in Iraq in sweeping democratic terms. But most of American democracy-promotion machinery was not government operated. Instead, it was run by a loose network of NGOs that focused on political-party development, free press, and human rights simply because they believed, as corny as it sounds, that those are worthy goals to pursue, without any geopolitical ulterior motives. They in fact detested President Bush for confounding regime change with democracy promotion.

At the time, the United States was making a push to expand its influence across the former Soviet Union, and people like Akayev, and the former leaders of Georgia and the Ukraine, were perceived to hew closer to Moscow. The idea was that a democratic opposition, if it attained power, would be friendlier toward the United States. So democracy promotion of the altruistic NGO kind did coincide with a more calculated policy goal of the American administration. None of the Western support would have meant a thing if strong homegrown opposition movements hadn't taken root in places like Georgia, the Ukraine, and Kyrgyzstan. Revolutions there were not American plots but were entirely local in nature, as tempting as it was for the incumbent regimes to cast them as American conspiracies. But the U.S. assistance, moral and financial, did help the local activists and nonprofits. "It's a big network operating on the American funds, and it's a huge resource for the opposition that can be activated at any time," Valentin Bogatyrev, an advisor to President Akayev, told me. Then he lamented, half jokingly, that it was too bad that Chinese money wasn't sloshing around in the system to support local politics. "If you brought Chinese money here, they'd be working on democracy-*de*motion projects."

Ironically, Akayev was now falling prey to the very freedoms he had allowed in Kyrgyzstan in the 1990s. The seeds of the civil society planted in those Switzerland-of-the-East days had taken root and emboldened the opposition. Other post-Soviet regimes, such as Uzbekistan, Turkmenistan, and Belarus, drove antiregime activists into a deep underground or out of the country, or simply put them in jail. They also curtailed the operations of NGOs, foreign and domestic, and kicked many of them out of the country. But Kyrgyzstan, by one estimate, was home to some five thousand NGOs promoting everything from rural health care to civic institutions. President Akayev himself once joked that if the Netherlands is a land of tulips, then Kyrgyzstan is a land of NGOs.

"People started registering NGOs like crazy because they thought it's easy money," Edil Baisalov, twenty-seven-year-old president of the Coalition for Democracy and Civil Rights, told me one day in his cramped office in downtown Bishkek, across the square from the presidential palace. His group operated on a $110,000 annual budget from the U.S.

Agency for International Development and the National Democratic Institute.

A lanky, animated overachiever, Baisalov wore a loose-hanging suit and a pair of black-rimmed glasses that kept sliding down his nose, causing him to keep pushing them up as we spoke. He had just returned from the Ukraine, where he had worked as an election observer. As a souvenir of the Ukraine's Orange Revolution, Baisalov had brought home an orange scarf, which was now draped over his office chair. He was clearly fired up by the Ukrainian uprising, and he spoke fast, his eyes aglow with excitement. "Ukraine was a formative experience for me. I saw what the result of our work could be." Baisalov would go on to become an important character at several painful junctures of modern Kyrgyz history.

He was born in the small town of Naryn near the Chinese border. With one main street meandering through town, flanked on either side by low-slung Soviet apartment blocks and ramshackle wooden huts, Naryn is famous in Kyrgyzstan for its insanely cold winters. Baisalov came of age in the early years of Kyrgyzstan's independence, and he took full advantage of the new opportunities. He studied in Turkey and the United States and eventually landed a job with Kyrgyzstan's national Olympic committee just in time to travel to the 1996 Atlanta Olympics, where he remembers snagging Andre Agassi's sweaty towel. Baisalov also ran into some Swiss businessmen who worked for an operator of duty-free shops, those airport islands of booze, cigarettes, and perfume. The former Soviet Union was virgin territory for such stores, and Baisalov talked himself into becoming the Swiss firm's Kyrgyz representative.

Back in Bishkek, he helped the Swiss negotiate an exclusive license to run a duty-free shop at Manas International Airport and worked on opening another store at the main land crossing between Kyrgyzstan and Kazakhstan. He hobnobbed with customs officials, one of the most corrupt species of post-Soviet officialdom. Only eighteen at the time, Baisalov had a job many in Kyrgyzstan would have killed for. He made $1,200 a month, a princely sum. His life had a glamorous aspect to it. There was frequent international travel at a time when it was still a novelty or a luxury for most of his compatriots. There were bottles of high-end liquor, the mainstay of duty-free trade. It seemed as if Baisalov was destined for corporate glory, for a steady climb up the salesman's ranks and into middle management, maybe an MBA, and onward and upward.

But then, annoying questions started creeping into his head. "What am I going do? Sell vodka for a living now? Am I going to wine and dine customs people from now on? I was bored." Baisalov went back to school looking for a master's degree and a better résumé. It was a time of great tumult in Kyrgyzstan's politics, and Baisalov jumped in with political papers and student debates. One afternoon he was leafing through a newspaper and stumbled upon a small help-wanted ad. An outfit with the grandiose name "Coalition for Democracy and Civil Rights" was looking for a coordinator. It looked vaguely interesting and Baisalov tore the ad out of the paper, put it in his pocket, and forgot all about it for a few days. Then he came across the crumpled piece of paper again and made the phone call. He was soon offered the job, and a salary of $400 a month, a third of what he made cutting booze deals with customs officials. In an inspired exercise of rationalization, Baisalov calculated that he only really needed about $200 a month to live comfortably, and this NGO salary was twice that amount.

Ahead of Kyrgyzstan's parliamentary elections, Baisalov set up ten regional offices and sixty cells across the country involved in promoting local self-rule, election monitoring, and other grassroots activism that would prove crucial in spotting election fraud and triggering the revolution.

A key candidate in those elections was Roza Otunbayeva, a petite, friendly woman with a helmetlike haircut and a quiet tenacity that allowed her to achieve big things in the Soviet Union, and even bigger things in independent Kyrgyzstan. One of eight siblings, Otunbayeva went to college in Moscow, where she studied German philosophy. It was the hoary era of stagnation and economic decay presided over by the buffoonish, unibrowed Soviet leader Leonid Brezhnev. Armed with a philosophy degree, Otunbayeva returned home to teach dialectic materialism at Kyrgyzstan's main university. That was a particularly obtuse branch of Marxism that became a required and hated subject for generations of Soviet students.

Otunbayeva didn't linger too long in the dead-end labyrinth of Marxist thought. She escaped to climb the ladder of the Communist Party hierarchy, rising to the post of deputy prime minister of Soviet Kyrgyzstan. She then held a string of high-profile jobs at the Soviet Foreign Affairs Ministry, serving as Moscow's envoy to the UN cultural arm in Paris and becoming the first woman to enter the rarefied top rung of Moscow's foreign-policy establishment. In independent Kyrgyzstan, Otunbayeva's star shot even higher. She was her country's first ambassador to Washington and later a foreign minister.

In 2003, she worked in Georgia as second-in-command of a UN peacekeeping mission in a local separatist conflict. She was there to witness Georgia's Revolution of the Roses, which deposed the country's longtime president, Eduard Shevarnadze. A former Soviet foreign minister, Shevarnadze had once been Otunbayeva's boss and mentor when the two worked in Moscow in the final years of the USSR.

One winter evening in 2005, I went to see Otunbayeva in her mother's small apartment in a Soviet-era building in Bishkek. For dinner, she served homemade *manti* dumplings stuffed with pumpkin—the gentler cousin of the traditional meat-and-fat bomb—and she insisted I try them. They were excellent. Otunbayeva had returned from Georgia a few months earlier, throwing herself into opposition politics with the same focus and discipline that had worked so well for her in her government career. Scenes from the Georgian revolution were still fresh in her mind. "Nothing terrible happened there; not a single window was broken, blood wasn't spilled," she told me. "People overcame their fear and said 'enough.'"

Otunbayeva registered as a Parliament candidate in her old Bishkek university district. But that same day, five hours later, election authorities revoked her registration, citing a hastily issued ruling that seemed tailor-made to trip up her candidacy. Having lived abroad for so long, Otunbayeva didn't meet the residency requirements to run for public office—never mind that her stint overseas was a government assignment. The American equivalent of that would be if Jon Huntsman were disqualified from running against President Obama only because he'd lived in China as the U.S. ambassador—nominated by Obama.

The Otunbayeva ban was absurd, but the government made no apologies about it. "Why should diplomats be allowed to run for office, and other people who were away from Kyrgyzstan be banned?" Osmonakun Ibraimov, the president's advisor, asked me rhetorically. "And this is not a lifetime ban; let those ambassadors live here for five years first. Then they can try to get elected."

Otunbayeva's removal from the ballot eased the task for another high-profile candidate running in the same district: Bermet Akayeva, the president's daughter. One evening in Bishkek, she addressed an auditorium packed with university students. After a few softballs during the question-and-answer session, a young woman in the back of the hall raised her hand and asked, "Why are you running for Parliament if you already have everything?" A wave of quiet laughter rolled through the rows of students. Bermet laughed too and said she had decided to enter politics so that "the life's work of my father doesn't disappear." Facing her from the back wall of the auditorium was President Akayev's enigmatic quotation in big block letters: "The world year of physics — optimism and hope." In the lobby downstairs hung a huge poster of her father's latest book with his smiling face on the cover. Akayev's son Aidar was also running for Parliament, as was the son of the prime minister.

A few days later, I went to see Bermet in her gleaming campaign headquarters. Ornate Kyrgyz wall hangings decorated the hallways, and the wide airy spaces well stocked with computers gave the place the feel of an Internet start-up. With jet black hair flowing down past her shoulders, Bermet wore a dark business pantsuit and stylish glasses. Pretty and intense, Bermet was married to a Kazakh businessman whose holdings in Kyrgyzstan increased dramatically after his induction into the president's family. He controlled fuel deliveries to the American base and was reported to be involved in many other lucrative ventures. But Bermet played down his wealth and influence. "It's true that my husband is a businessman, but he only has one or two projects here," she told me. "There's no reason to talk about the monopolization of power or business by our family."

Even unelected, Bermet wielded significant political power alongside her mother. And here again it's worth paying a brief visit to Medet Sadyrkulov, the former chief of staff who had clashed with the president's family and was exiled to Iran as an ambassador. By early 2005, his diplomatic stint was ending, and he was eager to get back home. His embassy colleagues threw him a party in Tehran. They composed and performed a song whose lyrics captured the departing ambassador's mood:

> Everything was great in the big city of Tehran
> But my dreams are of home where my mountains are.[4]

By the time he landed in Bishkek in 2005, Sadyrkulov had little time to admire those mountains. Kyrgyzstan was quickly careening into a deep political crisis. President Akayev, scrambling to shore up his power, invited his former advisor for a chat. There were rumors that Sadyrkulov might be appointed head of the national security council, an all-purpose fix-it man. But instead the president asked him to go talk to Bermet so the two could hash something out. To Sadyrkulov, who never lacked in pride, the visit felt uncomfortably like a job interview. The fact that Bermet was about the age of his own daughter didn't make the chat go any smoother. "You haven't quite reached the age for me to be talking to you," Sadyrkulov snapped at Bermet.[5] And that was that. It was, of course, a blessing in disguise. By avoiding the taint of the Akayev regime's final convulsions, Sadyrkulov positioned himself for a remarkable political comeback after the revolution.

Meanwhile, having been stricken from the ballot, Otunbayeva, another former ambassador, was battling the Akayev system on the streets. She and her fellow protesters chose yellow as their symbolic color and pitched a tent downtown, emulating their Ukrainian counterparts, who had earlier flooded Kiev's main square with tents and orange banners. Otunbayeva's political party set up a youth movement. Similar groups in Georgia, the Ukraine, and Serbia were instrumental in boosting support for the opposition among the young and the hip, lashing their generally contrarian mood to a political goal. As one of its first tasks, the Kyrgyz youth group, called Kel-Kel, or "Come Join Us," set out on an important mission: buying forty pounds of lemons to distribute to passersby. Such gimmicks were popularized by Gene Sharp's revolution manual *From Dictatorship to Democracy,* which was circulating among the young protesters.

A few days after Kel-Kel announced its existence, a mysterious youth group with the same name appeared out of nowhere. Its leaders claimed they were the real Kel-Kel, gave a press conference, and invited people to come on a free skiing trip to the countryside, where they spoke against street protests. "They copied our logo, they cloned us!" Kazbek Abali-yev, one of the original Kel-Kel's founders, told me. When we spoke, the two groups were fighting in court over the rights to the domain name www.kelkel.kg.

The president and his entourage spared no effort to tar the spreading protest movement. Making fun of the colors adopted by the protesters, Akayev called the opposition a "yellow-brown plague." Orange dollar signs were spray-painted on the homes of leading opposition activists, including Otunbayeva's, to insinuate they were in the pocket of the Americans. An editorial in a pro-government newspaper said, "For the Kyrgyz, yellow is the color of treason, and green is the color of the money that pays for it." A month before the revolution, Ibraimov, the president's advisor, told me that the "yellow-brown plague hasn't spread—we managed to build up the immunity against it."

The parliamentary elections took place amid massive fraud. Establishment candidates, like the president's children, all made it into Parliament, but many opposition candidates did not. The protest machinery constructed over the previous few years roared into action across the country. Baisalov's election monitors rang alarm bells about fraud; Otunbayeva's lemon youth army organized rallies in Bishkek. And influential southern populists, like Beknazarov, the bulldozer of the revolution, worked the crowds in their home provinces. The existence of Mike Stone's printing press allowed the opposition papers to cover it all in scathing detail that whipped up the protesters' passions even further.

The president hailed from northern Kyrgyzstan, a more urban, more developed part of the country clustered around the capital. In the Soviet days, Moscow also favored the northern elites because they were better educated and, in effect, were more like the Russians themselves because of their long exposure to Russian colonization, which was more visible in the north.

In building a top-heavy system that enriched a small circle of allies,

President Akayev cut off from power and money influential southern elites who now turned on him. The south of Kyrgyzstan was poorer, more rural, and more clannish, and it birthed a generation of kingpins who felt it was their turn to run the country. It's no coincidence that the uprising began in the south, where protesters seized government buildings and chased out local authorities.

On what would be the final day of President Akayev's fifteen years in office, crowds of protesters began gathering early in the morning on the edge of Bishkek, right in front of a psychiatric and substance-abuse clinic. Many arrived in buses from the south of the country, where uprisings had already toppled local authorities. The clinic was owned by one of the most colorful personalities ever to have walked the streets of Bishkek: Jenishbek Nazaraliyev, a self-styled witch doctor who built a lucrative business out of treating addiction to heroin smuggled into Central Asia from Afghanistan. (We'll meet him again later in the book.)

The location of the rally was peculiar and perhaps appropriate, given the crazy, feverish, and unruly mood settling over the capital. "As a psychiatrist, I can tell you this: the regime is losing its marbles," Nazaraliyev told me one day.

On the morning of the revolution, as protesters were gathering around the clinic, a short, stocky man in a button-down short-sleeved shirt appeared on the periphery of the crowd. He just stood there shuffling his feet, trying to make sense of the mass of humanity swelling in front of him.

"I was told there's a rally going on here, so I was interested in taking a look for myself," the man said. Upon further questioning, it turned out that he was the new interior minister of Kyrgyzstan, appointed to that job just a day earlier. As the guy in charge of the police, he needed to decide what to do, and he was clearly flummoxed by what he saw.

"I decided to face the people, talk to them, you know. Do we always have to confront each other with fists only?" the minister, Keneshbek Dushebayev, was saying to a small scrum of people gathering around him. But he really seemed to be addressing himself, working out in his own mind what he was supposed to do. Order a crackdown? Reason with the protesters? Or do nothing at all and hope this thing would melt away?

"I'm ready to get down on all fours and crawl from Bishkek to any point on the globe if that would help achieve peace and calm," Dushebayev carried on. The display of penitence conflicted with the government's earlier, more muscular statements about the brewing revolt and the need to crush it. Perhaps Dushebayev was mindful of his audience, many of whom were now tying yellow and pink ribbons around their heads, the twin colors of the revolution. Some of them booed and whistled as Dushebayev spoke.

"If you use force against us one more time, the fate of Ceaușescu awaits you!" someone screamed at the interior minister, in an apparent reference to the police shootings during the China land-transfer riots. Nicolae Ceaușescu was the longtime Romanian strongman who was shot by a firing squad, together with his wife, after protesters overthrew the country's Communist dictatorship in 1989.

"Just don't break windows, don't make too much noise, don't destroy things," Dushebayev was saying. "I won't issue an order to shoot at peaceful protesters." He complained that a few of his foot soldiers had already shed their uniforms and defected to the protesters, and he was eager for them to return to his command. "I won't punish anybody, please come back. We live in a difficult time, and we'll understand."

Behind him, protest leaders took turns addressing the crowd from a makeshift podium mounted on the roof of a low-slung boxy building. Otunbayeva spoke there, and then a man stepped up to the loudspeaker. Kurmanbek Bakiyev, an electrical engineer by training, had climbed the ladder of Soviet factory management all the way to the post of prime minister in the Akayev government. In 2002, Akayev sacked him as a scapegoat for the China land-transfer violence. Hailing from a powerful southern clan, Bakiyev refashioned himself as an opposition leader, and was now warming up the crowds and urging them to rise against his former boss. Akayev would later lament that it was all sour grapes on Bakiyev's part, that Bakiyev was "offended" to have been fired and was looking to exact revenge. "I raised him myself," the deposed Akayev would say after Bakiyev succeeded him as president.[6] For the time being, Bakiyev was shouting a string of hackneyed slogans about dictatorship into the loudspeaker, and the crowd below loved it all and hoisted banners telling President Akayev to resign.

At that point, having heard so many similar slogans over the previous few months, I decided to go back to a friend's apartment where I was staying and take a nap. The revolution might happen someday, but it wouldn't be on this particular day, I told myself in a highly prescient display of journalistic judgment. I lay down on the couch and read a few pages of Mario Vargas Llosa's *The Feast of the Goat,* a novel about life under the sadistic Dominican dictator Rafael Trujillo, assassinated in 1961. While I was reading the fictionalized account of the Dominican dictatorship, interesting nonfiction developments were taking place in front of Bishkek's drug-abuse clinic, about three miles away from my couch. No longer content to wave banners solely for the amusement of recovering addicts glued to the clinic's windows, the Kyrgyz protesters decided to take their fight straight to the heart of their own dictatorship and march on the White House, as the president's headquarters was informally known. I had no way of knowing any of this, of course, so I put down my book and fell asleep.

I was woken up by a phone call and reluctantly reached for my cell phone. It was Jamilla, a young Kel-Kel activist I knew.

"Where are you?" she asked.

"I'm working from home," I said, reluctant to own up to a midday nap.

"Well, you better get over here, because things are happening."

"What exactly is happening?" I asked, still groggy.

She told me, and I ran out of the building, feeling like the biggest fool alive. A cab dropped me off a block from the White House, and I walked out to the main square just in time to see a shower of rocks thrown at the police by the massive crowd of protesters. The police, thankfully, never opened fire. Because of the direction from which I approached the square, I found myself in a posse of young revolutionaries who had run out in front of the main crowd and were now trapped between the rows of riot police ahead of them and their stone-throwing brethren behind them. These unfortunate protesters were now dodging both friendly fire and rocks thrown back at them by plainclothes pro-government men. Like others around me, I had no choice but to run. I kept looking up and over my shoulder so that I could track the flying rocks, some of which appeared to be cobblestones pried out of the pavement. Sprinting across a lawn, I tripped on a sprinkler, fell, and then limped away from the line of fire, feeling once again like an idiot.

The White House is a big box of a building resembling an alien spaceship surrounded by an ornate cast-iron fence. A few bushy fir trees grow behind the fence. As they approached the White House, the protesters first faced helmeted riot police holding shields. After the rock barrage, the cops dispersed, leaving behind some bloodstains on the pavement. The blood belonged to the cops and probably to some protesters too who, like me, got caught in the cross fire. Some scuffles took place but no one got killed. I saw a few revolutionaries parading around with plastic shields and helmets they'd taken from the police. With the cops scattering away, the protesters crashed through the cast-iron fence and faced the last line of defense: an army unit charged with protecting the White House.

"You need to resign, right now!" a woman protester told the commanding officer, and then turned around to her fellow protesters and said, "This man refuses to order the army to withdraw, he says he swore an oath."

"Resign, resign!" Others picked up the refrain.

The officer, General Abdigul Chotbayev, was in a tough spot. Behind him, his soldiers formed a human shield around the White House. They waited for some sort of guidance from their commander. In front of him were the irate protesters telling him to take a walk. The commander stalled for time.

"You need to calm down, my dear sister," General Chotbayev told the woman protester. Then he moved away from the crowd and pondered his choices some more. Maybe he got in touch with his superiors, or maybe he made his own decision, but within minutes the soldiers formed a neat line and trotted behind the White House, never to be seen again.

All that separated the protesters from the palace now were a dry fountain bed and a few feet of pavement strewn with debris, abandoned riot shields, and cobblestones. The revolutionaries began their final approach with yet more stone throwing, now aimed at the White House windows. Shattered glass rained down on the jubilant protesters, and a few diehards pried open an entrance door and climbed inside. Soon enough, their grinning faces poked through the broken windows on the other side. The crowd cheered. More protesters entered the White House through the breach and began rifling through offices and throwing things out of windows. A round military hat flew out of one window like a Frisbee. It painted an arc through the air, landed on its rim, and rolled into the fountain. A coffee table flew out next, crashing with a loud thud that snapped its wooden legs. Computer monitors followed. A couple of teenagers next to me were playing soccer with a white riot-police helmet.

Some protesters were ambivalent about the vandalism. "We are a hardworking, peaceful people, we shouldn't be doing this," a man named Suleiman told me. Bakyt Murzaliyev, a thirty-five-year-old engineer from Bishkek, told me he hadn't received his $40 monthly salary in eight months and was very happy to see the government go. "We've been waiting for this for ten years." But he had no time to stand there and talk, so he excused himself and dashed inside the White House. I followed him.

A mixture of emotions propelled the people toward the White House: growing poverty, anger with a government that seemed increasingly disconnected from its own people, plain curiosity, the adrenaline of a revolution, and, in some cases, a desire to steal something useful. As I entered the White House, a man ran down the stairs hugging a computer monitor. "It's a gift for my brother," he said. A few more militant protesters paraded around with looted police riot-control gear. One of them tapped me on the shoulder and said, "Good job, man!"

"What do you mean?" I asked.

"You beat up a cop, so that's great," he said, and pointed at my right shin with a police truncheon. I looked down and saw that a bloodstain had spread over the spot where I hit the sprinkler while running away from the rocks. The guy assumed I had injured my leg kicking a cop.

In a darkened hallway, amid a melee of festive protesters breaking things in some kind of an animalistic urge, I bumped into Roza Otunbayeva, the former foreign minister and one of the uprising's leaders. It was an incongruous sight—a small woman in a headscarf walking shell-shocked through throngs of excited young men. She tried telling them they needed to stop and think about what they were doing, that they were hurting the cause of the uprising. "We worked so hard to achieve this, you must control yourselves, don't devalue the revolution," she was saying, but no one was really listening. This was not a time for diplomats and professors, or for thinking. And then she wandered off.

President Akayev had fled the White House right before the storm, and now his torn portrait floated in a shallow puddle fed by a leaking fire hose. Near his office on the seventh floor a protester was running around with an urgent errand. "I'd like to hang up a portrait of Bakiyev, but I can't find a good spot," he said and scurried away. Bakiyev, the former factory manager and prime minister, was fast emerging as a compromise figure who would lead the interim government after the revolution. On a hallway wall, someone scrawled a message: "The White House is a snake pit." Celebration continued in the president's old office, with wine being uncorked.

Later that night, I walked over to a place called Beta Stores. It was Bishkek's first Western-style department store, a four-story emporium stocked with groceries, clothes, electronics, and furniture. It had a food court and an indoor playground. With its distinctive facade of reflective glass, Beta Stores lay less than a mile away from the White House on Bishkek's main thoroughfare. The store had been built by a Turkish company. But somehow in the chaotic hours after the revolution, the store landed on the protesters' target list of the properties owned by the old regime. Having ransacked the White House, groups of young men roamed the city's streets, their mission accomplished. Many of them came from remote villages and had never seen a store like Beta before. The massive retreat of the police from the streets gave them a free rein. Located so close to the White House, Beta presented a fat, shiny target, and it didn't really matter who owned it.

By the time I walked up to Beta, it was gripped by an orgy of looting. A man ran out of the store and looked around. He seemed unsure what to do next. His nose stuck out above a big bundle of brand-new women's underwear he was hugging with both hands. Like me, he'd arrived here too late—all the good, expensive stuff had already been taken by quicker thinkers. The man wore house slippers, suggesting that he probably lived nearby and hadn't even bothered to put his shoes on. "Would you like to buy some panties, wholesale?" he asked me. I passed, and he shuffled away with his big bundle, dropping the occasional undergarment.

Inside, the store smelled of detergent and crushed-up cookies. Men were rolling up big Turkish carpets and helping themselves to packs of cigarettes from plastic dispensers above the cash registers. Someone hurried toward the exit with a grill oven. A couple of volunteers were telling the looters to stop, but just like Otunbayeva's earlier appeals in the White House, their feeble entreaties went unheeded. "We never thought it would come to this. All we wanted is for Akayev to resign," Maksud Mambekov, one of the volunteers mobilizing across Bishkek to stop the vandalism, told me. He stood next to a cash register, the one fixture of Beta that seemed utterly useless that evening. Someone eventually ripped out the cash register and made off with it.

The revolution here was so fast and surreal that a man who woke up on a prison bunk became the nation's security czar by the time he went to bed. Shortly after protesters took over the presidential palace, Felix Kulov, a former police chief and mayor of Bishkek, was sprung from jail and found himself cruising the city's mad streets in a white sport-utility vehicle, appealing to crazed crowds to stop the looting. "This turn of events was of course unusual," Kulov, clad in blue jeans and sporting a buzz cut, said the next morning in front of his new digs at the Interior Ministry.

A career police officer who rose to the rank of general, Kulov served as vice president, interior minister, and head of the National Security Service. Just as his personal popularity began to threaten President Akayev, Kulov was convicted of corruption in a dubious trial that Western observers considered politically motivated. It is not that he was necessarily blameless. It is just that he was no worse than the average, so picking on him smacked of selective justice.

For the next five years, Kulov languished in jail with six hundred other inmates. Comrades from his political party, Ar-Namys, supplied the whole prison with food, books, exercise equipment, woodworking lathes, soccer balls, and even special trucks to pump out the sewage.

Kulov's party once gave the cash-strapped prison twenty tons of potatoes. The party wanted to keep its leader fit and healthy, and the easiest way to do it was to support the whole prison. Behind bars, Kulov kept himself busy. He once gave his party comrades a wooden scale model of a ship carved by him and his jail buddies.

The day of the revolution, his supporters drove forty miles to the prison, where the superintendent promptly released him. "This man will be promoted," Kulov joked shortly afterward. The liberated general sprang into action that very evening, as looters rampaged through the capital, ransacking stores. The police had retreated into their precincts after the storming of the palace and were in no mood to venture out again. Bloodstains were still drying on the spots where the cops had come under a shower of rocks from the protesters. "They were so demoralized," Kulov recalled. "I could do little more than appeal to the conscience of every officer."

One evening after the uprising, Kulov addressed the crowds massing in front of the city's landmark Central Department Store, begging them not to loot. Several other popular shops, like Beta Stores, were overrun, vandalized, and emptied of merchandise.

The hordes of looters and thugs roaming the streets the first two postrevolutionary nights scared most peaceful residents into their homes, where some dusted off old shotguns and vowed to shoot if the marauding crowds approached. But the main department store survived with just a couple of cracked windows, an important moral victory of law and order in the capital.

The police, having absorbed the emotional shocks of being attacked by the protesters, came back to the streets, at one point shooting rounds into the air to keep looters at bay. Thousands of Bishkek residents responded to televised calls by Kulov and others to form militias and patrol their neighborhoods and the city's landmarks. "We came out because it's our city," said Igor Fadeyev, a print-shop worker, who donned the citizens' militia red armband and came to stand guard in front of the Central Department Store, a concrete cube stuffed with hundreds of shops. "If we don't protect it, who will?"

A Kulov aide told me his boss wished to return to prison after he was done mopping up the revolutionary mess, so that he could wait for an acquittal behind bars. But Kulov, of course, never went back to jail. Instead, he became prime minister.

On a blustery afternoon the day after the revolt, a man climbed on top of a children's slide in a village outside Bishkek, hunting for a better cell-phone signal. Standing there like an overgrown kid, the man screamed into the phone, cupping his mouth with his hand to block out the whipping wind. It was none other than Keneshbek Dushebayev, who'd served as the interior minister of Kyrgyzstan for two days and was now unemployed, though still very busy.

The countryside around him was the birthplace of President Akayev, and a large portrait of him was hanging intact on the side of a building. Hundreds of his compatriots congregated here for a rally to defend the honor of the local hero who had achieved so much and then was robbed of it all and had to flee the country. Two horsemen raced through an open field trailing a fluttering banner, like a biplane buzzing over a beach with a Budweiser ad in tow. "Akayev should go, but not like this," the horsemen's banner read.

A man in a green headband walked up to me and said, "They told us the revolution was carried out by the people, and who are we, not the people?" The folks in Kemin, Akayev's home village, were eager to march to Bishkek and, in the words of one agitated man, to "deal with the unconstitutional coup d'état" and to punish the looters and revolutionaries. Since many of those revolutionaries had come to Bishkek from southern Kyrgyzstan, the arrival of these disgruntled northerners would inevitably lead to street fighting and risk cleaving the country along the old north-south fault line. The interim government with Bakiyev at the helm desperately wanted to prevent Akayev's village people from entering Bishkek.

And that is why Dushebayev stood on the children's slide, shouting into his mobile phone. The former interior minister was one of the star speakers at the rally, and on the other side of that phone call was Kurmanbek Bakiyev himself. The interim leader got in touch to plead with Dushebayev to talk sense into the northern vigilantes and prevent them from marching to the jittery Kyrgyz capital. Nothing but trouble would come of it. Bakiyev informed Dushebayev that he was dispatching a trusted emissary to reason with the former interior minister in person. At that very moment, the emissary was getting into her chauffer-driven luxury sedan for a drive toward Kemin. Dushebayev, it was suggested, should get into his own car and drive toward Bishkek, so that the two could meet in some quiet spot along the highway, away from the crowds, and have a chat. Dushabayev dismounted the slide in such a hurry I thought for a moment he was going to slide down. He jumped into his car and raced toward Bishkek. I followed him in a taxi.

Revolutions are hard on everyone, but they are particularly difficult for the police and the military. Sworn to protect the state, cops and soldiers face a dilemma: stick with the government and face the wrath of protesters, or side with the protesters and face charges of treason. The situation gets even trickier if the government orders the army and the police to shoot the protesters. Few other segments of society have to make this choice with quite the same urgency and consequences. And that's why, I think, Dushebayev seemed indecisive as he flipped through various unpalatable scenarios both before the revolt and right afterward.

At the moment, his car was flying toward Bishkek on a nearly empty highway, passing occasional motorists. We could barely keep up. Soon enough, we saw a car heading toward us. It flashed its headlights and honked. Dushebayev slowed down and pulled over to the curb. The other car swerved to the curb as well, and the emissary stepped out. It was Cholpon Bayekova, a petite chairwoman of Kyrgyzstan's constitutional court.

Chief justice since the early 1990s, Bayekova became popular among opposition activists because of a key ruling. The Akayev administration was harassing protesters by requiring them to seek advance permission for rallies, and Bayekova struck down that requirement as unconstitutional. Her ruling was prompted in part by the government's moves to disperse demonstrations calling for Kulov's release from prison. After the revolution, she became a legal advisor to the interim leaders, helping them shoehorn the patently unconstitutional regime change into some semblance of legality. "I could not imagine this scenario even in my wildest dreams," she told me.

Now Bayekova, her head wrapped in a scarf against the cold wind, greeted the former interior minister, and the two walked slowly into the open field by the side of the road. They stopped by an outcropping of trees near a small pond and talked for about forty minutes. Her bodyguards and I shivered by the parked cars, the weather suddenly turning after the warm spring day of the revolution. It would soon snow. I don't know what the two talked about, but by the time they returned to the cars they seemed to have reached some kind of an understanding.

"Now, it's very important to cool down the hotheads," the judge told the former minister as they were about to get into their respective cars and drive in opposite directions.

Dushebayev nodded. He wore the traditional Kyrgyz *kolpak,* a tall hat made of white felt embroidered with black and gold thread and topped with a small tassel. When he nodded, the tassel jiggled. "I'll try my best," he said.

And he did. The northern vigilantes ended up calling off their ominous Bishkek incursion. With that, the revolution was over, and the unglamorous job of governing the country began. Inspired by flowers that bloom in Kyrgyzstan at that time of the year, activists called their uprising the Tulip Revolution. But the tulip would start to wilt very soon.

CHAPTER 2 *On the Heroin Highway*

One April morning a few days after the Tulip Revolution, I drove up a mountain just outside the Kyrgyz capital. On the otherwise deserted woodsy plateau near the top, someone had pitched an ornately embroidered tent. Its sole occupant, a gaunt young man in faded blue jeans, was sitting on a wooden bench right next to the tent. He had the world-weary bearing of a hermit, lost in thought and oblivious to the scenery around him. Down below, under the gauzy cover of low-hanging clouds, the city of Bishkek was recovering from the shocks of the uprising. From this height, the city appeared tiny, orderly, and serene. When I approached him, the man on the bench looked up with a wan smile, and then extended his hand for a limp handshake. His name was Alexander Stumpf, and he had traveled to this mountain all the way from Germany.

Stumpf was a hard-core heroin addict, his arms raked with bluish-red streaks where needles had burrowed under his skin in search of increasingly elusive veins. After all other treatments had failed, Stumpf heard about a mysterious Kyrgyz doctor who promised to cure substance abuse with a set of highly unorthodox methods. Maybe it all sounded too good to be true, but Stumpf had nothing to lose. He'd pretty much lost everything already: friends, money, a shot at a decent future. Even family support had begun to wear thin as Stumpf kept falling off the wagon, his promises to stay clean as short-lived as the cash he cadged from relatives.

So now, as part of the Kyrgyz doctor's regimen, Stumpf secluded himself on this mountaintop in a final attempt to escape heroin's grip. In his lap, he was cradling a large rock, the size and shape of a honeydew melon. Stumpf's lips were moving in a barely audible whisper. On the doctor's advice, he was talking to the rock, trying to transfer into it all the bad things from his life. There was plenty of talking to be done. "After working with the rock, my spirits rise," Stumpf told me.

The rock treatment was the brainchild of Jenishbek Nazaraliyev, the flamboyant Kyrgyz physician who counted underworld kingpins and yoga masters among his acquaintances, scrawled his musings about life with a crayon on his office walls, and considered the "witch doctor" label a compliment. Nazaraliyev blended conventional medicine with the mystical ways of his nomadic ancestors to build a lucrative private clinic catering to drug addicts and alcoholics. His clinic, as we've already seen, was the staging ground for the rallies that swelled into the Tulip Revolution. For Stumpf, though, the only uprising that mattered was his own private battle against heroin, and it was too early to tell which way it was going to go. The addiction that ground down Stumpf and hundreds of thousands of other junkies across Europe and Central Asia was nurtured by the booming heroin industry in Afghanistan. Addicts like Stumpf are the final link in a sophisticated supply chain that begins in the remote Afghan poppy fields and stretches through a network of heroin cooks, smugglers, and corrupt officials.

Making heroin is not that hard. A lab requires no sophisticated technology, just a couple of barrels, opium, firewood, acid, and recipes passed by word of mouth from cook to cook. You could stand next to a heroin lab or fly directly above one without discovering it, though if the wind is right you might pick up the cloyingly heavy scent of heated opium. Most of the gear can be carted away at a moment's notice, or even abandoned and easily replaced. "They can move very fast, and we are chasing them," General Mohammed Daud, Afghanistan's deputy interior minister for counter-narcotics, told me in Kabul.

I asked Ismatullah, a pensive police chief in a remote village in northern Afghanistan, to take me to see some heroin labs. "The ones that were destroyed or the ones that weren't?" he deadpanned back.

We drove down rutted roads flanked by mud huts. A billowing plume of dust hovered behind our jeep. Stacks of dried-out poppy stalks were piled up high on every roof, and at one point we passed a donkey laden with bundles of poppy plants. It was mid-August, well past the poppy harvesting season, so the plants we saw had already been wrung free of their precious contents and were now used as firewood or roofing material. Ismatullah was sympathetic to the poppy farmers. "We don't have real roads, we don't have electricity, or even candles to burn, and you ask us why we grow opium." I hadn't asked, but he felt he needed to answer anyway.

We stopped in front of a mud-walled house that didn't look particularly suspicious. In this remote corner of northern Afghanistan, the hut appeared to rise straight out of the tamped brown earth beneath it, like a sand castle on the beach. The place had a shaded terrace overlooking a patch of tomato plants. A child's boot lay forgotten in the backyard shrubbery. In a nearby stone enclosure splattered with dung, an emaciated cow sought respite from the afternoon sun by chasing tiny specks of shade. It was hard to imagine that up until a few weeks ago this had been a narcotics lab where people cooked heroin, one of the most addictive and destructive drugs known to man, and Afghanistan's most lucrative export.

The first sign that the mud hut was more than a simple home of a farming family lay right behind the cow: eight steel barrels used to make heroin out of the plentiful poppy plants that have become the primary cash crop here. More twisted barrels with gunshot and shrapnel holes were piled up in the backyard next to a mound of dried yellow poppy stalks, their bulbous tops slashed open to free the prized opium, heroin's key ingredient.

A few miles away, I saw another abandoned lab. It was hidden from prying eyes on a platform cut into the side of a deep, tree-covered gorge. Both labs had been recently raided by counter-narcotics forces from

Kabul. But the heroin cooks had fled well before the commandos arrived, abandoning both the house, rented from a local farmer, and their secluded canyon-side lab. A heavy scent of opium still permeated the canyon, and I saw a pair of rubber gloves crumpled in the dirt. It was reasonable to assume, as everyone here did, that the cooks had found employment in one of the many other labs sprinkled throughout the countryside.

Historically, most poppy cultivation and heroin production in Afghanistan has taken place in the south of the country, in vast unruly provinces like Helmand and Kandahar, where the West has been fighting the Taliban insurgency for years without much success. Pressured both by the competition and by the war, some southern drug dealers wanted to expand their business, and the north provided an ideal stage. Secluded and peaceful, at least by the rapidly deteriorating standards of Afghanistan, the northern province of Badakshan boasts solid poppy harvests and proximity to a key heroin market: post-Soviet Central Asia, which serves both as a voracious consumer of heroin and as an important transit point for shipping the drug onward to Russia and Europe.

In its waning days in power, the Taliban tried to curry world favor by imposing a ban on poppy growing. These days though, Taliban insurgents have no qualms about exploiting the opium trade to replenish their war chest. Ever since the 2001 invasion, Washington and its NATO allies have attempted a variety of approaches to the poppy problem. Initially, the West settled on doing nothing at all in the flawed belief that one could fight insurgents without fighting drugs. Later, the West worked from the usual counter-narcotics menu, which includes eradicating crops, urging farmers to grow innocuous things like wheat instead, and hitting drug traffickers. Though nominally committed to fighting drugs, the Afghan government and police are riddled with corruption and have extensive links to the drug trade. The results are grim: in 2001, Afghan farmers planted eight thousand hectares with poppy. Nearly a decade later, the poppy-growing area swelled more than fifteenfold. Occasional year-to-year decreases in cultivation are as likely to be attributed to plant bugs and inclement weather as they are to any concerted counter-narcotics strategy.

I grew up in the final years of the Soviet Union, and the withdrawal of Soviet troops from Afghanistan is an indelible childhood memory. There they were on our television screens, tired and happy, waving from the turrets of tanks and sitting cross-legged on their coffinlike armored infantry vehicles. They were marching back into their—our—disintegrating country across the curiously named Friendship Bridge connecting Afghanistan with the Soviet Central Asia. The bridge had been built to facilitate the invasion a few years earlier. Unperturbed by a strong whiff of defeat, the Soviet propaganda machine announced a glorious end to the mission of the "warrior-internationalist," whatever that meant.

The realities of the Soviet foray into Afghanistan began to hit home only later, and nothing captured the sheer absurdity of it better than Storm-333. That was the codename given to the 1979 Soviet plot to assassinate Hafizullah Amin, the violent and mercurial president of Afghanistan. After seizing power, Amin arranged for his predecessor to be smothered to death, setting the tone for the rest of his brief tenure. Amin managed to alienate most Afghan factions, had a lot of people killed, and retreated to a secluded palace. He had started out as a Moscow protégé, but then became too independent, erratic and possibly entangled with the CIA. Despite the violence he unleashed, he couldn't control Afghanistan. He had to go.

The 1979 assault was so secret that even the Soviet doctors who were in Amin's palace at the time thought the place was being attacked by a rival Afghan faction, according to an absorbing account by a Russian military historian.[1] The doctors had been called in because Amin and his family and friends had succumbed to a food poisoning that evening. Unable to trust fellow Afghans, Amin trusted only Soviet doctors, and he also employed Soviet chefs. Did those cooks try to poison him that day? It's not clear. But just weeks earlier, Soviet operatives had spiked a glass of Pepsi that was intended for Amin but was instead downed by his nephew. Stricken with hepatitis, the nephew was airlifted to Moscow, where Soviet doctors nursed him back to health. He was later executed in Afghanistan. The mysterious mass poisoning of a few weeks later was so bad that the Soviet doctors dispatched to the palace found Amin near death, lying in his underwear, mouth open, eyeballs rolled far back in his eye sockets. He barely had any pulse. The doctors pumped his stomach and hydrated him through IV drippers. They revived Amin just in time for him to regain consciousness and hear Soviet Special Forces fighting their way into his palace to kill him. Amin refused to believe this subterfuge until his very last moments. He threw an ashtray at his aide when the aide had the temerity to suggest that it was the Soviets who were coming to take him out, not some rogue Afghan faction. Amin was killed that evening. His body was wrapped in a carpet.

Now, thirty years later, the Russians were no longer killing Afghans, but Afghanistan was still killing many Russians—by heroin. Perhaps there's an irony in this unwitting revenge. On the drug front, Afghanistan has become Russia's Mexico. One summer a couple of years ago, I arranged to travel on the heroin production and smuggling trail. The idea was to drive from Kabul to Dushanbe, Tajikistan, three hundred miles to the north. The trip nearly fell apart before it could begin because I became a target of a counter-terrorism investigation in Brussels, where I lived at the time. I'd been on the road so often for work that I'd neglected to pay a utility bill, and missed a few reminders too. Unbeknownst to me, a Belgian court dispatched a bailiff and a beat cop to serve me with a final notice and take inventory of my belongings in case they needed to be sold to cover the arrears. On the morning of their visit, I was out interviewing the secretary-general of NATO. My landlord called, his voice a little shaky, to tell me a cop had just forced his way into my apartment. The landlord, who lived in the same building, had offered to let him in with a spare key. But the urgency to collect the debt (about $250, including interest) was such that the corpulent Belgian policeman refused to wait and busted open the door, breaking a floor lamp in the process. He jotted down descriptions and price estimates of various unglamorous things I owned: a Sony DVD player, a coffeemaker, and so on. (I was later given a copy.)

And then he saw something that transformed the mission in his mind's eye. No longer was he dealing with the malicious dodger of a utility bill but with a potential terrorist. I had maps of Afghanistan and Central Asia on my coffee table, and NATO printouts describing the nature and the size of the mission in Afghanistan. I was learning Arabic at the time, so I had a dictionary out too. There was a bulky satellite phone on my dining-room table. The beat cop, perhaps bored with his desk-jockey job, saw a chance to shine and out a sleeper agent. In fairness, Europe was on edge at the time, with various terror plots popping up from London to Madrid. The cop hurried out of the apartment, told my landlord he'd seen some disturbing things inside, and vowed to be back. My landlord called to give me a heads-up. I thanked him and laughed off the matter. But when I approached my townhouse that evening, I saw a dozen people milling about on the street. Some loitered in front of the building, others strolled back and forth on the other side of the road. Yet others were standing next to an unmarked van, maybe getting ready to pack me in. All wore civilian clothes. It looked like a bad police movie.

They encircled me and flashed badges, identifying themselves as members of an elite counter-terrorism squad of the federal police. The beat cop had painted such a dire picture of me that a judge issued a search warrant that very day. Eager to avoid any more broken doors, I let them in, and they swabbed for explosives, rifled through my books and DVDs (looking for Jihadi propaganda), and interviewed my landlord. Soon enough, they knew it was all a mistake, but they had to go through the motions. I was told that the beat cop, his imagination firing away, had reported that I might be hatching a plan to attack NATO troops in Afghanistan. The next day, I had to go to the police headquarters, where the police told me the investigation was now closed. For a while afterward, I worried that the unpaid utility bill would land me on some no-fly list, from which there's no easy escape.

Having convinced the Belgians I was no terrorist, I flew to Afghanistan. Qais, my enterprising translator, met me at the Kabul airport, built by Soviet engineers and now occupied by NATO. The Soviets had also built a clutch of five-story residential buildings in Kabul that looked as if they'd been airlifted straight out of a provincial Soviet town. The Afghans even referred to the settlement as *microraion,* the Soviet municipal designation meaning "subdistrict." Though in Russia this kind of housing now evoked the worst of Soviet shortages, in Afghanistan this was still prime residential real estate. Qais had an apartment there. He taught himself English to earn a living helping Western journalists. But he could still string together a potent chain of obscenities in Russian. That's all he remembered from his toddler days when his dad ran a small store where Soviet soldiers were frequent customers.

The Russian military footprint in Afghanistan, once gigantic, was now little more than a gaggle of guards assigned to the Russian embassy in Kabul. I knocked on the door of the compound once and was greeted by a burly Russian officer. It turned out he was from my hometown, where he'd studied to be a chef. In the compound's kitchen, crisscrossed by a web of clotheslines to which identical black socks were clipped in a pendulous infinity, the officer was in the process of whipping up a massive pot of rice and chicken stew.

As luck would have it, I'd walked into a party. A new set of guards had flown in that very morning to relieve the team currently in the compound. The new guards had come armed with an ominous supply of vodka and Russian delicacies, which were now being unpacked in preparation for the welcome-and-farewell party. The new arrivals were lounging on a lawn in the sun, cleaning their weapons. Later that evening, the chef served the stew, and the first shots of vodka were poured in the dusty gazebo in the compound's backyard. Perched on a plastic lawn chair, a CD player blasted Russian pop music. After exchanging the homophobic jokes requisite in an all-male company, the men began dancing—first awkwardly, then with a little more dedication. A few minutes later, a soldier who wasn't at the party because he had guard duty that night ran into the backyard. "Turn this down, now. Are you guys crazy? A Talib hears this shit, throws a grenade over the fence, and this party is over!" I staggered to my guesthouse way past midnight.

Before driving up north to explore the heroin economy, Qais and I spent a few days in Kabul, where we arranged to have lunch with a heroin cook who had just returned from a stint in Badakshan. Those were the kinds of people Qais's connections allowed him to produce. In his late twenties, the cook had a gaunt, goateed face and was wearing the traditional attire of baggy pants and a long shirt that had once been white.

He was an ethnic Pashtun from the Shinwar plains of eastern Afghanistan, and he insisted I refer to him simply as "Shinwari," a man from Shinwar.

This was his R & R break in the big city, and he was planning to head back to his heroin job a few days later. Shinwari spoke of the job so matter-of-factly that he could have been talking about packaging coffee or refining sugar. He ordered a Pepsi and chicken pizza, and told me he'd followed his cousin to Badakshan. A few years earlier, the cousin, who already had some heroin experience, borrowed money and ventured up north to set up his own shop. "Back home he was really poor, but in Badakshan he became rich," Shinwari said, paused to have a bite of pizza, and added: "Unbelievably rich." The cousin's northern operation grew, and he eventually recruited eleven cooks from his home village.

Shinwari was one of the recruits. The cooks worked in the backyard of a simple house rented from a local farmer, much like the busted drug lab I would see later. The process was fairly straightforward: the cooks dropped poppy seeds into a barrel and heated it over an open fire, mixing the brew with long wooden sticks. Then the cooks filtered the hot seeds through the mesh of a simple flour sack, collecting the opium juice underneath and letting it dry in the sun. Using electric mixers, they blended the hardened opium with two kinds of acid.

"And what you get in the end is a beautiful thing—pure heroin," Shinwari summed up with a smile on his face. "It sounds simple, but you have to know how long to boil it, how much acid to add; if you overcook, it's really bad."

People in Badakshan tend to be ethnic Tajiks and Uzbeks, so the expat Pashtun heroin contingent stood out. The Pashtun cooks treated their heroin recipes as a trade secret and pledged not to divulge them outside the lab. In the famously strict Pashtun tribal code, a promise is a promise. Shinwari told me a Pashtun joke. A guest asks a Pashtun how old he is. The Pashtun says he's thirty. Ten years later, the same guest puts the same question to the same Pashtun. The answer is also the same—thirty. The punch line: when a Pashtun says something, he sticks to it. "It's the same with the promise not to share the heroin recipes," Shinwari said.

A few days later, we packed our jeep with biscuits and drinking water and drove north. Unlike the badlands of the south, the Taliban traditional stronghold, the north at the time was a relatively peaceful place. But when our Toyota jeep rolled into Faizabad, the sleepy capital of the Badakshan province, we noticed that a strange car was trailing us. We tried to make sure we were not being paranoid or simply influenced by too many bad movies, so we drove around aimlessly in the back streets of Faizabad where traffic was light to nonexistent. Sure enough, the car kept on our tail. Qais noticed that it had license plates from another province, unusual considering that the closest province was a seven-hour drive away. We figured we were being followed because we were asking too many questions about heroin, a source of huge fortunes here.

That gave us some comfort. We thought we'd rather be followed by drug traffickers than by religious fanatics. The former, we hoped, were more rational. Before we left Kabul, Qais secured a handwritten note from General Mohammed Daud, the Afghan government's point man for counter-narcotics. The note consisted of squiggles and a stamp, and it said, basically, "Help these people," or so I hoped. When we visited Faizabad's police headquarters to see the chief, we mentioned the suspicious car and produced the note. The chief read it, nodded gravely, and summoned a young cop. He looked to be no older than his late teens and was so skinny that his police uniform hung in folds over his arms and legs. He had a wispy mustache, the kind that seemed to have never been touched by a razor. He wore white sneakers, a few sizes too large, and carried an AK-47 submachine gun.

For the next few days, he would be our bodyguard. He took his job so seriously that once, when I was looking for a bathroom and was told to just find a spot behind the police precinct, he ran behind me, his AK at the ready. When I went swimming in a mountain river, he watched me with concern. I don't know if he made us any safer. But he was good company. The suspicious car eventually fell back and never reappeared, its occupants probably judging us to be of no risk to anyone except ourselves. (It turned out that the person who really needed protection was General Daud himself. He had been a close ally of Ahmad Shah Massoud, the storied anti-Taliban commander assassinated in 2001 by hit men dis-patched by the Islamist militia. In 2011, the Taliban finally caught up with Daud too, killing him in a bomb blast not far from Badakshan.)

In Badakshan, people have grown poppy since ancient times, at one point enjoying a special dispensation from the Afghan king. Poppy is a versatile plant prized in this isolated and destitute part of Afghanistan for its medicinal and other qualities. In a strict Islamic society where alcohol remains a rarity, opium provides an easy substitute. Though it's just as *haram*, or forbidden by religious law, to get high as it is to get drunk, for those willing to skirt the injunction opium is far easier to obtain than liquor. On any given evening you can see huddles of men squatting on a riverbank here with clouds of smoke hovering over their heads. The morphine content means it's also a good though dangerously addictive painkiller. It wasn't long ago that people here gave it to sick children: an adult would light an opium bowl, inhale, and then puff the smoke in the face of a child.

In a small, dirty drug-abuse clinic in Badakshan's capital Faizabad, I met a patient named Mohammed Reza. He told me his wife had fallen ill with a debilitating case of rheumatism four years ago. So Reza started giving her opium to smoke, to relieve the pain. To keep her company, Reza picked up the habit too. The wife passed away, but Reza kept smok-ing three times a day to blunt the loss, developing an addiction so strong that his body shook and itched all over demanding the drug. He was eventually brought to this clinic, where he shared a room with a dozen other recovering addicts. As we were talking, another patient, Abdul Bek, piped up from a nearby bunk. "Opium is our only doctor," he bellowed. Bek, it turned out, had been smoking for twenty-five years in his remote village to alleviate various maladies, including headaches and back pains. "We don't have hospitals, medicine, or real doctors, so opium is it."

The poppy plant can also be used to make decent cooking oil and even soap, neither of which has narcotic qualities. And the poppy flower in full bloom makes a rose look a garden weed. Heroin is the latest addi-tion to the poppy plant's already formidable arsenal.

The breadth of Badakshan's intractable heroin economy was easy to see in the town of Argu. Ismatullah, the same police chief who'd shown me the heroin labs, now gave me a tour of his town. The main street wound through a haphazard collection of wooden kiosks selling groceries, clothes, and assorted other merchandise. Until a recent raid by Afghan special forces from Kabul, many shopkeepers acted as intermediaries in the heroin trade, stashing burlap sacks of poppy behind their more mundane wares.

I met with Haji Firouz, a shopkeeper, over melon slices in the office of the local police chief. "Poppy farmers used opium as currency," he said. "They came to the Argu shops and exchanged their opium for wheat, for instance. Then the heroin makers came to the shops, bought the opium, gave us cash, and we would buy more goods for the shops."

Mohammad Nahim, the head of Argu's counter-narcotics squad, nodded and added dejectedly: "The drug trade became so normal here that everyone is involved."

A bucket of padlocks, pried off the kiosks in the recent raid, sat on the windowsill. The Kabul commandos came, burned the opium in a big bonfire, and left. But the shopkeepers now fidgeted in their chairs and interrupted one another with complaints: some owed money to drug merchants; others said they were missing wads of cash from the shops and suspected the commandoes had stolen them. They demanded compensation from town authorities, and the local police were clearly sympathetic to the shopkeepers. It seemed everyone, including the cops, was eager to just go back to the old way of doing business.

A few miles from Argu, in a verdant valley bisected by a river, I met a group of poppy farmers. They too were angry. It turned out local government officials had urged them to grow something else instead of poppy, even promising financial help. The farmers believed them and planted wheat. But no help materialized.

"The government promised cash, equipment, fertilizer, tractors, seeds, but they didn't keep their promises," said a farmer named Abder Rahim. A black turban wrapped tight over his head, Rahim peered at me with steely-eyed rage, three deep creases running down his forehead. His meager wheat crop was now riddled with diseases. The next planting season was just a month away, and Rahim knew exactly what he was going to plant. Opium dealers were much better at keeping their promises than

Afghan poppy farmer Abder Rahim. (© Philip Shishkin)

the government. In the previous years, they brought Rahim seeds, told him exactly how much poppy to plant, and gave him a big advance on the future crop. Rahim said the dealers—he called them "businessmen"— were coming any day now to make arrangements for this year's growing season, and he couldn't wait. "I'm a poor farmer," he said. "I need the money."

His neighbor Abdel Jalil was also eager to go back to planting poppy and forget about the ill-advised foray into wheat. "I used to have two donkeys, now I have a truck. Wheat is nothing," Jalil said.

How could you argue with that? Kuchar, another local farmer, defied government orders to plant wheat and stubbornly continued to grow poppy even as his neighbors switched to the legal crop. Just as his poppy stalks stretched out and the bulbs swelled with opium, govern- ment troops showed up and scythed everything down. It was too late in the season to try planting something else, so Kuchar was really screwed. Now he's making plans to plant poppy again. "Even if they kill us, we will grow poppy because otherwise we'll die of hunger," Kuchar told me. "And it's better to die of a bullet."

The next day, I met a local police chief for an early breakfast of kebabs in a dinghy smoke-filled mud hut. The chief, Abdel Wahud, confirmed that the farmers felt cheated by the government. "Next year we'll be in big trouble with the poppy farmers," he said, "because the government lied to them." And why would the farmers obey a government stacked with corrupt officials, some of whom maintained well-publicized links to the drug industry?

The real money, of course, isn't in raw poppies, or even in opium. Both of these are fine if you are a farmer looking to plant something

The remnants of a clandestine heroin lab in northern Afghanistan. (© Philip Shishkin)

more profitable than wheat or a stoner looking to get high. But if you have serious drug-trafficking ambitions, you have to move into heroin. The business started developing in the 1990s as traffickers realized they could make more money by converting opium into heroin inside Afghanistan, instead of letting foreigners do the conversion outside—and reap the profits. By locating heroin labs close to the poppy source, they were also able to save on transportation of the bulky opium, according to people in the business and counter-narcotics officials. From the Badakshan poppy fields, the traffickers move the crop straight to the labs.

One evening in a guesthouse just outside Faizabad, Badakshan's capital, I arranged to meet a young trafficker who introduced himself as Qais, no relation to my translator. He said he'd been in the business for about three years, running newly manufactured heroin from labs to intermediaries in other parts of the country. Qais told me the labs had become more sophisticated over the years. Some now featured well-guarded guesthouses where traffickers could watch satellite television while they waited for their opium to be converted into heroin. The more advanced labs featured custom-made opium presses and could refine heroin to two levels of purity. The higher level was more expensive and destined for more discerning and wealthier users in Europe. The lower grade usually found the needles and veins of poorer junkies in Central Asia. Some labs stamped their heroin bags with a quality seal, usually featuring an animal of some sort. I was skeptical of this detail until a few days later I saw just such a stamp on a one-kilo bag of heroin in Central Asia. The bigger traffickers moved their product in well-armed convoys, paying off police and planning routes using satellite phones. Qais told me the heroin business in Badakshan was "bigger than you think," but that he personally was ready for a calmer life. "You worry all the time," he said.

He wasn't the only one who'd welcome a career change. "I can tell you I'm really tired of this job," Major Ghulam Muheddin, the counter-narcotics police chief in Faizabad, told me one day. He'd received plenty of death threats and had been shot at. Gray haired and soft spoken, Muheddin wore a mildly concerned expression, as if he thought he may have forgotten to unplug an iron back home. "I make plans to arrest people, and they find out in advance." One day, Muheddin arrested a man named Abdel who carried several kilos of heroin. Abdel was bounced between various police offices and soon released. Muheddin saw him ambling down a Faizabad street without a care in the world. The major lives on roughly $90 a month. A kilo of heroin here costs $900 and up. Muheddin was supposed to have twenty-two cops under his command, but he could find only twelve for the thankless job. Of those, none had working radios, and one was missing an arm. Muheddin was circumspect in their presence, and he later told me he suspected some of them of collusion with traffickers.

I met him in his dingy office behind a short wooden door that could take your head off if you didn't bend down in time. There was a map of Afghanistan on the wall, with a collage of a boot stomping on a bright red poppy flower. Strewn about the office were souvenirs of the trade: a couple of bags of viscous opium putty and a dozen canisters of acid, a key heroin ingredient. Acid is brought to Afghanistan using the same cross-border smuggling routes that later carry heroin out of the country. Industrial acid is not illegal, but if you see a big truck loaded with barrels of acid drive into the mountains, you can guess they are not making plastics or tanning leather up there. Muheddin seemed oddly committed to the job even in the face of high-level corruption that shielded traffickers from arrest or prosecution. Another police chief in the neighboring province told me he was lobbying his superiors for authorization to stop and search police cars—because they often carried heroin for the traffickers. No such authorization was forthcoming. Traffickers also controlled a key checkpoint leading to an important transit bridge to Central Asia. "The police there are all smugglers' people," Muheddin said.

One afternoon, he showed up in my guesthouse with a brick of heroin shrink-wrapped in clear plastic. It was light brown in color and cost about $1,000. "There's a lot of demand for this shit over there," Muheddin said, pointing generically behind his head toward the mountains, past which lay post-Soviet Central Asia.

Afghanistan's long border with Tajikistan follows the Panj River through rugged mountain terrain that's difficult to police. It's the first step on Afghan heroin's northward journey through post-Soviet Central

Asia toward Europe. One morning, I came to the ferry crossing to find a desolate shack that looked unlikely to produce any transportation. But I was soon told a dinghy was on its way from the other side to fetch me and the other passenger. "Who's the other passenger?" I asked.

The attendant pointed toward the riverbank, where I saw a man sitting cross-legged on a chair reading a book. Right next to him stood a Harley-Davidson motorcycle covered in travel stickers. The man was tall and bearded, and Australian. He wore black boots laced up midshin. He gazed up at the calm waters of the Panj and then down at his book again, serene as the sky above him. He was in the midst of some crazy solitary motorcycle tour that had already taken him many months. The current leg of the trip ran from Pakistan all the way into Central Asia. As we talked, locals came by to gawk at the bike, which had a distinct extraterrestrial feel in its present setting, much like the rider himself. An hour or so later, the promised dinghy sputtered across the river and took us to Tajikistan.

The Tajik guards frisked me and my backpack thoroughly. A lonely traveler on this river was always assumed to be a mule. Having cleared customs, I met with Abdullah, a former Tajik police colonel with an old white Mercedes. Abdullah now juggled a variety of part-time jobs, and he liked to boast of his exploits as a cop. I'd arranged for him to drive me around Tajikistan. As the first order of business, Abdullah suggested we celebrate my exit from near-dry Afghanistan by drinking cold beers at a roadside café. Here was the thing: I'd traveled only a couple of miles from northern Afghanistan—the people are ethnic Tajiks on both sides of the border—but the dinghy that took me across the river may as well have been a time capsule. I arrived from the Middle Ages straight into the Soviet Union circa 1970. The clothes, the food, the buildings, the cars—everything was Soviet.

After the beer, I went to meet Tajik border guards manning a small outpost on the Panj. The night before, they'd heard the suspicious whirring of a motor coming from somewhere in the dark skies above the river. They followed the sound down a craggy riverbank, shouted warnings, and then opened fire. What fell out of the sky was a motorized parachute carrying eighteen kilograms of Afghan heroin. For nearly two years, the guards had been hunting for this elusive airborne contraption used to transport heroin from Afghanistan to Tajikistan. They'd shot it down once before, but it fell on the Afghan side, out of their reach. This time, they had better luck.

The machine was all laid out in the courtyard of the border guards' barracks: a red, blue, and white French-made parachute outfitted with a harness ring, a German-made motor, a small propeller, a plastic gas canister—and eighteen one-kilo plastic bags of Afghan heroin. The harness ring was to hold a pilot, and the propeller to give him control of his direction after he jumped from a mountain on the Afghan side. The soldiers' bullets had pierced the gas tank, forcing an emergency landing, but the guards never found the pilot.

Earlier that day, the guards at the same outpost intercepted a waterborne heroin vehicle—an inner tube from a heavy truck with wooden boards placed on top for the smuggler to sit on. Shudi Nurasov, a skinny thirty-seven-year-old citizen of Tajikistan, was navigating the calm waters of the Panj with twenty one-kilo bags of heroin worth $24,000, each bearing a neat oval stamp reading, "AZAD PRIVATE FACTORY. The Best of All Export. Super White." But his raft was greeted by armed soldiers when it beached in Tajikistan. Wearing a glittery green skullcap and a dirty knee-length Afghan shirt, a bedraggled Nurasov told his story. A few months earlier, he'd befriended an Afghan man in a Tajik prison where he was serving a short drug-related sentence. The Afghan eventually entrusted him with the heroin under a typical deal: within a month, Nurasov would sell the heroin in Tajikistan and then pay his patron $16,000, keeping the rest. Nurasov, an opium addict, told me he picked up the heroin in Faizabad. He looked dejected and lost. A Border Guard commander told me Afghan traffickers have a persuasive tactic to make sure they don't get stiffed by the Tajik couriers: they hold their relatives hostage until the couriers sell the heroin and pay off their debts.

Sliced up with lightly guarded borders and full of avaricious officials, Central Asia is a trafficker's paradise. The region emerged destitute from the collapse of the Soviet Union, and Tajikistan faced particular hardship. A civil war in the 1990s took fifty thousand lives and weakened the already fragile state, empowering various warlords and armed groups that could now turn their expertise to running drugs. In the past decade, Kyrgyzstan meandered from one crisis to another, while corruption and organized crime flourished. In the meantime, to the south, Afghanistan churned out heroin in ever-greater quantities. It was the perfect storm.

As we barreled down from the border toward Dushanbe in our white Mercedes, Abdullah insisted we make a quick detour to buy some salt.

"Salt?" I asked.

"You'll see, don't worry," Abdullah said.

The white mountain rose like a mirage, sparkling in the sun. It took me a minute to realize it was made entirely out of salt. It has its own cave systems, rivers, and natural springs. Marco Polo, the intrepid Venetian traveler who traversed these lands in the Middle Ages, stopped to gawk at this mountain. "There's so much salt here it will be enough for the whole world, until the end of days," he wrote.

You could ski down this mountain. Workmen shoveled salt into wheelbarrows and took it to a large shack in the foothills. In the shack, women refined the salt and packaged it into plastic bags using a conveyor belt that spewed the large-grained powder out of a sieve. Outside, salt cracked and squished under my feet, leaving white residue on my shoes that never fully came off. Abdullah opened the trunk of his Mercedes and loaded it up with clear bags of salt. There was something wrong with this picture: a former Tajik police colonel and a Russian guy driving to Dushanbe from the Afghan border—one of the busiest drug highways in the world—with a trunk full of white powder.

"You sure it's salt?" I asked Abdullah.

He laughed. "The salt is much cheaper here than in Dushanbe." I guess so.

In Dushanbe, I went to check out a drug-rehab center, tucked away in a corner of a hospital. The center was run by Batir Zalimov, a thirty-six-year-old former heroin addict who walked with a cane and had discovered God. He'd been clean for a couple of years, having gone through the worst of withdrawal symptoms on a long-distance train ride to Siberia. There he worked odd jobs, figuring the cold and the need to survive would help displace the cravings. It worked. He was now back managing the rehab center. We talked in a small gazebo outside. "This is worse than a nuclear bomb," Zalimov said. "The addicts are getting younger and younger." These days, he told me, there are users as young as fourteen years old. When the first wave of heroin washed over from Afghanistan, Tajik youths had no idea how dangerous and addictive the drug was, especially when taken intravenously. "It was very prestigious, we saw drugs in movies," one of the rehab patients told me.

The explosion of heroin production in Afghanistan caught the weak government of this fractured nation completely unprepared. "We never imagined there would be heroin in Tajikistan," General Rustam Nazarov, who headed the country's Drug Control Agency, told me. "We weren't ready." The number of Tajik drug addicts seeking treatment has increased eightfold in ten years, according to government statistics. Intravenous drug use has touched off a serious AIDS problem. When I visited, Tajikistan had just negotiated its first-ever order of antiretroviral drugs. In a recent report, a UN agency concluded that "in the past ten years, Central Asia has experienced the highest increase in prevalence of drug abuse worldwide."

Smugglers find ever more creative ways to push the product toward the lucrative markets in Russia and Western Europe. A couple of years ago, Tajik investigators got a tip-off about a train car with heroin departing from Tajikistan to a Russian town in western Siberia. The train was eventually impounded in Russia. Hidden deep inside a shipment of onions in one car were seventy-four kilos of heroin packaged into round rubber containers made to resemble real onions. What's left of the contraband after the Russian journey pushes on to Western Europe. The Afghan heroin is starting to make inroads on the U.S. market too, though Latin America remains the primary source.

At the very end of the smuggling pipeline are addicts like Alexander Stumpf, the gaunt young German who was talking to a rock on top of a Kyrgyz mountain one morning a few years ago. Stumpf was so desperate to kick the habit that he traveled to Kyrgyzstan to subject himself to the strange methods of Jenishbek Nazarliyev, perhaps the most unconventional drug doctor in the world.

A blue baseball hat pulled tight over his broad face, Nazaraliyev cut an unusual figure in Kyrgyzstan, where he became a household name. For a time, he was a perennial presidential candidate, a life guru, restaurateur, and revolutionary who enmeshed himself in the opposition movement that toppled the Kyrgyz government. He owned two expensive restaurants in the capital; his rapid-fire political rants could be heard on the radio; he plastered Bishkek with ads for his eateries and for his clinic, along with antialcoholism posters stylized to resemble a child's handwriting: "Daddy, don't drink." It was an empire built, essentially, on heroin, rare for being benevolent.

Heroin casts an all-consuming spell on its victims. People who have tried it speak of it in sexual terms. One heroin-abuse doctor told me: "Imagine making love to a beautiful woman you are in love with. Then multiply that by a thousand. You'll get a rough idea." The chemical and psychological dependency is so strong that heroin addiction is notoriously hard to treat. In the medical field, and among his compatriots, Nazaraliyev inspired mixed feelings: respect for what he has achieved tinged with suspicions about the true effectiveness of his unconventional approach—which has grown ever more mystical over the years, as has the doctor himself. Nazaraliyev freely admitted that his mainstream colleagues have little regard for his witch-doctor methods and said that some Russian clerics even accused him of devil worship.

Nazaraliyev grew up in the southern Kyrgyz city of Osh, one of Central Asia's busiest trafficking hubs. Addicts who end up in his clinic probably used drugs that passed near his childhood home, hidden in backpacks or stashed inside vehicle tires. As a kid, Nazaraliyev absorbed the local lore about traditional healers who would dress in ceremonial garb, enter a trance, and attempt to cure a variety of maladies through strange hand motions and dances. He once saw his father, a trained psychiatrist, talk a woman out of a stress-induced paralysis in her legs—a scene that smacked of sorcery and magic. As a young man, Nazaraliyev occasionally smoked pot, plentiful in these parts, and once lost a friend to a heroin overdose. After getting his medical degree, he started working with alcoholics, and eventually opened his own clinic treating all kinds of substance abuse.

When I visited his clinic, five addicts squirmed in a deep medication-induced coma, designed to blunt the cravings. After going through other standard procedures, such as blood purification, the patients entered Nazaraliyev's surreal world. One signature treatment, known as stress therapy, featured the doctor with a scowl on his face and beads of sweat on his forehead waving his hands around the hypnotized, moaning patient. "Squeeze it all out, work harder!" Nazaraliyev said in a loud, guttural voice. He scurried around the room, clapped his hands, tapped his feet, and gave an occasional light slap to the shaking patient, who was leaning backward, head tilted, eyes closed, and arms outstretched. This technique was inspired by the traditional tribal healers of Kyrgyzstan's past.

A few years ago, Nazaraliyev, under the influence of Eastern philosophy, developed a fascination with rocks, which are imbued with mystical powers in traditional Chinese and Japanese beliefs. He scoured Kyrgyzstan's mountainous terrain in search of truly unusual stones featuring funky shapes, grooves, ridges, and colors, sometimes paying thousands of dollars for them. Small round stones littered his desk. "The legend has it that in the past people used them to fight the demons," he said. Medium-sized rocks were artfully arranged on combed beds of sand in his newly opened Japanese restaurant, called Sui-Seki, "The Stone in the Water." (Nazaraliyev also owned a steakhouse.) Gigantic rocks were assembled in an eerily scenic garden, complete with a stone-ornamented waterfall, outside of Bishkek where the doctor ran his second clinic.

It is there that Stumpf, the twenty-six-year-old heroin addict from Germany, was having conversations with a stone. Patients were free to pick a rock they liked from a pile of different shapes and sizes provided by Nazaraliyev. Stumpf had been shooting up for seven years, and traditional treatments in Europe inevitably led to remissions, so he turned to Nazaraliyev as "my last hope."

Most patients came here from the former Soviet Union, though addicts from Germany, the United States, and Israel—mostly post-Soviet immigrants—were frequent clients too. The Russian criminal underworld was also a steady source of patients, and Nazaraliyev had wide-ranging connections there. But he told me he preferred to hang out with yoga masters and that few of his closest friends were younger than seventy.

After his fellow patients burned their pretreatment clothes—slippers, T-shirts, pants—in a large campfire to symbolize a break with their drug-ridden past, Stumpf bounded up a mountainside to a lonely yurt—the traditional tentlike dwelling of the Kyrgyz nomads. When I visited, Stumpf was getting ready to spend forty-eight hours there alone, observing the oath of silence and reflecting upon his life, one of Nazaraliyev's recent innovations.

"Do you know what the silence is for?" Andrei Dobrydnev, one of the clinic's doctors, asked Stumpf.

"So that I can think . . ." Stumpf answered, tentatively, after a brief pause. He sat on a carpet inside the yurt and leafed through a Bible. (A Koran was also on hand, as was a notepad with some crayons, but nothing else.)

"Yes, so that you can think about problems—and there will be a lot of problems when you return home," the doctor said.

An even more intense voluntary procedure required the patient to walk in solitude for two hundred miles carrying a rock. A car from the clinic would trail him at a distance. Even some of Nazaraliyev's closest colleagues—all trained doctors in fields including narcology, psychiatry, and anesthesiology—were initially bewildered by the bizarre rituals, though they say they eventually came to understand their "Chief," which is how Nazaraliyev is universally referred to by his employees. "What is this? Why do we need these rocks?" Erkin Kubatov, one of the center's senior physicians, asked the Chief when the stones were first incorporated into the treatment regimen.

Many of Nazaraliyev's patients were hard-core addicts, who heard about his clinic by word of mouth. Dmitrii Dyo had been injecting himself with a homemade brew of poppy seeds and aspirin boiled in an industrial solvent, developing an addiction so strong that he wouldn't even spare pocket change to buy a chocolate bar for his eight-year-old daughter. "I feel reborn," he said after a recent stress-therapy session.

A three-week course in his clinic cost about $5,000, a steep price tag that eventually made Nazaraliyev a rich man. After a while he was able to delegate much of the treatment to his employees, which gave him time to focus on other pursuits. He traveled around the world, learning about drug cultures and writing a book called *Fatal Red Poppies*. He planned to open two more restaurants. And then there was the elusive presidency of Kyrgyzstan.

I first met him during the Tulip Revolution, which began with a massive rally right in front of his clinic. The noise and commotion of protesters chanting below bothered some doctors and patients, who threatened to pack up and leave the hospital. "Of course, it was very difficult to work," recalled Dolon Zaripov, head of intensive therapy. Other employees feared that their boss's antigovernment plotting would spell the end of the clinic. Amid all of this, a group of drug addicts from Georgia, whose own revolution inspired the Kyrgyz opposition, somehow got hold of Georgia's revolutionary red and white flag, which they hung outside their window in solidarity with the Kyrgyz protesters chanting below.

Nazaraliyev sat inside with an automatic rifle and bulletproof vest, ready for battle. With a black marker, he had written feverish notes right on his office walls, and I couldn't suppress the thought that perhaps the doctor occasionally partook of some of the substances that brought people to his clinic. Seated in front of me, Nazaraliyev compared the entire country to a drug addict who needed to receive "shock therapy," which he was ready to administer. He never used his rifle. In a newspaper op-ed a few days later, he compared himself to another doctor turned revolutionary: Che Guevara.

Meanwhile, high up on the mountain, Stumpf finished his forty-eight-hour meditation and threw his rock into a mound of other stones cast earlier by other addicts. Then he flew back to Germany, hoping the Kyrgyz magic was going to last.

CHAPTER 3

Anatomy of a Massacre

*T*he site of the massacre lay just beyond the mountains, but getting there wouldn't be easy. The already narrow highway narrowed even more until it was blocked by a gaggle of cops bundled up against the late-night chill. One of them shone a flashlight into my taxi. This was Uzbekistan, a big Central Asian dictatorship with a key role in America's war in the neighboring Afghanistan. Out on the desolate road, I sat in the car squinting and grinning into the beam of light, trying to project a non-threatening demeanor to the cops, but probably managing nothing more than a demented wince. It was May 2005, and I was eager to get past the police checkpoint and reach Andijan, a town in the valley behind the mountains. All I knew at the time was that something very violent had happened there a few hours earlier. There was a prison break, a rally, and shooting.

The Uzbek regime quickly blamed radical Islamists. But it faulted them for a lot of things that went wrong in Uzbekistan, a convenient scapegoat in a country with an impoverished rural populace and a bizarre command economy largely unchanged since the Soviet days. Having pinned the blame for the Andijan bloodshed on Islamists, the Uzbek authorities blocked all major roads there to make sure no one could reach the town and figure out what really happened.

It was a sensitive moment. The United States and Germany both had military bases inside Uzbekistan to ferry troops and supplies to the war in Afghanistan, then in its fourth year and about to take a turn for the worse. The Uzbeks were allies of convenience, almost of necessity. The implicit compact was that in return for the Uzbek leaders' help, Washington wouldn't press them on awkward things like torture, stolen elections, and the jailing of political opponents. Now with word trickling out about the killings of civilians in Andijan, this compact was going to be hard to maintain.

Islam Karimov, Uzbekistan's only ruler since independence in 1991, wasn't going to take any chances with domestic disturbances. Barely two months earlier, President Akayev of Kyrgyzstan had been overthrown in the Tulip Revolution, an event that jolted his fellow Central Asian autocrats. A consummate strongman, Karimov disdained Akayev for his flirtation with civil society and thought he was too spineless to ward off his own doom. "I asked him once: 'Why aren't you pushing back, taking certain countermeasures?'" Karimov recalled. "His answer: 'I can't.' What can you say to that?"[1] Another neighbor, Tajikistan, had been torn asunder by a civil war and an Islamist insurgency. So as far as Karimov was concerned, he had no choice but to be ruthless.

Karimov followed in the well-established tradition of the despots who have ruled these arid lands long coveted by empires. In the nineteenth century, for instance, Russia's territorial crawl eastward was threatening to bump into Britain's colonies in India, with Central Asia literally caught in the middle. Emissaries from both empires used diplomacy, threats, and bribes to compete for the attention of Central Asia's kingpins. In one particularly bloody episode in 1842, the emir of Bukhara, part of modern-day Uzbekistan, threw two British envoys into a rat-infested dungeon and then had them publicly beheaded on the main square. Within decades, the Russians conquered Bukhara along with most of the rest of Central Asia, a dominion that would last until the breakup of the Soviet Union.

A veteran Soviet functionary, Karimov grew up in an orphanage in Samarkand, the ancient Silk Road town once ruled by the emirs of Bukhara. After an engineering stint at an aviation plant, Karimov climbed the pole of the Communist Party hierarchy and was in a perfect position to grab the reins of independent Uzbekistan. A survivor, he created a political system that would tolerate no challengers, in a marked contrast to Kyrgyzstan, where a physics professor was bragging about his Switzerland of the East.

One of Karimov's main preoccupations was the challenge of political Islam. Under Soviet rule, Uzbekistan was a fairly secular place, but independence helped unleash an Islamic awakening in the predominantly Muslim nation of 27 million people. In the late 1990s, the Islamic Movement of Uzbekistan, a militant group battle hardened in the civil war in Tajikistan, set its sights on toppling the government in Tashkent and allied itself with the Taliban regime in Kabul. By then, the Taliban had extended its reach into northern Afghanistan, all the way up to the river border with Uzbekistan—and it seemed that water wasn't going to stop the holy war. "We were getting reports that Taliban fighters were mooning our border guards," recalls Farkhad Tolipov, a political scientist who worked in Karimov's administration at the time. One morning in early 1999, six car bombs rocked downtown Tashkent just as Karimov was heading to work.

Furious, Karimov blamed the blasts on Islamists, although there are whispered rumors in Tashkent that the explosions were staged by Uzbek security services as a pretext for the purges that followed. Whatever the case, Islam Karimov wasted no time in declaring a holy war of his own. Never has a man worn his first name with such irony. Massive roundups of Muslims that began then continue to this day. A Western official in Tashkent told me, "The Uzbek approach is there can be no perception of weakness here: you grow your beard a little bit, pray a little too fervently, you are going to be in trouble. They whack these people, put them in prisons, and of course these are incubators for radicalism. This is a serious problem that they have. In this part of the world what's perceived as a recipe for survival is you have to look tough."

Karimov was chasing Islamist conspiracies, some real but many of them imagined, when 9/11 happened, and his own private war became conglomerated with the Global War on Terror. Just like President Akayev in Kyrgyzstan, Karimov allowed the Americans in. They occupied an old

Soviet air base near the Afghan border. The Germans were given use of another base.

Not only did the war in Afghanistan help legitimize Karimov's own domestic crackdowns, it also gave the savvy politician a strategic counterweight against the rising Russian influence in the region. In a way, Karimov was playing the same empire-juggling game his predecessor, the emir of Bukhara, had played a century and a half earlier.

An interesting subchapter here is the crusading approach taken by Craig Murray, Britain's ambassador to Uzbekistan between 2002 and 2005. While the West cultivated the Uzbek regime, Murray talked openly about torture and abuse. In one instance, he obtained photographs of an inmate's disfigured corpse delivered to his family for burial. He forwarded the photos to a Scottish pathology lab, which reported back that the body had likely been submerged in scalding water. This detail became forever etched into the human rights lore of Uzbekistan. When critics talk about "a regime that boils its opponents alive," as they frequently do today, they are referring to these photos. In the nineteenth century, the emir of Bukhara got rid of troublesome British envoys by cutting their heads off. But the current regime didn't need to do much because Murray self-destructed. A married father of two, he fell for a dancer in Tashkent as policy disagreements with his London bosses grew. The maverick ambassador fell into a depression and ended up on suicide watch. He was eventually fired. All of this is chronicled in his memoir, *Dirty Diplomacy: The Rough-and-Tumble Adventures of a Scotch-Drinking, Skirt-Chasing, Dictator-Busting and Thoroughly Unrepentant Ambassador Stuck on the Frontline of the War against Terror.*

And now, in May of 2005, Karimov's carefully constructed political edifice seemed to teeter in the ancient town of Andijan. At the police checkpoint on the way there, I did my best to pretend I was not a journalist. Journalists were the last people the Uzbeks wanted there. Nothing could be allowed to chip away at the official version of events that the Uzbek spin masters were busy packaging for global consumption: a terrorist revolt, swiftly dealt with. In the car, I hurriedly invented a grandmother, on whose well-being in Andijan I desperately needed to check.

The fiction of a worried grandson fell apart on the highway's shoulder, where the cops made me unpack my bags and quizzed me about my laptop and satellite phone as well as my passport stamps—all of which suggested, possibly, journalism. So I offered a bribe. I identified a friendly, middle-aged policeman and, when his buddies stepped away, I inquired about the possibility of using a toll road. The thing about bribes in the former Soviet Union is that you rarely offer one up front. Even those who are prepared to accept it—a disturbingly large chunk of officialdom—want to maintain a facade of decorum and plausible deniability.

"What do you mean, 'a toll road'?" he asked. But even before he finished the question, a half smile of comprehension crossed his lips. He offered me tea, stepped away, and got on the radio. A few minutes later he returned. "We are under strict orders not to let anyone through, I just can't help you." I picked up my belongings from the curbside and drove back to Tashkent. The city had been leveled in a 1966 earthquake and then rebuilt in a bland Soviet style of wide avenues and Lego-like clusters of apartment blocks.

Later that day, out of pure desperation, I decided to try something else. If I couldn't drive to Andijan, could I possibly fly there? Tashkent's main airline office was a cavernous hall filled with chaotic throngs of people mobbing a couple of open ticket windows. The concept of a line was just that, a concept. Behind those windows, menacing-looking matrons wielded enormous power over travel. After some jostling and pushing, I succeeded in presenting myself to one such matron. "No tickets" was her curt reply when I told her of my proposed destination.

"But I really need to get there and I can pay double," I said. The matron—short black hair, fifties, lots of makeup—shot me an evaluating look, jotted down a phone number on a piece of paper, and told me to call during her lunch break.

We met on a plaza outside of the ticket office. I came prepared with several thick bricks of bills. Years of inflation kept adding zeros to the Uzbek currency, but the government never bothered to redenominate the som. So even small purchases, like cigarettes or bread, required multiple bills. Anything bigger required wads of soms held together by thin rubber bands. The Uzbeks are great experts at carrying, counting, and hiding voluminous stacks of bills. Fingers twirling, lips moving silently, they count their cash with robotic speed and dexterity, impervious to distraction. They can even participate in conversation by nodding or shaking their heads, or mumbling, without tripping up. But whenever I tried to count money, no matter how hard I concentrated, I always lost count and had to start all over again.

The airline woman sold me a ticket to fly to Ferghana, a town very close to Andijan. Ferghana was on the other side of the dreaded police checkpoints guarding the mountain pass. So the state-owned airline was going to carry me over the state-imposed blockade of Andijan. In a police state, incompetence is a virtue. Once in Ferghana, I found a local driver who took me to Andijan using unpaved back roads where we didn't encounter any more trouble.

Andijan is best known as the birthplace of Zahirrudin Babur, a descendant of Genghis Khan and the progenitor of the Mughal dynasty that ruled the Indian subcontinent for centuries. A restless conqueror, Babur picked fights all over Central Asia and Afghanistan before setting his sights on India and its riches. For a man who died at forty-seven, Babur accomplished a lot. But then he had an early start. His memoir begins like this: "In the month of Ramadan in the year 899, in the province of Ferghana, in my 12th year I became king." Even after his conquests took him far away from Andijan, Babur retained a special fondness for his birthplace. "No pears are better than those from Andijan," he wrote. Local wildlife was memorable too. "The pheasants get extremely fat, and it is said that not even four people can finish a stew made from just one."[2]

For centuries, the rolling hills and vistas of the Ferghana Valley, where Andijan is located, have seen a tragic succession of invasions, revolts, and heavy-handed government policies. Chinese, Turkic, and Mongol armies took turns invading the valley; the Arabs brought here the religion of Islam. In the late nineteenth century, the Russians conquered much of Central Asia. They soon faced revolts in several towns including Andijan, where two dozen Russian soldiers were killed by rebels, prompting a violent Russian crackdown. Later, Soviet dictator Joseph Stalin—known for resettling entire peoples to suppress dissent and national consciousness—

sliced up the Ferghana Valley in a fit of creative mapmaking, dividing clans and ethnic groups among three newly created Soviet republics: Uzbekistan, Kyrgyzstan, and Tajikistan.

In the early evening when I arrived in Andijan, its streets were quiet and empty of people. I stopped by a teashop for a bowl of green tea. It was a typical Uzbek place, raised platforms covered with carpets, trees planted between them. The seating arrangement always presented problems. After you kicked off your shoes and climbed up, you had to fight the temptation to take a nap. If lunch was involved, it wasn't a fight I could easily win. Out on the sidewalk, I struck up a conversation with a man whose eyes darted left and right as if he wanted to make sure no one saw him talking. "Everything is quiet, nothing really happened here, it's all exaggerated," he stammered and hurried away. I walked toward Babur Square, Andijan's central plaza, but the whole downtown area was blocked off. From a very big poster, Uzbekistan's president smiled and waved his hand at several military trucks and an armored personnel carrier parked across the street.

Trouble in Andijan had started a few months earlier when the government rounded up twenty-three prominent local businessmen and charged them with an Islamist conspiracy. In the 1990s, after Uzbekistan emerged as an independent state from the ruins of the Soviet Union, the country began to reconnect with its Muslim faith, long suppressed by the Communists. Islamist diehards also popped up on the scene and, inspired by the Taliban's success in Afghanistan, agitated for the creation of an Islamic state in Uzbekistan. The country's secular dictator took no chances and cracked down. Over the years, his targets grew ever more esoteric, encompassing anything that carried a faint whiff of organized religion.

The twenty-three Andijan entrepreneurs never hid their Muslim faith, but what set them apart was their business acumen. Glossy brochures for their network of companies featured shoes, furniture, suits, candy, bread, and even shovels and hinges. The businessmen were respected in the city because they provided jobs and paid decent wages. Their companies spawned subcontractors, suppliers, and dealers, further deepening their economic power. "They were good businessmen, they never cheated anyone, they did charity work, they paid their taxes," said Muzafar Itzhakov, an Andijan human-rights activist. "They gave employment to thousands of people here, and in our economic crisis not everyone can do this."

The Andijan 23 were accused of belonging to an obscure and heretofore unknown Islamist group inspired by a treatise called *Path to Faith*, which prosecutors said showed their violent intentions. "It's not the Rotary Club of Andijan," an American supporter of the Uzbek regime would say later.[3] In the pamphlet, the alleged author, then already serving a seventeen-year jail sentence, offered his convoluted musings on personal betterment and Islam, devoid of any political appeals. I'd found a copy on the Internet and printed it out before coming to Uzbekistan. It nearly put me to sleep when I read it in my hotel room in Tashkent. When I finally finished it, I tore it up and flushed it down the toilet. In Uzbekistan, you don't want the cops to find *Path to Faith* in your bag. It might ruin your day.

None of the charges against the 23 detailed any specific plot but rather accused them of undermining the constitutional order—a fuzzy line that sent a lot of people to prison in Uzbekistan, in the same way the "enemy of the people" tag condemned thousands in Stalin's Soviet Union. If the jailed Andijan group wasn't the Rotary Club, it wasn't al-Qaeda either. Having jailed the 23, the government went after their business associates and nabbed thirteen more people, including Bahtiyor Muhtarov, who worked as a confectionary wholesaler at a large Andijan bazaar. The hounding of the businessmen became a hot issue within Uzbekistan's tiny but surprisingly feisty circle of human-rights defenders.

While the businessmen awaited trial, their relatives, friends, and supporters held vigils in front of the courthouse. And at some point desperation began to set in. Their businesses crumbled and became worthless. The extremism charges could easily earn them fifteen years in jail, and torture is a well-documented feature of Uzbek jails. There was little doubt that the businessmen would be found guilty—Uzbek courts generally do not acquit people. So a plan was hatched to free them by force.

The merchants were held in a high-security prison perched behind an incongruously pink wall on the edge of Andijan. On May 12, a group of men broke into a garrison building in town, captured weapons, and moved swiftly toward the prison. Some of the attackers were relatives and friends of the jailed businessmen. You could look at it as Uzbekistan's own version of France's Bastille Day, when angry mobs stormed the infamous Paris jail, a symbol of government oppression. Or you could look at it as a desperado escapade by armed thugs. Something similar was happening throughout the country: government repression was pushing people to the brink, and even those who weren't militant were becoming militant. This was the nasty self-fulfilling prophecy of Uzbekistan's campaign against assorted enemies of the state.

Inside the prison on a warm May evening, Muhtarov, the jailed confectionary wholesaler, was getting ready for a nap on his narrow bunk when his cellmates told him the jail seemed to be under attack. "Let me rest, don't tell me fairy tales," Muhtarov snapped back.

Soon after, cell doors were blasted off their hinges, and hundreds of sleepy inmates shuffled this way and that, unsure of where to go. By the time I arrived in Andijan, Muhtarov was a fugitive from Uzbek justice, lurking somewhere in the no-man's-land of the Ferghana Valley's confluence of borders. Our paths never crossed at the time. I spoke to him years later when I began to interview Andijan refugees. His account helped round out the picture of those bloody, chaotic days of May 2005.

As Muhtarov gave up on the nap idea in his cell, his fellow inmates ran toward the exits. Not everyone was eager to be liberated. Escaping in an armed jailbreak means putting yourself permanently outside the law, and some inmates would rather serve out their sentences and leave the prison the conventional way. Two days after the prison break, I sat in my hotel's dingy cafeteria nursing a warm, sour beer for lack of other recreational opportunities. I was the only customer, so it was easy to strike up a conversation with one of the women behind the counter. Her nephew, an inmate in Andijan's prison, had rashly escaped in the melee, and was now pondering how to negotiate a return to jail to complete the few months left on his robbery sentence. In a cult Soviet comedy *Gentlemen of Fortune*, there's a scene of four inmates escaping from prison inside a cement truck. Later, when three of them dry their solidified clothes by the fire, they ask the fourth why he'd followed them into the cement tank despite having only months left till legal freedom. The man deadpans: "Everyone ran, so I ran too."

Outside the Andijan prison, freed inmates wearing drab government-issue overalls and slippers soon scurried across the neighboring streets, alarming local residents. Government forces sprayed an old car with gunfire, on suspicion it was carrying weapons to the militants inside. When I visited, the car was still there, riddled with holes. It was like a bizarre modern-art installation: a bright yellow colander of a car sitting on flat tires by the pink prison wall. Muhtarov, the freed wholesaler, later told me that he'd shuffled off in search of his wife and six kids. The gunmen took a few local officials hostage and moved toward Babur Square for an impromptu rally. With the prison break complete, the events of the day entered a crucial second phase. Thousands of local residents who had nothing to do with the inmates or the gunmen flocked to the central square. An old loudspeaker went around the crowd, and people took turns shouting into it. They talked about the dismal economy, about oppressive government policies, about everything, it seems, except Islamism. Theirs were the same types of complaints that I'd heard in my earlier travels in Uzbekistan—from dispossessed farmers, from traders, from relatives of prisoners.

Rumors rippled through the crowd that high-ranking Uzbek officials, perhaps even the president himself, were on their way to address the rally and somehow make things better.[4] Such was the enduring appeal of the myth of the good czar. Through centuries of misrule and repression, people in the Russian and then the Soviet empire held out hope that all the abuse was orchestrated by midlevel bureaucrats while the man at the top was kept in the dark. If only you could bypass the evil entourage and tell the czar directly what horrible injustices were being visited upon his subjects, he would open his eyes in shock, punish the abusers, and make things right. You read accounts of victims of Stalin's purges dragged into dungeons and forced by their interrogators to sign wholly fabricated admissions of guilt before getting shot like dogs, and the victims, incredulous to the last, say things like, "Does Comrade Stalin know about this?" or "It's all a mistake, you must tell Comrade Stalin." The myth of the good czar is a coping mechanism, a refusal to believe that the political system is really as rotten from the top as it seems. In Andijan that day, as protesters were expecting the Uzbek president to alight on the square and talk to them, security forces quietly cut off all retreats and prepared to turn the square into a kill zone.

On the other side of town, in a quaint old quarter of low-slung adobe houses with airy courtyards, Yogdorbek Mamajonov was having a great day. He'd just turned sixteen, and his mother, Rahima, was planning to throw a dinner party for family and friends that weekend. At around 5:00 p.m., Rahima realized she didn't have enough meat for the party. Yogdorbek volunteered to go buy more, picked up a friend, and the two wandered off down a maze of winding alleys. Many others that evening set off on similarly mundane journeys—to buy bread, to paint a house, or to go home from work—only to be sucked into the widening vortex of events on Babur Square.

Back in the chaos of the square, Muhtarov, the freed confectionary wholesaler, succeeded in finding his wife, who came to look for him when she heard of the jailbreak. After months of captivity, Muhtarov was anxious to get home to see their six kids. But it was hard to find an escape hatch from the square. Military vehicles converged on the place, and their occupants began taking potshots at the crowd of protesters. "A military vehicle rolled in from the direction of the theater [a few blocks away], fired off a few random rounds, and drove away," Muhtarov recalled. "Then it rolled back in and did the same thing." As the intensity of the shooting increased, people around him started dropping dead. Many had come to the square out of sheer curiosity. "All the kids wanted to see what was happening, you know how kids are," a relative of a seventeen-year-old boy named Sardarbek Hasanov told me. The teenager died of a bullet wound to the head.

Muhtarov and other men encircled the women in the crowd within a human shield. Huddling in that formation, all unarmed, they moved down one of the main streets leading from the square. Heavy rain was falling on Andijan. Muhtarov's huddle reached the Cholpon movie theater, in front of which sat several armored personnel carriers. Their machine guns rattled with gunfire. Muhtarov's brother-in-law was by his side, having come to the square to help his sister look for Muhtarov. "A bullet hit him in the head and he died right away; we moved him to the side of the road," Muhtarov recalled.

One of the first people I met in Andijan was Muzafar Itzhakov, a local human-rights activist with an office not far from the notorious prison. Human-rights defenders are a species peculiar to dictatorships, where all the usual animals of a civil society have been exterminated. In a way, these defenders are a mutant species that has soaked up the vestigial DNA from all those extinct animals. Human-rights defenders are government watchdogs, investigative journalists, pundits, legal advocates, charity workers, and shrinks all wrapped into one. Though they come in many shapes, sizes, and ideological stripes, they have one common quality: they are all insanely brave. Itzhakov hit the streets in the hours after the prison break to collect eyewitness testimony. Security forces, he told me, kept firing indiscriminately as people, alone and in groups similar to Muhtarov's, dispersed from the square, or were unlucky enough to be passing through the neighborhood. One such group contained some gunmen, but also their hostages and many innocent civilians. "An armored personnel carrier came up and started shooting without warning at the hostages, at onlookers, at women and children," Itzhakov said. "There was no return fire." By that point it was already dark, and soldiers pursued the protesters on foot.

In one case Itzhakov was able to document, a fleeing man took cover behind an outdoor clay oven used to bake *samsa,* a delicious Uzbek layered pastry. He was already wounded in the leg. Soldiers cornered him there and shouted, "Get up!" The man rose slowly, yelling, "I'm unarmed and I'm wounded." When his head cleared the top of the oven, the soldiers shot and killed him. In fact, Itzhakov continued, "many people had bullet holes in the back of their heads, like a control shot." He was using Russian gangland slang for a hit man's way of ascertaining that his mark is definitely dead. But I didn't have to take his word for it, he said, and he gave me a couple of victims' addresses to check out.

As my taxi rolled into the maze of streets in old town Andijan, I was worried it would be difficult to find their homes. I was wrong. In an old Uzbek mourning custom, relatives throw an ornate carpet over a bench

A funeral in Andijan. (Yola Monakhov, courtesy of Sasha Wolf Gallery)

in front of their house and just sit there dazed, receiving condolences. At first, I used Itzhakov's list of addresses, but soon enough I realized I didn't need it. After I'd visited one grieving family, all I had to do was just look around for other mourning benches. Those benches were everywhere. It would have been harder to find families who *weren't* grieving or didn't have a neighbor who was. As I walked through the streets, I began to understand the true extent of the massacre. It was also then that I recalled, in one of those irrelevant flicks of memory, the Hollywood-worthy date of the bloodbath. It took place on Friday the 13th.

When I met her, Rahima Mamajonova was sitting on her mourning bench. On her lap she held an open ninth-grade yearbook of her son Yogdorbek, who'd gone missing on an errand to buy meat for his birthday dinner. Wearing a dress shirt and tie, Yogdorbek looked stern and very, very young in his photo. Rahima recounted the search for her son. Early on Saturday morning, after a sleepless night, she ventured into town, which by then really did look like a gory set of a slasher movie. "There were all these bodies piled up on the side of the road. I saw more than a hundred in one spot, covered with sheets. I pulled the sheet from every single one to try to find my child." Mamajonova paused to collect herself. "Some bodies had guts, brains spilling out. There was a corpse clutching a loaf of bread, and another lying on top of a bicycle." But Yogdorbek wasn't among them. Rahima and her older son Kadyrjon visited the local hospital—no Yogdorbek there either—and then went to the town's main morgue. Soldiers were guarding the entrance, and they wouldn't let Rahima in. She cried. So Kadyrjon went inside instead. There were so many bodies in there that workers had to stack the overflow in the courtyard. Kadyrjon estimated the number at about seven hundred. He eventually found his younger brother—he had five bullet holes in his body. The friend who had accompanied Yogdorbek on the meat-buying errand was dead too.

Outside, a call to prayer, sonorous and plaintive, rang out across a stunned neighborhood. I walked for a while to clear my head, and then went into the house of Tulkun Ergashev. That Friday, Tulkun was later than usual in returning home from work. His younger brother Jaboron, a car mechanic, had already come home and was worried about Tulkun. He could hear distant bursts of gunfire. As the evening progressed and the gunfire intensified, Jaboron couldn't handle the inaction and went looking for Tulkun. An hour later, Tulkun finally got home—the commotion downtown had forced him to take a detour. But Jaboron never returned. "For me, that's the heaviest thing—knowing that he died looking for me," Tulkun told me. He found Jaboron's body the next day. He had six gunshot wounds, including one to the back of his head. Jaboron didn't die in a single burst of gunfire but appeared to have been finished off after he was already wounded. He'd had time to tie a rag around a bullet wound in his leg. As I spoke with Tulkun, Jaboron's six-year-old son played nearby. He waved a toy gun, pretending to shoot.

Down the street from Tulkun's house, Fasadjon Khudorberdiev stared blankly into the distance from his own mourning bench. At 4:00 p.m. that Friday, his thirty-three-year-old son Kasim packed his toolkit and left home on a bicycle to help paint a friend's house. Fasadjon found his body on the street the next day. "He had one bullet in the leg, another in the neck," Fasadjon said. There were many others around him. "The whole street was splattered with brains and blood."

Kids play in front of a bullet-riddled wall in Andijan.
(Yola Monakhov, courtesy of Sasha Wolf Gallery)

Exactly how many people were killed that night may never be known. The Uzbek government insisted on a laughably low figure that mostly included militants, blocking all suggestions of an independent inquiry. Gulbahor Turayeva, a pathologist who ran a local NGO, told me she saw about five hundred bodies in a local schoolyard. "Many were in terrible condition, with gunshots to the head, wounds in the legs, multiple wounds all over," she said. "There were not stains, there were pools of blood." Several relatives of victims showed me death certificates issued by the local morgue. They were all numbered—one said 314, another 334. But there was no way to tell whether those figures represented the tally of those who were killed on May 13 or referred to a more general count of deaths in Andijan, perhaps since the beginning of the year. A lot of people in Andijan were also convinced that the government dumped many victims in secret mass graves. But no evidence has emerged to back up those rumors. Still, from the anecdotal evidence collected on the ground, it is reasonable to assume that several hundred people lost their lives, virtually none of them involved in any way in the prison break.

As I read through my notes in my rundown hotel, I wondered how much longer I'd be able to escape government scrutiny. Andijan, I was told, swarmed with plainclothes security men tasked with ferreting out journalists, among other unsavory elements. A few local ones had been escorted out of Andijan already. Within days of the massacre, the Uzbek government organized a tightly controlled propaganda tour of the city for a small group of foreign journalists and diplomats. They were driven around like schoolchildren on a daytrip, not allowed to talk to anyone except their official guides. When I snuck into Andijan and checked into my hotel, I asked the woman at the reception desk not to report me to the local police precinct—the hotel was required to do so by law for all of its guests. The receptionist, a middle-aged Russian woman, took pity on me and told me she'd give me twenty-four hours before giving the photocopy of my passport to the police. This small act of kindness probably helped me avoid detection and enabled me to interview people.

Before I left Andijan, I went to see another human-rights defender, Saidjahon Zainabitdinov. He had a round face and almond-shaped eyes whose outer corners pointed sharply downward, giving him a perpetually melancholic expression. Saidjahon met me in his spacious front yard, and we sat down at a wooden table shaded by trees. I wanted to know more about the motivations and identities of the gunmen who stormed the prison and provoked the government into unleashing the massacre. As chairman of a small NGO called Appeal, Saidjahon had followed the case of the twenty-three arrested merchants from the very beginning, studied whatever evidence he could get his hands on, and met a few of their relatives, friends, and employees at the numerous rallies in front of the courthouse.

One of the men he met there was Sharavjon Shakirov, who had two brothers among the twenty-three jailed merchants. In the photo Saidjahon showed me, Shakirov looked to be in his midthirties and had pointy ears. He worked in a textile factory belonging to his brothers. Shakirov was a practicing Muslim—most people in the Ferghana Valley are—and he was also no Boy Scout. In 1998, he was accused of illicit storage of ordnance, though Saidjahon said the case appeared fabricated, which wouldn't be unusual in Uzbekistan. As he spoke, Saidjahon suddenly tugged at the white button-down short-sleeved shirt he was wearing: "He gave me this shirt as a gift." In the weeks leading up to the jailbreak, Shakirov and his friends and coworkers were getting restless and desperate. "If they'd waited just a little longer maybe the merchants would have been acquitted," Saidjahon said. "But then again, I doubt the government would have made any concessions in this case." Saidjahon still seemed stunned that Shakirov and his buddies pulled off the armed raid. "I never thought they were capable of something like this," he said. At some point on May 13, Sharavjon called him on his cell phone. In a very brief conversation, Shakirov asked him to come to the rally on the square. "We'd be offended if you didn't." But Saidjahon didn't go. Though he didn't sugarcoat or justify what the gunmen did that night, he tried to understand their actions. The hostages they took, about twenty, were representatives, in their eyes, of the state apparatus of repression—judges, prosecutors, taxmen, intelligence men. "They just couldn't take it anymore; they snapped."

The government's subsequent slaughter of Andijan residents made sense in the cold logic of a dictatorship. If you are a dictator and want to remain in power, you eventually have to go all the way because there's nothing more ridiculous than being a half-ass dictator. You piss off a lot of people, and make them want to get rid of you. Yet, as a half-ass despot, you don't kill, jail, or scare enough people to make others think twice about getting rid of you. So, eventually, you fall. At the time of Andijan, this wasn't a hypothetical risk for the longtime ruler of Uzbekistan. In neighboring Kyrgyzstan (just thirty miles south of Andijan), a half-ass dictator had just been overthrown and chased out of the country in a popular uprising. The Uzbek leader decided not to show any weakness in the face of a challenge.

As news of Andijan reached Washington, U.S. officials faced a dilemma. Should they speak out against the atrocities and jeopardize the American military base in Uzbekistan or keep quiet to safeguard American strategic interests? Doves within the administration argued that Washington had no choice but to condemn the massacre, that human rights had to trump security considerations. Hawks viewed that approach as naïve and dangerous. "If we took such a good-and-evil view of the world, we wouldn't be able to count on support from any non-democratic country," Donald Rumsfeld, the defense secretary at the time, recalls in his memoir.[5] The doves won the debate. Washington publicly rebuked the Uzbek regime, and Karimov soon retaliated by evicting the Americans from the base. But as we'll see later in this book, Washington would soon pursue a rapprochement with Tashkent, guided by the same unsentimental thinking articulated by Rumsfeld.

Early on Saturday morning after the bloodbath, Saidjahon Zainabitdinov walked the streets of Andijan collecting bullet casings. In his courtyard, he poured the casings out of a metal tin onto the wooden table between us. They clanked and tumbled over each other. They were all about five inches long. I picked one up and traced its base in my notebook with a pen. It was larger than a quarter. The use of machine guns was consistent with the multiple bullet wounds of many victims. On his morning walk, Saidjahon also collected loose slippers and sandals. They were now piled up in a basket, some with caked brownish bloodstains. Saidjahon walked me to his metal gate and told me to be careful because Andijan was full of plainclothes security operatives. A few days later, Saidjahon was arrested and sentenced to seven years in prison for slander and extremism.

Leaving Andijan, I headed to the small town of Kara Suu (Black Water), right on the border with Kyrgyzstan in the heart of the Ferghana Valley. There were chaotic reports that people there had chased out the police and all other local officials, in effect setting up the Free Republic of Kara Suu, though of course they didn't use that name.

Kara Suu was a straight shot down the main road from Andijan. But it couldn't be that easy. At a highway checkpoint, heavily armed and helmeted cops pulled me and my Uzbek colleague out of the car, then searched and interrogated us. Uncertain of what to do with us, they drove us to their headquarters in a police precinct a few miles away. There, we were presented to a pudgy and angry colonel, whose belly spilled over the belt of his green pants. Since it was pointless to lie, I told him the truth about who I was and where I was going. "Where's your temporary registration?" he yelled. All visitors to Uzbekistan needed to be registered somewhere, usually a hotel, which then issued little scraps of paper as evidence. I checked my pockets and fished out a crumpled square with the stamp "Tashkent Palace" on it. It was the place where I had stayed for a night a couple of days earlier. The colonel examined it and noted it was a few days out of date. "I strongly suggest that you go back to Tashkent, because you can't go to Kara Suu."

The cops drove us back to our car. A crane was lowering a concrete bar onto the highway. The government was sealing off the Free Republic of Kara Suu. We decided to take another road to Kara Suu—it would be a detour, but perhaps there would be no checkpoints there. The same thing happened again: armed cops, a thorough search, and a trip to headquarters. It turned out to be the same headquarters. And the same colonel strode out to meet us, angrier and pudgier than an hour ago. He smoked and smirked and couldn't believe how stupid we were. He yelled and threatened to throw us in the brig in the back of his precinct. Eventually, the colonel let us go, though he made it clear in language amply salted with swear words that he didn't want to see us again.

Back in the car, I looked at the map of the Ferghana Valley. Kara Suu straddled the border between Uzbekistan and Kyrgyzstan. So another way to get to Black Water town would be to cross the border into Kyrgyzstan about twenty miles from the spot where I now was, then approach Kara Suu from the Kyrgyz side and cross into Uzbekistan again. It was a convoluted plan, but why not give it a shot?

The fundamental problem with the plan was that the border crossing I was going to use was closed. After Andijan, hundreds of refugees tried to flee to Kyrgyzstan, so the Uzbek government shuttered the crossing. Once again, I benefited from the kindness of strangers. An Uzbek border guard agreed to let me through, in clear violation of his orders. I didn't tell him about my plan to reenter Uzbekistan. Two hours later I approached Kara Suu from the Kyrgyz side. Uzbekistan lay right across the river.

Back in the Soviet days, the Kyrgyz and Uzbek parts of Kara Suu were a single town with a river running through it. With independence from the Soviet Union in 1991, Kyrgyzstan and Uzbekistan were left with an absurdly jagged border, a legacy of Stalin's artificial divisions. In 2001, the countries punished each other's citizens with visa requirements.

Then, Uzbek authorities decided to tear asunder the two parts of Kara Suu in a more physical away. They destroyed the Kara Suu bridge and closed the border crossing. That decision deprived the residents on the Uzbek side of an easy way to see relatives in Kyrgyzstan and of a chance to earn money at a big outdoor bazaar in Kyrgyz Kara Suu. Many used to go there to buy goods from clothes to flour and then resell them back in Uzbekistan, where customs duties made similar merchandise far more expensive. Used to adversity, the Uzbeks found creative ways of dealing with the problem of the destroyed bridge. They strung thick ropes across the river and then used pulleys and baskets to haul cisterns of fuel and clothes, and sometimes themselves.

About twenty-four hours after the Andijan massacre, Kara Suu erupted in its own uprising. It was as if the antigovernment bug was contagious. More than a thousand people gathered on the main square to demand the reopening of the bridge. The crowd then burned a local police precinct and several other government buildings. Police and border guards fled. There were no reported casualties.

Having evicted the government, Kara Suu residents got down to business. As I stood on the Kyrgyz side of the river, I saw workmen welding thick metal sheets onto the skeleton of the old bridge. Once there were enough sheets to form an unbroken path across the river, people began to cross the bridge, first cautiously, as if expecting to be yelled at to stop, then more confidently. In the space of one hour, four boys wearing skullcaps crossed the bridge back and forth at least five times, carting heavy sacks of flour to the Uzbek side. "Now, these people have a chance to earn money, to feed their families," said Bakyt, a Kyrgyz border guard watching over the pedestrian traffic. There were no guards on the Uzbek side, so I walked back into Uzbekistan.

Life without government proceeded at a leisurely pace. Someone was cutting down an old tree; a group of old men drank tea at an outdoor cafe; people shopped for meat and vegetables at the riverside market. There were no armed people on the streets, no rallies, and no police. Even though the government blamed Islamists for the unrest here, just as it did in Andijan, there was little evidence of that on the ground. "Our only wish was for this bridge to be reopened," Abubakir Atahonov, who earned his living as a porter, told me. It was a five-minute walk with the bridge, a twenty-mile drive without it. You could see why the bridge mattered so much to him.

I made my way to the central square and went into a small café for some green tea. Three employees lounged around there, and we started to talk. One of them, a pudgy, chatty guy in his late forties, introduced himself as Odiljon. Without the government, "it's been so easy to live, so easy to breathe," he said. When the riots began, "the cops just ran away, like rabbits from wolves. When they come back, it will be a complete *pizdets.*" The Russian swearword, derived from a female body part, packs an emotional punch best expressed in English with words like *disaster, collapse,* and *tragedy.* Yet there's also a devil-may-care subtext to it, a tone of resignation, or mockery, and sometimes even of humor. "How great and powerful is the Russian language," novelist Ivan Turgenev famously wrote. Odiljon kept going: "When the cops or tax people come to this café, they act like kings. Once the cops ordered *plov* [a Central Asian staple of rice and lamb] for about $70; they ate and left without paying, so we had to cover it from our own pockets." During the rioting, he said, "people talked about Andijan; we heard that a lot of innocent people died there, maybe the military killed them."

At that point in the conversation, the three men asked me if I'd like to drink some vodka with them. It was only lunchtime, it was hot outside, I was working, they were complete strangers, and I had just entered a police state illegally. Yet none of these very solid reasons prevented me from accepting the invitation. Later I told myself I did it to maintain the camaraderie and keep the conversation flowing. Warm vodka was poured. We drank, and then we drank again because these things never stop with one shot. It was then that I noticed two men approach the café. Something in their faces spelled trouble. More specifically, it spelled SNB, the Uzbek National Security Service. I got up, a little surprised by how tipsy I was (I hadn't eaten lunch), and all of us stepped outside. One of the two men, wearing a grotesquely bad brown suit, asked to see my passport. I demurred and said I was just visiting. "Are you aware that you are breaking Uzbekistan law by being here?" he asked. My drinking buddies were on my side. Odiljon whispered to me to run while he launched into a long, mildly drunk speech in Uzbek, complete with backslapping and laughter.

I took a few steps back, and then started walking fast toward the bridge. It was about a mile away. The brown suit yelled at me to stop. So I took off running. I didn't look back until I reached the bridge, so I don't even know if he pursued me. It was the fastest and drunkest mile I'd ever run. Workmen had finished welding the bridge, and the Kyrgyz border guards let me back into Kyrgyzstan. The next day, Uzbek special forces and the military took control of Kara Suu. The free republic was no more. The feared *pizdets* had arrived.

But the Andijan saga wasn't over yet. Hundreds of refugees from the massacre walked all night toward the border with Kyrgyzstan. Bahtiyor Muhtarov, the wholesaler freed in the jailbreak, was among them. His wife was with him. But their six children remained in Andijan—when she left to look for her husband, she never intended to be away for more than a couple of hours. On a borrowed cell phone, the Muhtarovs called a relative to ask him to look after the children because now it didn't look like they'd be back anytime soon.

Crossing into Kyrgyzstan, Muhtarov's wife landed in a squalid tent camp erected to hold more than 400 Andijan refugees. Muhtarov and about thirty other men involved in the prison break were singled out for extra scrutiny and put in jail while the Kyrgyz investigated their past. Muhtarov's wife and the other low-risk refugees were soon herded onto a UN plane chartered to take them to Romania for further international resettlement. For hours, the plane sat on the tarmac at the Manas airport, while Kyrgyz officials weighed whether to allow the other 30 men to board the aircraft too.

Uzbek authorities put enormous pressure on the fledgling Kyrgyz government to extradite those thirty, including Muhtarov, to Uzbekistan, where they would inevitably be convicted as terrorists and spend the rest of their lives behind bars. Whether to send them to Western exile or to Uzbek hell was largely up to Azimbek Beknazarov, the bulldozer of the revolution, who had just been catapulted to the post of prosecutor general in the new Kyrgyz government. Beknazarov was sympathetic to the Uzbek demands. "The UN didn't really coordinate with us, they just sent the plane. Just because the plane is there doesn't mean we have to let everyone out," he told me.

While the plane sat at the gate, the U.S. envoy to Kyrgyzstan went to see Beknazarov to plead with him to let the refugees go. The West, having broken off ties with the Uzbek strongman, now threw its weight behind the Andijan refugees, lobbying heavily for their freedom. Finally, Beknazarov relented and allowed half of the thirty men to board the UN plane. Around 5.30 a.m., it took off for Romania. "My friend, I did it for you," Beknazarov later jokingly told the U.S. envoy.[6] But Muhtarov wasn't among the lucky half. He lingered in jail for another two months until he and a dozen remaining inmates were hustled to the waiting room of the Manas airport. There was a plan afoot to fly them out to England, but Muhtarov wasn't quite sure whether his final destination would be London or Tashkent. "We had to check every single one of them," Beknazarov later recalled. Under armed guard, Muhtarov and his buddies took frequent trips to the airport bathroom where they chain-smoked to soothe their jangling nerves. Finally word came down from on high: London it was.

In Europe, Muhtarov, with all of $50 to his name, rejoined his wife, who had flown out earlier with other low-risk refugees. In the international resettlement crapshoot, the Muhtarovs drew Finland, a placid Nordic land that was to be their new home. Muhtarov now runs a support group for Andijan refugees. It's a tight-knit community scattered across Western Europe and America. There's a pocket of Andijan farmers outside Phoenix, Arizona.

The escape from Uzbekistan was bittersweet. The Muhtarovs' six children—then aged three to seventeen, five boys and a girl—were stuck in Andijan, waiting for their parents. A network of friends and relatives eventually began to look after them. The Muhtarovs filed family-reunification papers, but the Uzbek authorities wouldn't let the kids out, at one point insisting that the eldest son serve in the conscript Uzbek military first. When the son protested that he was flat-footed and medically exempt from service, authorities ordered a new barrage of tests to examine his feet in greater detail. Years went by, and other bureaucratic hurdles to reunification followed. The kids lingered in Andijan. Meanwhile, in Finland, the Muhtarovs had a baby daughter and appeared to be steeling themselves for a very long, if not permanent, separation from their Andijan children.

There were some wrenching decisions. In Andijan, a friend's wife fell ill and couldn't have more children. The couple already had a daughter, but they wanted a son too. The Muhtarovs had been blessed with no fewer than five sons, all of them technically orphans now living on the beneficence of relatives and earning spare change serving tea at the cattle market. So it seemed only natural that the friend asked if he could adopt one of Muhtarov's sons. After some deliberation, the Muhtarovs agreed. What emotions went into that decision, I couldn't quite tell. "Of course it was difficult, but we did it for a friend" is all Muhtarov would say on the matter.

CHAPTER 4 *The Dark Years in Kyrgyzstan*

The Rise and Fall of the Gray Cardinal

*I*t was well past midnight when a luxury Lexus SUV joined the line of cars waiting to cross the border from Kazakhstan into Kyrgyzstan. Sheltered under blue archways, the Korday border checkpoint sits next to a bridge over a meandering river called Chu. At any hour of day or night, scores of cars, trucks, minibuses, and pedestrians laden with heavy bags clog the approaches to the border crossing between the two Central Asian countries. Bishkek, Kyrgyzstan's placid capital, and Almaty, Kazakhstan's glittering commercial hub, are only 140 miles apart, an easy drive if it weren't for the wildcards of the border.

Fidgeting in the backseat upholstered in plush leather on that chilly night in early 2009, the main passenger of the white Lexus was not accustomed to waiting in line, at border crossings or anywhere else. He wore a suit, carried a titanium-encased Vertu cell phone that cost at least $7,000, and had a leather briefcase whose precise contents would later invite furious speculation, including a rumor that it contained $2 or $3 million in cash. He was hatching a plot to topple Kyrgyzstan's president, the man who'd been swept into office in the euphoria of the 2005 Tulip Revolution.

Back when he was the president's top aide, the Lexus passenger would speed past this checkpoint with nary a slowdown, his assistant calling the head of Kyrgyzstan's Border Guard Service ahead of time to warn him of the approaching big shot. Now, the border guards not only refused to wave the Lexus through but forced the car to pull over for extra scrutiny, a development that irritated the main passenger to no end.

The man in a hurry to get home that night was Medet Sadyrkulov, the most intriguing figure in modern Kyrgyz history, and a one-man distillation of its twists, absurdities, and disappointments. He first appeared in our narrative in 1999 when Sadyrkulov, then chief of staff to President Akayev, scrounged up half a million dollars for a clandestine mission, never fully explained but possibly involving a hostage ransom. The wildly ambitious chief of staff then clashed with the equally ambitious first lady, a confrontation he was doomed to lose. Bending to his wife's will, President Akayev sent Sadyrkulov into a gilded political exile, as Kyrgyzstan's ambassador to Iran. After the Tulip Revolution, Sadyrkulov managed to get reincarnated as the chief of staff to the man who overthrew President Akayev.

Initially seen as Kyrgyzstan's democratic savior, the new president, Kurmanbek Bakiyev, instead built a regime that quickly matched and then surpassed the worst of its predecessor's excesses. Sadyrkulov resigned as chief of staff in early 2009, frustrated by the erosion of his influence within Bakiyev's inner circle and dismayed by the corrupt and authoritarian bent of the regime—a regime that he himself had helped create. So now Sadyrkulov was a private citizen with few perks of power. He worked out of a small office on the first floor of an obscure Bishkek museum. He'd borrowed the white Lexus from a wealthy friend.

Though his stature was diminished, his plans were big. The man who had once been known as the gray cardinal of Kyrgyzstan now redirected his formidable bureaucratic talents toward the goal of overthrowing President Bakiyev.

After his resignation, Sadyrkulov traveled widely and met with officials in Russia, Kazakhstan, China, and at the U.S. embassy in Bishkek. He powwowed with Kyrgyzstan's opposition politicians, many of whom were incredulous at the apparent transformation of a man who had only recently harassed them. He reached out to his allies within the government and in Parliament, a pocket institution whose elections he'd helped rig. And he looked for money and television support—two things that would be key if he wanted to succeed in pushing the president and his family from power.

It was as if Karl Rove abandoned George W. Bush toward the end of his first term, reached out to the Democrats, and tried to flip Fox News.

On the morning of March 12, 2009, Sadyrkulov went to Almaty for the day, a frequent stop in his plotting adventures. He invited a friend to keep him company—an intense, bearded political scientist named Sergei Slepchenko who often consulted the former chief of staff on matters of state reform. Sadyrkulov's longtime driver took the steering wheel. Although his exact schedule for the day is not known, he did spend a few hours holding court in the bar of a high-rise Almaty hotel, where he met with an influential Russian commentator on Central Asian affairs and perhaps with others. Later that evening, Sadyrkulov told his chauffeur to take him back to Bishkek.

As the Lexus sat stranded at the border crossing, Sadyrkulov placed a few calls attempting to clarify the delay. He also called his wife. "They are holding us here for too long, not letting us pass for some reason. We've been sitting here forty to fifty minutes already," he told her.[1] Unbeknownst to Sadyrkulov, the border guards were following orders they'd received earlier to report the rebellious former chief's arrival at the checkpoint up the chain of command. It was a reversal of the routine from Sadyrkulov's gray cardinal days, when news of his imminent arrival would trickle down the chain of command to assure him speedy passage.

At 2:30 a.m. the Lexus finally cleared customs and pushed out onto the highway, its passengers eager to make up for lost time. A few miles down the road, the Lexus's high beams snatched out of the darkness what appeared to be an impromptu police checkpoint. Things like this often pop up on roads throughout the former Soviet Union, as underpaid cops stop passing cars at random in the hope of finding a violation, no matter how minuscule, and then extract a bribe to ignore it. Annoyed as they must have been by yet another delay, Sadyrkulov and his companions would have had no reason to be overly suspicious when a uniformed officer flagged the Lexus down with a police baton. The driver pulled over.

A few hours later, as the first milky light began to settle over Kyrgyzstan, a panicking young man ran down a deserted mountain road, looking for help. With frequent switchbacks and sharp drop-offs, the road snaked through a popular resort area on the outskirts of Bishkek, about seventy miles east of the nocturnal police checkpoint. Old villages here jostle for prime roadside space with swanky new country homes, restaurants, small hotels, and clubs where the city's moneyed classes like to party. People celebrate weddings here; young couples come on dates; families bring picnics; and the business and political movers and shakers come to unwind, sometimes with financially motivated female company.

One of the older establishments here is a place called 12 Chimneys. It has a popular restaurant that serves fresh trout and barbecued meats. Out back, there's a collection of wooden cottages where you can stay overnight. A little stream and surrounding mountains provide a pleasant setting for strolls. The distraught young man running down the road in the wee hours of March 13 told the police he'd spent the previous evening at 12 Chimneys in the company of his girlfriend, who worked there. Bleary-eyed from all the revelry, the young man, Omurbek Osmonov, decided to drive back to Bishkek, just twenty minutes away. But as his Audi rounded the many bends in the road descending down the mountain, Osmonov dozed off behind the wheel. He awoke from a sharp jolt. His Audi came to a sudden stop as it rammed into a white Lexus parked on the shoulder. The Lexus caught fire. Osmonov flung open his door, jumped out of the Audi, and realized the flames were already too big and wild for him to try to extinguish on his own. Panicking, he ran down the road to get help.

By the time the cops arrived on the scene, the Lexus was so thoroughly burned that they couldn't even tell how many passengers were inside. Eventually, pathologists suggested there had been three people. A crime-scene photo from that morning shows three clumps of black coals with little resemblance to humans laid out on stretchers next to the Lexus, a light coat of snow covering the mountains behind the burned car. In the photo, the cops in square fake-fur hats take notes behind the yellow police line. Though it would take some time to reach full scientific certainty, all the initial evidence that morning pointed to the conclusion

Police examine the burned Lexus in which the former presidential chief of staff was traveling. The remains of three passengers are laid out on stretchers on the ground.
(Courtesy of Kanybek Imanaliyev)

that those three mounds of coals had once been Sadyrkulov and his traveling companions.

The police quickly concluded that it was a freak traffic accident, and Osmonov—visibly saddened by it all—was on hand to provide his confession. He was sentenced to twelve years in prison for manslaughter. Despite requests from Sadyrkulov's friends and allies, investigators ignored serious inconsistencies of their traffic-accident theory. How come, for instance, the remains of the Lexus driver were found not in the driver's seat, which was empty, but in the passenger seat?

Medet Sadyrkulov, whose photos often show a hint of a mischievous smile lurking under a drooping mustache, lived an intense life at the very pinnacle of Kyrgyzstan's power. Just like his country, he was a man of contradictions and rapid reversals of fortune. He engaged in headspinning intrigue but, like a particularly agile cat, always landed on his feet even when it looked like he was about to smash head first into the pavement.

He served as a consigliere to two Kyrgyz presidents who couldn't stomach each other because one overthrew the other. Yet somehow both presidents trusted him. Sadyrkulov wanted to strengthen the young Kyrgyz state, only to see state authority corrupted and misused time and time again. A savvy bureaucratic infighter, he fought to preserve and expand his own palace influence, an effort that pitted him against the powerful and avaricious families surrounding both Kyrgyz presidents.

His final grand intrigue that ended in a torched car on the edge of a cliff capped a career that had begun humbly enough. Born in a village outside Bishkek, young Medet got his first job as a laborer on a livestock farm. Soon he enrolled in the history department of the country's main university. A friend later recalled that Sadyrkulov looked like "a simple village guy": modest, friendly, and kind.

As was common back then for most Soviet students, Sadyrkulov and his classmates spent a few weeks each year helping farmers collect the harvest. During one such pastoral stint picking apples and grapes, the young college kids from the big city ran into trouble with the local tough guys, who enjoyed nothing more than hitting on the college girls. Scuffles and fights ensued in the dark alleys on the farm, and those usually ended badly for the college kids. One evening, a group of particularly aggressive and drunk local kids showed up at the college contingent's temporary quarters angling for a brawl and yelling insults. Though scared and disorganized, the college kids shuffled outside and responded with their own taunts. The two sides just stood there trying to stare each other down when Sadyrkulov, unnoticed by the brawlers, climbed up on a tall industrial oven and took a stage dive into the midst of the local kids' scrum. Landing punches, he yelled, "Attack them!" to his frozen friends. They shook off their surprise and followed Medet into battle. The local kids scattered.

The evening's heroics earned him respect not only from his peers but also from the toughest of the local kids, who would henceforth settle all their issues in direct and mostly amicable chats with Medet. "I often saw some of these local thugs around Medet, and they always behaved in a friendly way," Zainuddin Kurmanov, a lifelong friend of Sadyrkulov who first met him in those apple-and-grapes days, recalled later. "His authority rose steadily among us, and by the time we returned to Bishkek he was already famous."[2]

After graduating, Sadyrkulov landed a job teaching history at Bishkek's Medical Institute, and it was there that he first evinced serious political ambition. At the age of thirty-three, the young professor suddenly nominated himself as a candidate in the elections for the secretary of the school's Communist Party committee. The party bosses pressured him to step aside in favor of the establishment candidate, a much older department head with a PhD in economics. But in a noisy committee meeting that lasted all day, the insolent history teacher refused to obey and went on to win the ballot by just six votes. This was the only time Sadyrkulov would seek elected office—his subsequent career bypassed the pitfalls of electoral politics, although he proved adept at manipulating the ballot box.

The young party secretary caught the eye of the town's political elite. When Kyrgyzstan gained independence from the former Soviet Union, Sadyrkulov was recruited to join the administration of Kyrgyzstan's first president, Askar Akayev.

After the Tulip Revolution, Akayev settled in Moscow, where he soon resumed teaching physics at a university, almost relieved, one senses, to be out of the cauldron of plotting and intrigue that Kyrgyzstan had become.

Fresh from his Iranian exile, Sadyrkulov was less fortunate. In the postrevolution zeal to expose the many wrongdoings of the disgraced former regime, prosecutors quickly zeroed in on the financial machinations within Akayev's inner circle. Though there was certainly plenty to investigate, the sweeping inquiries gave off a strong whiff of a witch hunt that would allow no exonerations. The fervor to expose, accuse, and indict is a common psychological condition for all revolutionaries because every new accusation leveled at the old regime helps legitimize the revolution.

Leading the prosecutorial charge was Azimbek Beknazarov, a burly former court bailiff who became a key figure in the 2005 uprising. Kyrgyzstan had first learned of his existence three years earlier when Beknaz-arov organized the mass protests against the forfeiture of land to China. He became known as the bulldozer of the revolution. Later, when he be-came a permanent if somewhat tiresome fixture in Kyrgyzstan's whiplash of revolts, prosecutions, and intrigue, Beknazarov's nickname morphed into yet another fitting label: the Beknosaur.

In April of 2005, just a month after President Akayev flew into exile in Moscow, Sadyrkulov found himself in a crowded Bishkek courtroom as a defendant in a high-profile criminal case. "The financiers' case," as it became known on the front pages, sought to establish exactly what had happened with the $420,000 that Sadyrkulov had raised for the former president. "They are walking around the corridors of the White House with half a million dollars, and no one knows where the money went?" the bulldozer fumed later. "Isn't the court interested in finding out what happened with state money?"[3]

Deep in optical physics in the safety of Moscow, Akayev wasn't in-terested in supplying an answer. His lawyer later disavowed any knowl-edge of the episode altogether. That left Sadyrkulov quite literally hold-ing the bag. "Akayev kept his silence, and screwed him," his daughter Aijan recalled. In court, Sadyrkulov swore that he'd done nothing wrong. As a good civil servant, he simply followed the president's order to find money for a vital national-security mission in the Batken province.

Years later, when Sadyrkulov was already dead, a close friend of his said the national-security mission was of an entirely different nature. The friend, Kanybek Imanaliev, had served as President Akayev's press sec-retary at the time of the mad scramble to find $420,000. Imanaliev told me Akayev needed the money to pay a bribe to prevent publication of a damaging report that was going to dig deep into the first family's finances, including the business dealings of Akayev's controversially wealthy son-in-law. Akayev was about to seek reelection, and such a report would be inconvenient. The hush money, Imanaliev said, was destined for a for-eign journalist who'd flown into town to collect it.

It is true that Sadyrkulov cared deeply about the hostage crisis in Batken, and that his life at the time was consumed with endless meetings about how to end it, Imanaliev recalled. It is perhaps the reason Batken militants were chosen as a plausible target for the money when a public explanation was required. But it was, Imanaliev told me, "complete rubbish," a red herring tossed to the judge and the public. It is hard to gauge the veracity of this account, and I was not able to verify it independently. As fantastical as his allegations may sound, Imanaliev was close both to Akayev and to Sadyrkulov at the time. Whatever the truth, one conclusion is beyond dispute: shady things were going on in the White House at the time, and Sadyrkulov was right in the middle.

April in Bishkek is a wonderful time. Trees and flowers turn downtown streets into lush, canopied arcades where old ladies sell fizzy water out of similarly dated Soviet-made machines the size and shape of a phone booth. The machines shudder and hiss violently before giving up any liquid. The air is warm and fresh, retaining at night a fading memory of the winter chill. The skies are a piercing blue, and the sight of white mountain peaks rising in the distance always forces me into a pointless loop of thoughts about the frailty and smallness of human existence. April of 2005 was a particularly wonderful time in Bishkek. Unspoiled by the disappointments soon to come, the revolution was still young, and all the things that would soon become hackneyed clichés still sounded plausible — and yes, even inspiring. A corrupt regime had just fallen. And you could still say "democracy" and "freedom" without laughing out loud. People did say such silly things, myself included.

It is hard to imagine a person feeling more outcast at the time than Sadyrkulov. While the country was in a celebratory mood, there he was sitting on an uncomfortable court bench, cast as a villain, a shady financier, a bagman for a discredited president, a piñata in the big anticorruption campaign. Some so-called friends who once sought his attention abandoned him as tainted goods. Prosecutors wanted him jailed for twelve years, and threatened financial penalties that would have ruined him. "It was a very difficult time," Aijan, his daughter, recalled. On the day of the sentencing, the courtroom was packed beyond capacity. Overflow spectators crowded the stairways. And then a miracle: a judge began reading an acquittal decision. As the news registered with the hushed audience, someone stood up and paraphrased a line from a cult Soviet comedy: "Long live the Soviet court, the most humane court in the world!"[4]

What did just happen? In Kyrgyzstan, big decisions like that aren't usually made by judges. So it's plausible that someone high up in the new government didn't want the master bureaucrat slain on the altar of the revolution.

At a small celebration of his freedom held that evening in a Chinese restaurant, Sadyrkulov had a few drinks with family and friends. His mobile phone rang. It was a prominent Kyrgyz politician calling to congratulate him and to apologize for not coming to his rescue. "You must be angry at me?" the politician asked.

"Angry? No, I'm not just angry. I'm *very* angry," Sadyrkulov replied and hung up.

Then he turned to Imanaliev, the former press secretary, and said with liquor-enhanced panache, "I'm going to fire that guy." And a few months later, he did.

Instead of moving into a prison cell, Sadyrkulov moved back to his old digs in the presidential palace. Within a year, he clawed his way up to his old job: the chief of staff. Kyrgyzstan is a small country, and it feels even smaller in the upper reaches of the country's political elites. A dozen or so familiar faces rotate through stints in government, business, opposition, sometimes prison, then back in government, opposition, and so on. Still, Sadyrkulov's political survival was astonishing. In a grudging acknowledgment of the man's gumption, a presidential advisor at the time called him "a master of intrigue," a label that would turn up time and time again in descriptions of Sadyrkulov. "He was the most trusted man in Akayev's team," the advisor grumbled. "And here he is running the presidential administration again."[5]

The task, in Sadyrkulov's eyes, was an ambitious one: to strengthen the Kyrgyz state weakened by the 2005 revolution and to consolidate political power, diluted by the uprising, back where it rightfully belonged: within the government. Revolutions destroy the old order, but they don't do much else. A statist to the core, Sadyrkulov had plenty of work ahead of him. "He always tried to convince me that any president who comes to power through a revolution has a double responsibility. He must clear the debris and get rid of pseudo-revolutionaries who don't have any government experience. And that's why we have to help the president," his friend Kanybek Imanaliev recalled later. In practice, this meant shoring up the personal power of Bakiyev and his inner circle, and casting aside those who stood in the way. Sadyrkulov embraced the project with such vigor that it ruined some old friendships.

The strongest performance of political theater came in 2007. Sadyrkulov helped rewrite Kyrgyzstan's constitution, which had already been rejiggered plenty of times to match the constantly changing facts on the ground. Tinkering with the constitution would become Kyrgyzstan's national obsession, a way to impose reason and law on the irrational and of course illegal series of uprisings and coups. The 2007 version stripped the Parliament of many powers and strengthened the office of the president. It triggered the disbanding of the current Parliament and called for new elections, a chance to stack the freshly castrated assembly with figureheads and assure complete subjugation to the president.

To that end, the chief of staff helped create a new party using a well-rehearsed trick from the political playbook of Russia and neighboring Kazakhstan. In both of those countries, parliaments are dominated by parties whose only ideology lies in complete devotion to the president. These parties tend to have corny names, evoking a grand and hazy idea of national salvation that no sane, patriotic person would dare oppose. In Kazakhstan, it's Our Motherland. In Russia, it's United Russia. Kyrgyzstan's version was to be called Ak-Jol, or White Path, which had as its hastily created logo a red circle with a white squiggle of a path meandering toward the horizon.

There wasn't much time to consider the artwork more deeply. Between the party's creation and the election date lay only a couple of months. And the party needed to win big. Bakiyev gave it a resounding endorsement. "We are not a party of power, or a party of bosses. We are a party of doers, of people who work," Bakiyev thundered at the founding convention, his descriptions of what the party was not neatly summing up the party's very essence. Ak-Jol was a brainchild of Sadyrkulov.

With the full resources of the state at its disposal, the party swept the elections. Opposition groups were saddled with new requirements that set bizarre regional vote minimums on top of an overall national threshold a party needed to clear to be allowed into Parliament. "All the Parliament seats were being divided up and given out in a single place—in Medet's office," says Vadim Nochevkin, a journalist who knew him well.

The breathtaking fraud and insolence of it all pushed the opposition into the streets in the biggest antigovernment protests since the 2005 revolution. President Bakiyev flipped the opposition a giant birdie with a hugely ironic book published in 2007 under his name and with the clunky title *Reforming the Party System Is a Crucial Condition for the Democratic Development of Kyrgyzstan.*

Protesters pitched traditional Kyrgyz yurts on Bishkek's central square. The authorities sent in the police to crush the yurts and evict the protesters. A yurt is more than just a tent. It's a Kyrgyz national symbol that evokes the nomadic roots of the Kyrgyz tribes, a romanticized idea of itinerant horsemen still relevant for the Kyrgyz national identity today. The yurt's crisscrossed support beams appear on Kyrgyzstan's national flag.

So tearing down a yurt is both a bad omen and bad manners, and when the cops destroyed their yurts, protesters were furious. "The police acted as if they'd just won World War II," Kanybek Imanaliev, who was in the opposition, recalled. At a meeting with Sadyrkulov and the minister of the interior, opposition representatives complained about the police tactics. Sadyrkulov heard them all out, but then nodded toward the minister and said, "The minister is right." "Our relations were strained after that, we were on different sides of the barricades," Imanaliev said.

By then, most of the leaders of the 2005 revolution had already abandoned Bakiyev, a man whom they had thrust forward as the nation's best democratic hope but who now acted, well, like an asshole. Roza Otunbayeva, a key leader of the Tulip uprising, became foreign minister in the Bakiyev administration. Within months of assuming her new post, she began fielding strange requests from senior government officials. On a few occasions, President Bakiyev asked her to hire "several beautiful young women" so they could work in Kyrgyzstan's embassies abroad, a request whose provenance and urgency Otunbayeva never fully understood. Another senior official lobbied her to appoint his son-in-law ambassador to China. Otunbayeva also suspected corruption in the new multimillion-dollar contract to print new Kyrgyz passports. She eventu-

ally resigned and became a dogged presence in the halls of the Kyrgyz
Parliament. She often arrived at parliamentary debates armed with a loudspeaker so that she could be heard in case authorities cut off her microphone, which sometimes happened.

Following the revolution, Edil Baisalov, the lanky former duty-free
negotiator turned democracy campaigner, drifted for a while, giddy with
a sense of accomplishment. "After we overthrew Akayev, I was euphoric
and a bit lazy," he recalled. But a new target soon presented itself in the
form of organized crime creeping, unimpeded, into state institutions.

Across the former Soviet Union in the 1990s, the collapse of state
authority and the boom in private enterprise, both legal and less so, created a new breed of gangster specializing in protection rackets, extortion,
and the settling of business disputes. Organized crime, of course, existed
in the Soviet days too, but it was largely limited to the prison yard and to
the criminal underworld of thieves, crooks, fences, killers, and other riff-
raff about whom a law-abiding, 9-to-5 toiler had no reason to worry. In
the wild first post-Soviet decade, when laws couldn't keep pace with the
galloping beasts of capitalism and corruption, crime figures stepped out
of the shadows and entered the mainstream. They recruited foot soldiers
and muscle men from the ranks of underemployed boxers, martial-arts
experts, wrestlers, and veterans of elite military units. These were known
simply as *sportsmeny*, or "athletes," and a popular song from those days
captured their sudden metamorphosis from gym rats and soldiers into
gangsters.

> We are former sportsmen,
> And now we are racket men.
> If it weren't for all the changes,
> We'd get jobs moving furniture.

As time wore on and the qualified labor pool of athletic talent shrank,
the necessary brawn was provided by the so-called *otmorozky*, which
means something like "frozen brains" in Russian and denotes a willingness to do anything to anyone for a reasonable fee, or just for fun. Staffed
by athletes and frozen brains (sometimes these qualities would happily

coexist in the same person), rival gangs fought over spheres of influence and collected protection money from nascent businesses. Their proprietors, often young and inexperienced but eager to get rich in the commercial free-for-all, paid up their protection fees with the same grudging acceptance people in the West reserve for paying taxes: no one likes to do it, but the consequences of not doing it are potentially far greater, so most people pay.

The "bandits" or "brothers," as these enforcers were known, were alternately romanticized as fearless street fighters and ridiculed for their supposedly slow wits, the result of frequent poundings on the head. As their unofficial headgear, they adopted a flat woolen cap usually favored by retirees or by nineteenth-century country squires. The fashion spread beyond the brotherhood and allowed many young men to affect a quasi-criminal, tough-guy look.

For a few bizarre weeks in the early 1990s when I was in high school in Saint Petersburg, Russia, I worked for a small real-estate firm co-owned by my cousin—a stint I could describe as an internship, except the word isn't sufficiently flexible to capture the weirdness and complexity of the experience. For one thing, this ambitious real-estate operation was headquartered in an unused wing of a functioning kindergarten, the voices and footsteps of toddlers frequently interrupting the complex real-estate transactions being hatched by my cousin and his three colleagues. One of them was a mercurial Ukrainian who froze glistening white hunks of salted pork fat in our fridge and then sliced off wafers for snacks. A reminder of who had occupied this wing until recently greeted us every time we went to the bathroom: five miniature potties not designed for real-estate moguls.

My cousin, not even twenty years old at the time, rented the wing from the kindergarten director, an elderly woman with her hair trussed up into an enormous bun on top of her head. She needed the rent income to supplement the meager state funding for the school, or to pad her own salary; we never knew or cared. Our wing had a separate street entrance, a set of chipped stairs that clients could take to avoid the throngs of toddlers in the hallways. Our business plan was to buy up rooms in the so-called communal apartments once occupied by a single family but now owned by complete strangers. Theoretically, there was money to be made from reconstituting those once-opulent apartments under a single ownership, cleaning them up, and selling them. People did get rich doing this, but not us. I'm not even sure we managed to execute the business plan, but we did make enough money to buy booze and a desktop computer — and to attract attention from a local gang that insisted we pay for protection. Our defenders were three guys who always showed up together, in obligatory woolen caps.

Their leader was a short, squat man named Pasha. He had the makings of a potbelly, was missing a couple of teeth, spoke with a heavy lisp, dabbled in boxing, and liked to wear an ankle-length maroon overcoat, under which my cousin once spied the barrel of an AK-47. On fee-collection days, Pasha often planted himself in front of our solitary desktop and spent an hour or so playing a shoot-'em-up game and chain-smoking. Then there was Marat, a self-described wrestler, who spoke seldom but once had a few drinks in our office and entertained us with tales about his former, now deceased, brother-in-arms nicknamed Mosquito. A third guy I don't remember well, except that he was very tall.

We were small fish, too incompetent and inconsequential to get in real trouble. Soon enough I stopped showing up to work and my cousin went back to college. But people did get hurt in the nasty business disputes or fallings-out with their presumed protectors, or lost their lives because they owed someone too much money, or someone owed money to them, and it was cheaper to kill them than to pay. Many of the Pashas and Marats of the world died too, or went to jail, but some of them rose through the ranks to the top of their crime syndicates. As they prospered, they ditched their ridiculous maroon jackets and woolen caps, replaced missing teeth, and set about acquiring legitimate businesses and reputations, their wild shakedowns of the 1990s a distant echo of a past when anything went.

In Kyrgyzstan, the man who personified that evolution better than most was Ryspek Akhmatbayev, a possessor of an illustrious post-Soviet criminal résumé. A professionally trained boxer, Akhmatbayev served in the intelligence and sabotage unit of the Soviet paratroopers — the elite of the elite, the rough equivalent of the Navy Seals. By the late 1980s, the

Issyk-Kul native had gone into racketeering and extortion, earning himself his first criminal conviction. For much of the 1990s, he was wanted for several murders and attained fame as one of Kyrgyzstan's top mob leaders. He earned the nickname Robin Hood, presumably because of his talents in the area of wealth redistribution. After the Tulip Revolution, Ryspek's brother, a member of Parliament, paid a visit to one of Kyrgyzstan's prisons as part of a government inspection team. A riot broke out and the brother was killed, allegedly on the orders of a rival mob boss, a fierce Chechen who was incarcerated in that prison under unusual conditions that allowed his flunkies to grow marijuana next to their cells.

Ryspek, technically a fugitive from Kyrgyz justice, railed against high-ranking government officials for setting up his brother, and organized massive rallies in Bishkek demanding the resignation of the prime minister. He vowed to move into politics. As if on cue, a Bishkek court acquitted him of a triple-murder charge. Right in the courtroom, Ryspek declared his intention to run for Parliament. First, he got elected as the chairman of Kyrgyzstan's Fencing Federation, and then he won a Parliament seat with a whopping 79 percent of the vote in his home province. All doors seemed to be flying open in front of Robin Hood, a triumphant march from the woods that would have been impossible without the involvement of well-placed government protectors.[6] In fact, rumors swirled pointing to links between Ryspek and senior officials of the State Security Service.

A year after the Tulip Revolution staged in the name of democracy, a convicted extortionist and a suspected triple murderer, his slate wiped miraculously clean, was about to become a legislator, with an assist from the law-enforcement elite. The scenario jolted Kyrgyzstan's civil society just as it was waking up from the euphoric slumber that followed the Tulip Revolution. Ryspek's was the most extreme and visible case, but there were other examples of widespread corruption, of organized crime running unrestrained. Right around the time of Ryspek's election victory, in April of 2006, Edil Baisalov organized a big law-and-order rally in central Bishkek, the first major protest after the Tulip Revolution. A couple of days after that, Baisalov was crossing a downtown street when he received a blow to the head and crumpled to the ground. Before he slipped out of consciousness, Baisalov clung to one of those strange momentary thoughts that would sound ridiculous later: "Why is everyone else getting shot and I'm only getting punched? Why didn't they shoot me?" Baisalov had been hit with a piece of rebar that glanced off the back of his head as he turned left to look for approaching traffic. The attacker landed the blow with enough force to cause serious damage, but Baisalov's height and the last-minute flick of the head most likely saved him. He spent a few days in the hospital, bandaged and bloody. A month later, Ryspek died in a hail of bullets as he exited a mosque, his alleged government protectors having been removed from their jobs a few days earlier. Robin Hood was a victim of a contract hit that would clear the path for the ascendance of yet another underworld boss, whom we'll meet later.

Baisalov soon channeled his formidable reserves of energy toward criticizing the approaching 2007 parliamentary election, the one that would be rigged in favor of the ruling party. One day, he visited a printing plant and snapped a photo of the sample ballot with his mobile phone. He posted the photo on his widely read blog to ridicule the upcoming election. Next thing he knew, criminal charges against him were being considered, and the government announced plans to destroy the entire print run, at an enormous cost, because anyone could now ostensibly use Baisalov's photo to print high-quality fakes. Friends advised the indomitable campaigner that it would be better to leave the country than to risk prosecution, fines, or imprisonment, since he was clearly a marked man now. Baisalov, by then married with a year-old daughter, heeded their advice and applied for asylum. Within days, the German embassy helped him get out of Kyrgyzstan. On a winter night, bracing against the freezing wind and snow, Baisalov crossed the land border into Kazakhstan, his wife and infant daughter in tow. "I joked that the only thing we were missing was a goat on a leash," he told me. Baisalov resettled in Sweden, but he would eventually return to Kyrgyzstan and assume a prominent role once again.

The 2007 election, as we've already seen, was a watershed moment that alienated Bakiyev's former allies from the president. And Medet Sadyrkulov, the president's chief of staff, was doing much of his dirty work. "He was an evil man," says Temir Sariyev, a prominent Kyrgyz banker and politician. "He could have played it differently, he didn't have to help the Bakiyev clan. But he thought he could outsmart everyone. He thought he could be the puppeteer yanking all the strings and controlling everything. With Sadyrkulov's hands, Bakiyev destroyed the opposition."

This should have been the crowning moment of Sadyrkulov's tenure under Bakiyev, a point in time when the wily chief of staff should have emerged as the undisputed power behind the throne. But he was not the only one vying for supremacy within the president's inner circle. Bakiyev had six brothers and two sons, a posse of ambitious men who stampeded toward the throne once Bakiyev landed his posterior in it. "It's not my fault that we have a big family," Bakiyev would say later.[7] Some were content with ambassadorships and other small perks. But within that group, two relatives stood out for the sheer reach of their ambition. One was Janysh Bakiyev, the president's younger brother, who began his career as a small-town cop and eventually rose to high-profile police posts dealing with organized crime and drug trafficking—the two interrelated scourges of Kyrgyzstan. The other relative was Maxim Bakiyev, the president's younger son. The two men couldn't have been more different. Janysh was gruff and often monosyllabic in his answers, an old-school figure forged in grimy police precincts. Maxim was young and urbane and Western educated, prone to bouts of locution. As was fashionable among the young jet set, he was drawn to finance and business administration.

Janysh and Maxim drifted into fitting niches around the president. Janysh became chief of the State Protection Service, essentially a group of bodyguards for key government officials. Janysh interpreted his new remit broadly and built out his team into a lavishly financed security fiefdom on par with branches of the military, police, and intelligence services. He bought state-of-the-art wiretapping equipment and set up an elite special-forces unit whose exact purpose remained unclear. When a local journalist proposed a visit to the unit's training base so he could write about it, he was told to drop the story idea.

While his uncle dealt with thugs, guns, and spooks, Maxim focused on finer points of finance, bringing in a contingent of whiz kids to help him set up an all-purpose investment shop. They included a banking consultant from Latvia and an international finance impresario with a degree from Berkeley. Maxim declared to an interviewer that he was a person "removed from politics, a businessman."

The brother and the son became key players within the president's entourage, often competing for influence. Their prominence limited the power of Sadyrkulov. Perhaps mindful of his earlier attempt to compete head-to-head with the former first lady and the exile to Iran it earned him, Sadyrkulov now acted with more nuance and guile. Instead of confronting the powerful relatives, he decided to exploit their differences to his advantage and back one over the other. Between the thuggish uncle and the urbane nephew, the choice seemed obvious. Sadyrkulov set out to befriend and mentor Maxim, figuring he could mold the young businessman into a true statesman and perhaps prepare him to one day ascend to the throne now occupied by his father.

"Sadyrkulov always tried to act through Maxim, judging him to be progressive, young, and full of potential. He preferred Maxim to the retrograde Janysh. He taught him things, tried to connect him with smart people," recalled Elmira Ibraimova, a longtime friend who served as a deputy prime minister in the Bakiyev administration. At times, Maxim seemed to value Sadyrkulov too. He once gave the chief of staff an expensive Vertu mobile phone as a New Year's gift, the same phone that would be with Sadyrkulov at the time of his death.

When the family's influence in the affairs of the state became too big to ignore, Ibraimova says she asked Sadyrkulov, "Did we vote for the president, or for his son, or his brothers?" Sadyrkulov replied that he shared some of her misgivings about nepotism but that the only wise course of action was to work within the system, within the family. "What can one do?" he asked Ibraimova. "Maxim is a smart guy; we should try to manage the state through him."

If Sadyrkulov disliked the president's brothers, they didn't love him back either. Some viewed him as a pesky micromanager and a competitor for the boss's attention. "The brothers were hysterical about him, they kept pressing the president to remove him," recalls his daughter Aijan.

Sadyrkulov's face was dominated by one ubiquitous feature: an ample mustache lying like an inverted half moon over his upper lip. In a private diary, one presidential brother referred to him as "a cunt with a mustache."[8]

Eventually, Sadyrkulov's alliance with Maxim began to unravel too. The early hope that Maxim would mature into an enlightened statesman fizzled against the mounting evidence of his bare-knuckled tactics to usurp the country's most lucrative businesses for personal gain. Sadyrkulov watched his protégé with growing dismay, and began to share with friends and family his misgivings about Maxim. "You know, I made a mistake," he told Ibraimova. "Maxim is very greedy, for him the question of money trumps everything else." Sadyrkulov appeared "extremely disappointed" by this, and although the two men remained on cordial terms, the chief of staff no longer believed Maxim was good news for the country.

Inside the Business Empire of the President's Son

To get a sense of what kind of entrepreneur flourished in Kyrgyzstan during the Bakiyev era, let's make a stop in the San Francisco of the early 1990s and meet a bookish and ambitious teenager named Eugene Gourevitch.

He grew up in Moscow, and by the time he turned twelve, in 1990, the Soviet Union was crumbling into pieces. Eugene and his mother, like many Soviet Jews before them, emigrated to America. They settled in San Francisco where young Eugene established himself as a precocious student. In 1995, Gourevitch made a cameo appearance in a *New York Times* article about how overachieving immigrant students from Eastern Europe were making their U.S.-born counterparts uncomfortable and resentful because of their eager-beaver conduct in class and their success in winning academic honors. Gourevitch told the paper that sometimes if he answered a teacher's question, other students would say, "Oh God, how does he know that?" But Gourevitch made no apologies for it. "To me, that's part of education. I'm not willing to sacrifice my education because someone else feels inferior."

Years later, I asked Gourevitch if that know-it-all kid was indeed him, and he said that yes, it was: "I sound like such a fucking asshole. Perfect." When we met in a Manhattan café on an unseasonably warm February evening, Gourevitch didn't look or act the part. He is short and a little overweight, his plump face fringed by a five o'clock shadow. (When he bought himself a new iPad, a friend wisecracked on Twitter: "Tonight, Gourevitch became the largest app ever written for an iPad.") He wore a sweater and ordered a cappuccino and a glass of water, which, at one point in our conversation, he accidentally knocked over with a sweeping hand gesture. Mopping up the spill with napkins, he apologized for his clumsiness.

This polite, soft-spoken, articulate man in front of me was hard to square with a wild history of financial high jinks that began on the Horn of Africa, continued in the tangles of the Italian mafia, and blossomed in the shady business universe of Maxim Bakiyev's Kyrgyzstan, where he was sentenced in absentia to fifteen years in prison. Gourevitch seemed to wear that conviction as a badge of honor, mocking it on his Twitter profile: "Former banker. Trader. Atheist. Family man. Born to spread misery vicariously and viscerally. Kyrgyzstan's Most Wanted. Not even remotely gangsta." His Twitter photo runs with the 1930s gangster theme: he's wearing a dark pinstriped suit, a white shirt, and a black porkpie hat cocked over his right eye.

Gourevitch's transformation from just another immigrant kid striving to succeed in America into an international man of intrigue was triggered by boredom with the prospect of a conventional career. Gourevitch, in other words, was too ambitious for his own good. He got an MBA from Berkeley and, like many newly minted business administrators in the American boom years at the turn of the century, he had plenty of lucrative options. Attending a recruiting retreat for budding consultants, Gourevitch developed a queasy feeling in his stomach, an alienation from the cookie-cutter crop of square young men and women eager to climb the pole of corporate finance. "I was so incensed by the culture and the people, by the obsession with money and bonuses, working twenty-hour days," he recalled. "Not that I mind working hard, but it has to be for a purpose I understand." And let's be clear: Gourevitch didn't mind making money, either; in fact he loved it. It's just that he wanted to do it away from a nameless cubicle of some corporate headquarters.

An opportunity soon presented itself in the person of Ilya Karas, a family acquaintance from Moscow. Karas first showed his business acumen in the final years of the Soviet Union when he dabbled in computers and founded one of the country's first joint-stock companies. In the 1990s, Karas left Russia and lived in Hungary and Malta, setting up a string of business ventures. Among them was a small bank in Kyrgyzstan where Gourevitch did a summer internship while still at Berkeley. The bank would eventually grow into a financial behemoth under Maxim Bakiyev, and Gourevitch would return. But for now, Karas dangled in front of the young and eager master of business a career opportunity in another obscure land: Djibouti.

A former French colony on the eastern shore of Africa, Djibouti is surrounded by Somalia, Ethiopia, and Eritrea, a neighborhood fraught by perpetual strife. While Gourevitch was getting his business degree at Berkeley, Ethiopia and Eritrea were fighting a bitter border war. In another war a decade earlier, Eritrea had won independence from Ethiopia, which itself at the time was being consumed by a long-running civil war. And Somalia was a state in name only, riven by a never-ending series of internecine conflicts, its territorial waters infested by pirates. Where others might have seen only chaos and bloodshed, Karas and Gourevitch saw a business opportunity and decided to open a bank in Djibouti catering to Ethiopian companies. To bulk up the local currency, the Ethiopian government maintained strict foreign-exchange controls, meaning that many local firms had trouble accessing international markets since the Ethiopian birr was not freely convertible. So, for instance, if an Ethiopian construction firm wanted to import equipment from Germany, it had no easy way of paying for it, and would have to rely on the services of financial intermediaries as far afield as Dubai. Karas and Gourevitch wanted to give those Ethiopian firms a financial clearinghouse closer to home, and Djibouti was perfect for that. Unlike its neighbors, it was not at war with anyone and had a major port in the Gulf of Aden.

Gourevitch arrived in Djibouti in 2000 to run the bank and manage a team of a dozen fellow Russian finance whizzes. To give the startup an edge in the rough-and-tumble business world of Djibouti, Gourevitch sought out one of the president's nephews and put him on the board of directors, paying him about $5,000 a month. Despite the right connections, the bank didn't clinch many deals, aside from arranging a loan for an Ethiopian bitumen company. With expected profits failing to materialize, Gourevitch and his team grew despondent as they roamed the noisy port and the dusty streets of Djibouti looking for business. "There was nothing to do but work and drink; some people went nuts," Gourevitch recalled. The pasty white guys from Russia, with their promises of complex financial engineering, stood out and sowed some suspicion. "People on the street would shout, 'Russian mafia,'" Gourevitch said. After two years of this, Gourevitch decided he'd had enough and moved to New York. When I asked him if there were any upsides to his African adventure, Gourevitch smiled and said, "Well, I learned a little French." He also picked up business lessons that weren't taught at Berkeley, "an entirely different set of skills." In short, he emerged from his Djibouti foray a little banged up and humbled but with a thicker skin and the confidence to pursue unconventional business projects. In New York, he set up a consulting firm and began to look for new ideas. The name of the firm was Virage, Russified French for a sharp, high-speed turn, the kind that makes car tires screech.

If the Djibouti project skirted along the line of financial chicanery, Gourevitch's next venture crashed through that line in a spectacular mafia plot to swindle the Italian treasury out of hundreds of millions of dollars. Gourevitch was not a mastermind of that scheme but, according to a mind-numbingly detailed fifteen-hundred-page Italian indictment, our enterprising New York financier played an important role in setting up a string of offshore shell companies and bank accounts to make the ruse possible. The plot revolved around the value-added tax that Italian companies are required to pay on certain goods and services they sell.

For this particular scheme, the fraudsters picked Fastweb and Sparkle, two prominent Italian telecom firms, the latter of which was an Internet subsidiary of Telecom Italia, the country's old fixed-line monopoly. Next, the fraudsters set up fictitious firms based outside of Italy but still within the European Union. Let's call them "Companies A," as the Italian prosecutors did. The significance of that move lay in the fact that cross-border transactions within the EU were exempt from the national value-added tax, unlike deals between firms within the same country (Italy in this case), which were subject to VAT. Next, the fraudsters set up yet another layer of firms, this time in Italy. Let's call them "Companies B." Having done all this, the financial operatives launched a complex cascade of fictitious transactions, what Italian prosecutors called a carousel or merry-go-round fraud of "exceptional insidiousness."

It worked like this: Companies A sold to Companies B a telecom service, usually phone cards for downloading multimedia content from the Internet. Let's say the value of the service was €100. Because it was a cross-border EU transaction, it was exempt from VAT. Next, Companies B sold the same exact service to Fastweb and Sparkle. But this time the VAT applied because both Companies B and the two Italian firms were all based in Italy. Factoring in the tax, the transaction was now worth €120. Fastweb and Sparkle were on the hook to pay those extra €20 to the Italian Treasury. Then, Fastweb and Sparkle resold this same service to its originators: Companies A, based outside of Italy. This time, the sale was exempt from VAT and was worth, again, €100. And here comes the clincher: Fastweb and Sparkle could now claim a €20 tax refund from the Italian Treasury. The preceding transactions were mostly fictitious, the Italian prosecutors alleged, but the tax credits were real and ran far bigger than €20. In the course of three years, the merry-go-round succeeded in bilking the Italian state coffers of at least half a billion dollars.

To keep the carousel spinning, its operators bribed members of the financial police and engineered a fraudulent election of a national senator who provided another layer of official protection to the fraudsters. The proceeds were reinvested in real estate and funneled to offshore tax havens. Directing parts of the sweeping operation were members of the 'Ndragheta, a powerful mob that emerged in the fishing villages and agricultural groves of Calabria, a province that lies along the toe of the Italian boot jutting into the Mediterranean. The Calabrian family clans of the 'Ndragheta built their wealth by smuggling cocaine from South America to Europe, and were now looking to expand their financial and political influence.

One key figure in the merry-go-round was Gennaro Mokbel, a Rome businessman with ties to the 'Ndragheta. Mokbel helped rig the senator's election by tapping the Calabrian mob's pull among Italians living abroad who supplied the necessary absentee ballots to put the man in office. Buying political influence like that, the operators of the merry-go-round made "a quantum leap" into the heart of the Italian state, according to the indictment. Mokbel is portrayed by the investigators as a ruthless figure, at one point telling the senator in a phone call caught on a wiretap, "You can become president of Italy, but for me you will always be a doorman, meaning you are my slave."[9]

In the indictment, the prosecutors attempted to show the scope and sophistication of the merry-go-round by including a color-coded illustration complete with offshore firms, national flags, and a tangle of arrows for bank transfers, connecting them all in a Jackson Pollock–style blur. The immediate consequence of looking at the illustration is a deep sense of confusion followed by a headache, and that's precisely how the merry-go-round was built. The international finance whizzes tapped by the carousel masterminds wove a web of transfers specifically designed "to make it more difficult to reconstruct the paper trail of money," the prosecutors said. "Through these qualified international players, accustomed to such money laundering, [the masterminds] completed the complex financial circuit designed to simulate the existence of commercial operations [and] to support the transfer of proceeds of money-laundering to bank accounts."

Eugene Gourevitch, the precocious student from Moscow, Berkeley MBA, and veteran of Djibouti, was among those "qualified international players." His plump frame, decked out in a suit and a red tie, appears at meetings secretly photographed by the Italian investigators. When we spoke in Manhattan, he was reluctant to discuss his involvement in detail because he was still talking to the Italian authorities about a settlement. He did recall his brief interactions with Mokbel, the 'Ndragheta liaison. "The first time I met him was in an office building. He comes in with three huge guys. One of these guys blocks the exit." Mokbel was smoking a cigarette at the time, and when he finished, he deposited the butt into the outstretched cupped hand of one of his oversized bodyguards.

"I thought my life is over," Gourevitch said. After a few tense moments, he relaxed a bit, surmising that the ridiculous entrance was "just a show of force." Gourevitch got the message. "I had an honest belief that I was providing an innocuous service," he told me. "Until I was threatened and had no choice but to keep doing what they wanted."

For a while, Gourevitch's Italian shenanigans remained hidden in the thicket of Italian investigations, and the enterprising young man embarked on a new chapter in his cinematic career. He moved to Kyrgyzstan to work for the same small bank where he'd done a summer internship a few years earlier. By then Karas, the old Gourevitch family acquaintance who'd invited him to Djibouti, had sold the bank to Mikhail Nadel, another Russian-Jewish émigré financier operating out of London and Hungary. At the time of the sale, Asia Universal Bank (AUB) was registered in western Samoa and amounted to little more than an office space with a banking license in Bishkek. Nadel paid Karas about $150,000 for the whole thing.

The bank quickly established a checkered reputation as a place where Russian companies could hide profits and evade Russian taxes. In a highly unusual move, Moscow's Central Bank publicly censured the Kyrgyz startup for helping Russian firms engage in "gray import" operations and cautioned Russian banks against working with it. If a Russian company wanted to import a consignment of computers worth $1 million from China, for instance, it could cycle the transaction through a network of offshore firms, and disguise the true cost of the deal—and its tax liability—from Russian customs. Asia Universal Bank played a key role in the setup, taking advantage of Kyrgyzstan's liberal money-flow regulations. "If you recall, they used to call Kyrgyzstan the Switzerland of the East," Nadel told me on the phone from London, where he now spends most of his time. Nadel insists that he broke no laws, and that the tax evasion should be Russia's headache, not his. Besides, there's nothing wrong with looking for ways to lower one's tax bill. "People who don't think about tax planning should have their heads checked out," Nadel said.

Still, Moscow's official rebuke was a big blow for the bank's reputation at a time when Nadel was nurturing dreams of a major expansion and was cultivating ties with Western financial institutions. To buff the bank's image, Nadel commissioned a compliance audit and even claims he donated some of his personal money so that the Kyrgyz government could fund a new financial-intelligence service. In Nadel's telling, this is where Asia Universal Bank's shady history ended and a clean future began. Subsequent investigations, however, painted a different picture, alleging that after the Tulip Revolution the bank mutated into a money-laundering juggernaut operating under the protection of Maxim Bakiyev, the president's younger son.

At Nadel's invitation, Gourevitch moved to Bishkek to help Asia Universal Bank obtain correspondent lines at Western banks, bring in more foreign financing, and otherwise plug the Kyrgyz firm into the global financial network and raise its profile. His Italian entanglements still hidden from public view, Gourevitch served on the bank's board and held a 10 percent stake in the bank. Nadel praised his intelligence and drive. "He's a very nice guy, a professional with a smart head on his shoulders, and he's very brave," he told me. Gourevitch, for his part, also liked his new business partner. "I found him to have a dynamic and interesting personality," he said. Settling into his new gig, Gourevitch noticed that the bank continued laundering money on an ever more audacious scale, fine-tuning and building upon the earlier "gray-import" mechanism. "The volume of transactions increased exponentially," he recalled. Living in a large apartment in downtown Bishkek, Gourevitch didn't have moral qualms about the arrangement, reasoning that it didn't seem to involve truly dirty money, like drug proceeds, and didn't hurt anyone, unless you counted Russian tax collectors as victims. After the Bakiyevs came to power, "the floodgates were opened," Gourevitch continued. "Maxim and Nadel reached some kind of a deal. There was a profit-sharing agreement between them."

The banker and the president's son were friends, having met in 2002 at the Bishkek wedding of a mutual acquaintance. Back then, Nadel was a small-time facilitator of Russian tax evasion, and Maxim's father was Kyrgyzstan's prime minister. After the revolution, when Maxim's influence shot into the stratosphere with his father's ascendance to the presidency, Nadel and Maxim remained close, speaking every day and hanging out socially, Nadel recalled. In June of 2009, Maxim threw a lavish party to celebrate the opening of a gaudy new hotel on the shores of Lake Issyk-Kul, Kyrgyzstan's Riviera. Booze ran free and plentiful, while pop stars flown in from Russia and Europe provided the schmaltzy live soundtrack for the invitation-only gathering, according to a U.S. diplomatic cable.[10]

Before Maxim's arrival, the assorted business leaders and politicians, all wealthy and influential men in their own right, looked like schoolchildren waiting nervously for the principal. Maxim's private jet landed at a nearby airport, and a large motorcade carried him to the hotel, where he moved through the crowd with a large retinue of bodyguards. "The businessmen stood at attention when Maxim came near," the cable notes. But there was one entrepreneur who seemed completely at ease. Nadel, the dapper banker, "acted like the second host of the party, loudly toasting with the men and making advances at the women," the cable says. "He took a group of people to watch him swim in the lake, where his bodyguards followed him into the water."

Nadel insisted to me that his friendship with Maxim never crossed into business and that Maxim never received any money from Asia Universal Bank. Whether it was solely through Nadel's business genius or because of an assist from the president's son, the bank began to grow like a mushroom after a downpour. The Kyrgyz mushroom sprouted a web of links that reached as far as the United Kingdom, Belize, Panama, New Zealand, and Bulgaria, places where a bewilderingly large number of interconnected shell companies cropped up in a cloud of secrecy. With no employees, these shells engaged in a furious daisy chain of multimillion-dollar transfers that seemed to have no discernible business purpose and were all processed by Asia Universal Bank, according to an exhaustive investigation by Global Witness, a London-based group that digs into international corruption.

Between 2008 and 2010, for instance, one such shell, UK-registered Velcona Ltd., received transfers of $699 million and transferred out $700 million to similarly obscure firms with offshore registrations. On paper, Velcona belonged to a Russian man from a small town just outside Moscow. In 2008, corporate records indicated that the man traveled to London for the firm's shareholders' meeting—a remarkable feat considering that he appeared to have died three years earlier, Global Witness found.[11]

Another shell that did business with AUB was Vesatel United Ltd., a company registered in New Zealand whose director was a woman residing in Panama. Vesatel played a supporting role in the controversial takeover of Kyrgyzstan's largest cell-phone service provider, a deal overseen by Eugene Gourevitch, the peripatetic New York financier. We'll learn more about the intrigue surrounding the lucrative cell-phone company later. When Global Witness tracked down the Panamanian woman to inquire about Vesatel, she wrote back: "I live with my little baby in a small town in the interior of the country and I have no job. I've only been a nominal head of these corporations and I have nothing more to say about this topic."

Why such secrecy?

Temir Sariyev, who as finance minister a few years later helped investigate AUB's operations, told me this: "A lot of money came in from companies overseas, money that needed to be sterilized, several billion of dollars every month. There were all sorts of suspicious transactions. AUB was off-limits to regulators; in fact, the bank told clients, 'We control the state, so no one can interfere with us.' The clients needed guarantees that their cash wouldn't be seized or arrested. So their money would arrive at AUB, spend the night, and then get transferred out via six or seven shell companies overseas. AUB earned commissions on these transactions, hundreds of millions of dollars." Having sifted through thousands of transfers and corporate registration documents, Global Witness arrived at a similar conclusion, citing "alarming red flags for money laundering." Kyrgyz prosecutors later accused the bank of facilitating "large-scale embezzlement of state funds" to the tune of tens of millions of dollars. Nadel, for his part, denied all these allegations and claimed the bank was in strict compliance with all applicable laws.

Asia Universal Bank wasn't some Podunk entity operating on the margins of the global financial system. It had relationships with the world's best-known financial institutions, Citibank, Standard Chartered, and UBS among them. Inside Kyrgyzstan, AUB grew into a colossus that held the accounts of major Kyrgyz companies, such as the airport operator, the national railways, the gold-export monopoly, a major electricity distributor, and many others. On top of that, AUB managed key state assets, including the Treasury and the National Pension Fund. It was an astounding achievement for a bank that only a few years earlier had been a storefront registered in western Samoa, barely worth $150,000 and not even able to obtain a retail banking license.

There was more. Gourevitch, AUB's part owner and board member, set up his own shop in Kyrgyzstan, called MGN Group. Billed as the country's first investment bank, MGN scored an immediate coup: it won the contest to manage Kyrgyzstan's entire development fund, an all-purpose investment pot of money worth nearly $300 million. MGN's victory in that contest wasn't in any grave doubt because there were no other competitors. "If Goldman Sachs had bid on the contract, they might have gotten it," Gourevitch told me. "But we were the only ones there." Gourevitch parked the fund at AUB, and then transferred most of it to a Swiss branch of a Liechtenstein bank, where it was out of reach of auditors or regulators. Pricewaterhouse Coopers later reviewed the transfers and concluded that although the fund was eventually returned to Kyrgyzstan in its entirety, "there was a possibility that it had been used for money-laundering or other potentially illegal activities."[12] Gourevitch told me that all he did was exercise "sound cash management."

The man in charge of the development fund was Maxim Bakiyev, the president's son. His official job title was director of the Central Agency for Development and Investments, a government department custom-made for him to run. Gourevitch and Maxim were friendly, having met through Nadel, the super-banker. Gourevitch knew Kyrgyzstan's president too, and even translated for him during several private meetings with foreigners. Maxim, for his part, trusted Gourevitch with his own fortune and frequently checked in to see how his investments were faring at Gourevitch's boutique firm. "I had a few million of his personal money that we were running at MGN, so he wanted updates," Gourevitch told me. MGN, in turn, did most of its business through Asia Universal Bank.

In his early thirties, the well-connected Gourevitch became a ubiquitous presence in Kyrgyzstan's business circles. Besides his involvement with AUB, the New York financier sat on the boards of major local companies in which MGN Group had made investments. In 2009, Goure-vitch became deputy director of strategy at Megacom, Kyrgyzstan's larg-est cell-phone service provider. In a mere decade of existence, Megacom became a case study of how the country's successive ruling clans horned themselves into Kyrgyzstan's biggest businesses.

Founded in 1999, Megacom snatched the country's first GSM li-cense, granting it permission to operate within the promising but yet-untapped cellular band that would soon dominate the market. At the time, Megacom was purely a paper creation, but it had all the right papers. The local businessman set out to find investors, and he soon connected with people close to Aidar Akayev, the younger son of Kyrgyzstan's first president.

Whether by force, persuasion, or because of a mutually beneficial meeting of the minds born of some combination of the two, people affili-ated with Aidar gained control of Megacom, according to a well-placed insider who later investigated the company's history on behalf of the government. By 2005, Aidar's people sold Megacom to a Britain-based, offshore-registered firm called Penwell Business Ltd., which represented Russian telecom investors. With Penwell's money, Megacom started build-ing a network of cellular towers, in preparation for going live. But the Tulip Revolution disrupted those plans. The newly installed Bakiyev ad-ministration suspended Megacom's license. "New people came to power, and all work stopped," the Megacom insider told me. "They said the Kyr-gyz state must have an ownership stake in the company." Within months, Penwell sold 49 percent of Megacom to a Hong Kong–registered firm that acted as a front for Maxim Bakiyev, according to Kyrgyz prosecu-tors. The firm was nominally owned by a longtime friend of Maxim, who died two years later in a jet skiing accident on Lake Issyk-Kul.

With Maxim cut into the deal, Megacom resumed operations, its sus-pended license magically restored. Megacom plowed more money into its network of towers. Then, in 2009, entrepreneurs affiliated with Maxim made a bold move to push Penwell, Megacom's majority owner, out of the business altogether, according to Kyrgyz prosecutors. The alleged scheme followed the classic post-Soviet scenario known as "a raider's takeover," which makes a Western-style hostile takeover look amicable and cuddly by comparison.

In the 1990s, as private enterprise began to blossom across the former Soviet Union, business disputes quickly acquired a dark side. Say, you opened a popular restaurant in a choice location in downtown Moscow, and others took note of your lucrative business and the valuable real estate behind it. But you weren't interested in selling. One day, you show up at the restaurant to find that the locks have been changed. Someone you've never seen before tells you that you no longer own the place. You get upset and think it's all a prank or a mistake, and turn to the police and the courts, only to learn that the restaurant has indeed been sold, multiple times, and is now owned by a firm registered in Cyprus. There are court decisions and share-transfer records to back this up. You appear to have signed some of them. You can sue the new owners, but they will protest in court that they acquired the restaurant fair and square, not from you, but from another company you've never heard of. Good luck untangling what happened and getting your business back. Corporate raids like this take different shapes and colors, but what they all have in common is the raiders' ability to enlist the help of corrupt judges, cops, or taxmen to steal your business. And it has happened to companies far bigger than the hypothetical Moscow restaurant.

In the battle for control of Megacom in 2008, Maxim-affiliated Forntek sued Penwell, the carrier's majority owner, over a seemingly obscure development. Penwell's ownership structure, which included wealthy Russian telecom investors, had changed, and Forntek insisted it should have been consulted on those changes ahead of time. Since Penwell hadn't given any advance notice of its internal reshuffle, Forntek claimed in a Bishkek court that the Russian firm violated an agreement between the two owners of Megacom. As a penalty for this breach, the court should strip Penwell of its entire 51 percent ownership stake in Megacom and turn it over to Forntek, the Hong Kong firm said in its lawsuit. Perhaps unsurprisingly, the court agreed, and told Penwell to get lost. Never mind that the Russian investors had been plowing money and equipment into Megacom for years.

Corporate raids of this kind rarely stop with a single transaction or a favorable court order. What usually follows is chain of other deals designed to cover up the trail and complicate any subsequent attempts by the jilted owners to recover their assets. Kyrgyz prosecutors allege this is exactly what happened after the court squeezed Penwell out of Megacom. "Using the court decision, [people affiliated with Forntek] transferred 100 percent of Megacom shares to several straw buyers in the course of a single month, in order to eliminate the possibility of Penwell reclaiming those shares from their illegal possession," Kyrgyzstan's prosecutor's office said later.

Gourevitch, by then Megacom's deputy director of strategy, provided the final twist in this alleged plot. He arranged for Megacom to borrow $80 million from a local bank, money that was "later transferred out, in cash, via an offshore firm using a fake passport," according to prosecutors. When the bank demanded repayment of the loan, Megacom had no money, and another court pronounced the beleaguered cell-phone carrier bankrupt. Such forced bankruptcies are another common way for corporate raiders to artificially lower the price of a target company's assets and then sweep them up in a bankruptcy fire sale. In Megacom's case, the loan and the bankruptcy were designed to facilitate "the ultimate siphoning off" of the carrier's assets, the prosecutors said.

While Gourevitch worked on the Megacom loan, an associate of his registered two offshore companies that snapped up Megacom's assets in the bankruptcy auction. Those assets included expensive telecom equipment provided earlier by the jilted Russian investors. The two offshore firms then sold those assets to yet another company, Alpha Telecom, that appeared to have been set up for the sole purpose of absorbing the carrier's assets. Alpha, in turn, sold shares in itself to two other offshore shells. One of them, the New Zealand–registered Vesatel, had as its director the self-described unemployed single mother living in Panama. Kyrgyz prosecutors alleged that Maxim stood as the ultimate beneficiary behind the facade of the straw buyers. But the man who founded Alpha Telecom later told Global Witness that he represented a group of Kazakhstani investors. "It's difficult to tell if Maxim had anything to do with that group," he said. Gourevitch declined to discuss the matter with me, citing the ongoing Kyrgyz investigation. In an earlier blog post, he wrote that he'd been asked "to help optimize certain processes at [Megacom]. I did this. Nothing sensational."

Gourevitch did tell me about Maxim's general approach to commerce: "In the business world, he would be as ruthless as he could. If he didn't consider you to be in his circle of trust, then he would basically do whatever. He had interests or controlling interests in many businesses. But Asia Universal bank was how he amassed his wealth. Not only was it a way for him to make money, but it was also one of the few places he could trust to keep his money. And in a situation like his I don't know which is more important." Maxim has said little publicly about what he did during his dad's presidency. In the one statement he issued from exile in London, where he eventually fled, he called all charges against him "bogus" and designed "to divert the attention" from the misdeeds of Kyrgyzstan's new rulers.

Maxim's outsize business role prompted inevitable comparisons with Aidar Akayev, the influential son of the previous president, who was rumored to have a penchant for drink. Wags coined a joke comparing the two, and Maxim came out looking worse: "We'd rather have a drunk Aidar than a sober Maxim."

While Kyrgyzstan's premier mobile carrier dissipated through the offshore carousel only to be reconstituted in the hands of mysterious new owners, Gourevitch was hobnobbing with former U.S. senators. As director of Asia Universal Bank, Gourevitch was busy burnishing the bank's international image, in preparation for an initial public offering from which AUB's principals stood to reap enormous profits. Some valuations placed its market worth at close to half a billion dollars. As part of the whitewash, Nadel and Gourevitch retained APCO Worldwide, an American public-relations firm. Through APCO, Kyrgyzstan's bankers hired two former U.S. senators to serve on AUB's board of directors.

One was Bob Dole, the stentorian-voiced Kansas Republican and World War II hero who unsuccessfully ran for president against Bill Clinton in 1996, and who later starred in a television commercial for Viagra, the erection booster drug. The other was J. Bennett Johnston, a Louisiana Democrat and a veteran Washington lobbyist. According to a person familiar with their hiring, the senators were paid $175,000 each a year to serve on the AUB board, a job that entailed occasional board meetings in Bishkek and in Vienna, but little other work. The senators also received stock options that could be worth additional hundreds of thousands of dollars in the event of a successful initial public offering.

Back in Bishkek, Asia Universal Bank was flying high, its many lines of business running smoothly. Judging from photos taken at the time, a trim, youthful Nadel liked to wear his hair slicked back, which gave him a passing resemblance to Gordon Gekko from the movie *Wall Street*. He was a prominent presence in Bishkek, donating to charitable causes and winning international banking awards. "It would be simply inhumane to refuse aid to a seriously ill child, a war veteran or a single mother who has stumbled on financial hardship," Nadel told a Western trade publication at the time.

Behind the scenes, however, AUB engaged in strong-arm tactics and staged a Megacom-style corporate raid against a major local rival that had a large retail network coveted by AUB, according to Kyrgyz investigators. The target was PromStroiBank, one of Kyrgyzstan's oldest banks, founded by an elderly man who was known to harbor pro-opposition sentiments. Temir Sariyev, the prominent opposition figure who would later become finance minister, told me PromStroiBank was pushed into an artificial bankruptcy as the first step of the corporate raid. Officials at the state social fund, managed by PromStroiBank at the time, decided to withdraw the fund from the bank's accounts. "Contractually, they may pull the money out of the bank gradually, with advance notice. But they came to the bank and said, 'We need the money tomorrow.' The bank said, 'You should give us some time.' So they sued the bank, saying it failed to fulfill its obligations. The bank couldn't prove anything to the judge, and the court declared the bank bankrupt," Sariyev told me. In 2008, AUB swooped in to buy the weakened rival, cementing its position as Kyrgyzstan's biggest bank.

Nadel disputed this account and said PromStroiBank's bankruptcy was a natural outcome of the bank's financial difficulties, and that there was nothing artificial about it. "What should the state do in a situation like this, when a private bank is refusing to return state money?" Nadel told me. There was no corporate raid or a rigged court order, just a normal failure of a competitor, in which AUB spotted a business opportunity, Nadel said.

AUB wasn't the immediate first buyer of the bankrupt rival. A smaller Kyrgyz bank picked up PromStroiBank first, and then, within a month or so, flipped it to AUB. If Saryiev is right, and a raid had indeed taken place, then the presence of a straw buyer would be consistent with the general pattern of such takeovers. Nadel assured me that AUB's delay in stepping in had a simple explanation: AUB had to convene its far-flung board members and get their green light for the purchase. "I needed a month to obtain board approval," Nadel said. "As you know, we had former senators on the board, so we needed time."

Is it possible that prominent former U.S. legislators rubberstamped a dubious corporate takeover in faraway Kyrgyzstan and otherwise lent credibility to the allegedly massive money-laundering operation? I put the question to J. Bennett Johnston, the former Louisiana senator and a Washington lobbyist affiliated with the white-shoe law firm of Steptoe & Johnson. As far as he was concerned, AUB was a clean bank eager to improve its international reputation. Allegations of malfeasance sounded implausible to the former senator. "There was no factual basis for this, none," Johnston told me. Yet he conceded that he knew "amazingly little" about the bank's inner workings, having visited Bishkek only twice and stayed no longer than three days. "It's not like it was see-no-evil-hear-no-evil," Johnston continued, saying a major audit testified to the bank's integrity. "We would not have besmirched our reputations acquired over decades for some bank in Kyrgyzstan. That's just absurd to me." Johnston declined to comment on how much he was paid.

Gourevitch, who helped recruit the senators to AUB's board, told me, "They turned off common sense, but they were paid very well." Gourevitch made a small personal contribution too. One day, when he was talking to Bob Dole, the former presidential candidate mentioned that his wife, Elizabeth, a sitting U.S. senator from North Carolina, was running for office again. Gourevitch made a $4,600 contribution to Elizabeth Dole's reelection campaign. "I thought it was a nice gesture," he said. In a biting television ad around that time, Elizabeth Dole accused her opponent, a former Sunday school teacher named Kay Hagan, of accepting campaign donations from a political action committee representing "godless Americans." "She hid from cameras, took godless money," the voice-over said. "What did Hagan promise in return?" Elizabeth Dole lost to Hagan by a wide margin. I tried to contact Bob Dole directly and through his spokesman to discuss his involvement with AUB and Gourevitch. Neither responded.

Looming over Kyrgyzstan through it all was the steely presence of Maxim, who occupied a special place in the unofficial pecking order. The prime minister and scores of other senior officials, many of them old enough to be his father and outranking him in the formal hierarchy, flocked to him for advice, consultation, or approval of key decisions. "I believe he had this model in mind: the ruling family is rich and has absolute control over key policies and institutions; he wanted to rule with an iron fist," Gourevitch told me. In private conversations, Maxim showed a strong authoritarian streak too. "You'd be talking to him, and he'd cut you off, saying something like, 'Okay, I got it.' And you knew it was over; if you were going to keep pushing your opinion beyond that you were risking his wrath."

Sadyrkulov, the president's chief of staff, watched Maxim's rise with dismay, tainted as it was with widespread whispers of corruption and strong-arm tactics. According to friends, Sadyrkulov began to drift away from the young man he had once believed in and had big plans for. With the president's brothers and Sadyrkulov famously at odds, the relationship with Maxim was the major link keeping Sadyrkulov in the inner circle of the first family. As that relationship grew strained, the chief of staff was fast becoming an odd man out.

Mysterious Deaths

As the New Year's Eve of 2007–8 was approaching, Sadyrkulov received a stream of well-wishers and gift-bearers for that biggest of holidays on the old Soviet calendar. A massive secular Christmas that freezes all work for nearly two weeks of champagne-and-vodka-soaked overeating, the holiday is a time to give presents not only to family and friends but also to business associates and others whose good disposition might be desirable in the year to come. As a powerful man whose favor was sought nationwide, Sadyrkulov was the target of a veritable avalanche of presents, cards, flowers, and bottles of fine booze that were delivered by mail, messenger, or in person, both to his office next to the president's and to his city apartment.

New Year's Eve was a busy time for the women of the Sadyrkulov household. Ainagul, his wife of many years, was preparing a festive family dinner. A Christmas tree glittered in the living room. The door-bell rang with yet another delivery, and in the general commotion of the evening Sadyrkulov's twelve-year-old daughter accepted a small package festooned with holiday wrapping. There was an unsigned card that read: "On New Year's Eve, one's soul is filled with anticipation of a miracle. We wish you to have a wonderful celebration of the holiday and to re-main in an excellent mood for the rest of the year!"

The twelve-year-old ripped off the wrapping and peered into the package, not quite sure what she was looking at. Inside were two small purplish-black objects. She showed the package to her mother, who went pale when she saw the contents: a severed human ear and a finger. Within hours, the extended Sadyrkulov family would sit down for New Year's dinner, a never-ending marathon of toasts and banter. So Ainagul de-cided not to spoil the fun. Thankfully, her young daughter didn't under-stand what she'd just seen. Laughing off the matter, Ainagul put the box out on the balcony, where the winter cold kept the body parts intact while the family celebrated New Year's a few feet away. "It was a good party," recalled Aijan who, like everyone else around the table that night, had no idea about the macabre gift chilling outside. Shaken up, Ainagul nonetheless managed to keep a poker face through the evening as she watched her husband crack jokes and be his usual ebullient self.

On the morning of January 1, Ainagul showed Sadyrkulov the body parts. The chief of staff lost it. "Bastards!" But he quickly collected him-self and set about figuring out who could have sent the package. Since it was reasonable to assume that the mastermind was both crazy enough to dream up a stunt like that and powerful enough to think he could get

Medet Sadyrkulov with his wife, Ainagul. (Courtesy of Ainagul Sadyrkulova)

away with it, Sadyrkulov needed to approach the investigation carefully. He needed someone he could trust with this delicate matter.

Like the rest of the country, Melis Turganbayev was planning to sleep in on January 1. A police colonel in charge of the organized-crime unit in the Interior Ministry, Turganbayev let his subordinates go veg out for the first ten days of January, in keeping with the general celebratory somnolence. But at 10:00 a.m., Turganbayev was woken up by a phone call. Reluctantly, he shuffled over to the phone. "Sadyrkulov would like to see you now," the caller from the chief of staff's office informed the sleepy colonel. He wasn't offered any explanation for the urgent summons. "What a mess," Turganbayev thought as he got dressed and hit the deserted streets.

Later that morning, a somber Sadyrkulov showed Turganbayev the finger and the ear. The colonel and the chief of staff weren't close friends but they knew each other well from earlier in their careers when Sadyrkulov was head of a municipal district in Bishkek while Turganbayev ran the police department of the same district. Both men had risen through the ranks since then, and now Sadyrkulov asked his old cop buddy to investigate the provenance of the body parts, still sitting in their half-ripped gift box. "No one should know about this," Sadyrkulov told him. Leaving the meeting with the severed finger and ear in his bag, Turganbayev thought, "Something really bizarre is going on here." The matter would eventually cost him his job, and almost cost him his freedom and reputation.

The first thing that strikes you about Turganbayev are his own ears. Asymmetrical and misshapen, they resemble two squished dumplings flattened against a square head, on top of which sparse strands of black hair are combed strategically to camouflage a widening bald spot. Ears like that are usually a calling card of a wrestler. When I asked him about a possible athletic background, Turganbayev allowed that he'd "done some sports in the past, just like everyone else." It wasn't until I returned to the subject a couple more times that Turganbayev reluctantly revealed that he was a little more than a weekend ranger. Twice he'd won the Soviet Union's junior wrestling championship, a massive event stacked with burly hirsute men from all over the empire.

With an economics degree from a Bishkek college, Turganbayev had ambitions beyond the wrestling mat. After a short stint as a bookkeeper on a collective farm, he almost joined the KGB, but demurred at the last minute and became a beat cop instead. His caseload tended toward the brutal: assaults, murders, and rapes. In the early days on the beat, he arrested a man who confessed to having raped and killed a little girl. In the precinct, Turganbayev, who by then had kids of his own, snapped and threw a few heavy punches at the rapist. That was the only time in his career that he lost composure like that, although he claims the bloodied suspect later told him he probably deserved the extrajudicial beating. More complex cases soon followed, including the mysterious murders of the former head of the customs service and his wife.

In 2002, someone threw a grenade at the car of the secretary of the National Security Council. The secretary suffered fragmentation wounds but survived the explosion. A nationwide manhunt for the grenade lobber was launched. Turganbayev led the investigation. Within six months, the colonel arrested the main suspect: a young military veteran with a history of substance abuse. The man told Turganbayev he was merely a triggerman and that the contract to kill the security-council chief had come from on high. Turganbayev began untangling those threads, and soon enough was zeroing in on "some important people who may have ordered the hit," he recalled. Just as the inquiry entered its most sensitive stage, the case was taken away from Turganbayev without explanation and given to the National Security Service, the successor agency of the old Soviet KGB. Turganbayev was ordered to turn over all evidence he'd collected in the case and move on. "The higher you climb, the more politics and intrigue there are," Turganbayev said. "Those in power need flexible people in law enforcement, people who can do their bidding." His digging must have annoyed some powerful folks, because the pressure on him didn't stop there.

Relieved of the high-profile case, the colonel now had time to take care of a project that he'd long postponed: renovating the shabby building of his criminal-investigations unit. But with no money in the budget, he had to be creative about financing. An acquaintance in the construction business gave him some leftover fiber-optic cables, which Turganbayev then bartered elsewhere for new paint to throw on his precinct's peeling walls. The scheme may not have met squeaky-clean contracting rules, but it was the only way to get the cracks in the walls patched over. A corruption investigation into the matter soon followed, and Turganbayev was fired. While he fought in the courts to clear his name and get reinstated, the Tulip Revolution took place and demolished the government.

Within days of the revolt, the lone triggerman arrested in the 2002 grenade attack on the security chief's car met with a suspicious death in his prison cell. Back when Turganbayev was investigating the case, the man had told him he'd recorded a detailed tape naming names of those who ordered the assassination. He promised to reveal the whereabouts of the tape only at trial. But now, with the revolution tearing up the old law-enforcement and government hierarchies, there was a real risk that the triggerman's tape would never see the light of day, or that new investigators would not take his story seriously. One morning he was found hanged in his cell. The tape, if it existed, never surfaced. Though the official version was suicide, Turganbayev has little doubt that the man had been killed to shut him up for good. "So the case remained a mystery."

For the colonel himself, the revolution was good news. The old corruption charges against him were dropped, and he resumed his job on the police force. Turganbayev recalled those days immediately after the Tulip Revolution as a brief window of optimism. "We all thought the system would change for the better, that we would be able to work normally, but we were naïve."

This was the man who on January 1 of 2008 walked the empty streets of Bishkek with a human finger and ear in his bag and a lot of unanswered questions in his head.

To solve the mystery, Turganbayev and his small team of criminal investigators first needed to find the corpse that had supplied the contents of the New Year's gift. They scoured Bishkek's morgues and hospitals looking for a body with missing fingers and ears. They scrutinized police reports and death certificates, and finally stumbled upon a body that seemed to match the description. On January 3, in the foothills outside the city, police had found a male corpse missing both ears and three fingers on his left hand. Strangely, authorities didn't investigate foul play, on the assumption that the disfigurement had likely been inflicted by wild foxes. "Get over there quickly!" Turganbayev urged his underlings. They photographed the unidentified corpse and then fanned out across Bishkek's homeless shelters and others spots where the homeless were known to congregate in the winter to keep warm.

Shown the picture, the indigents shrugged their shoulders and shook their heads until one vagrant finally recognized the dead man. "That's Tolik the Singer," he exclaimed to investigators. Tolik played the accordion well and liked to sing.

"So where is he now?" one investigator asked.

"Oh, he died at the end of December, right over there in the lobby of that apartment block," the homeless man said, pointing his finger in that direction. Investigators found the dead man's sister, who told them Tolik had become a vagabond shortly after their parents passed away. Alone and cold one night, he died.

Next, Turganbayev's gumshoes found the local beat cop who had responded to the call about Tolik's death. The young cop said that just as he arrived on the scene he saw two other, more senior policemen from another precinct loading the dead Tolik into their car.

"Hey, where are you taking him?" the beat cop asked them.

"None of your business, forget about it," one of them said. Then the pair drove off with the body.[13]

By analyzing transcripts of police dispatch records and interviewing witnesses, Turganbayev's investigators eventually identified both of those policemen and established that they'd received an order from a higher-up to find a suitable corpse.

"Sir, are you joking?" one of those cops, Tynychbek Mamatov, asked his commanding officer when he gave him the bizarre order, according to his later testimony in court. But Mamatov and a colleague did as they were told. Thinking no one would miss a dead bum, they took Tolik's body and drove it out to a deserted field. Their commanding officer and three unidentified men trailed them in another car with tinted windows.

"Drop the body here and leave," the commanding officer snapped at the junior cops.

They were happy to oblige. Next, the men from the officer's car approached Tolik's body and cut off fingers and ears.

As Turganbayev pieced together the gory puzzle and moved up the police hierarchy, his team, like overzealous Internal Affairs sleuths everywhere, faced stonewalling and intimidation. From interviews, documents, and tips, Turganbayev began to form a suspicion that Janysh Bakiyev himself may have commissioned the New Year's gift to Sadyrkulov as a way to warn the ambitious chief of staff to know his place in the pecking order.

But Turganbayev wasn't given time to continue the investigation. Just as in 2003, when his probe of the high-profile grenade attack was blocked, the ear-and-finger inquiry hit a wall too. His superiors told Turganbayev to close the investigation and forward all case materials he'd collected so far to the prosecutor's office. The two cops who'd snatched Tolik's body eventually faced disciplinary action, but they weren't fired or jailed—indeed, they were reprimanded only for moving the corpse without authorization, with no mention made of the severed body parts.

Turganbayev's small team of investigators was disbanded, and the colonel was reassigned to the most boring part of the Interior Ministry—back-office operations and budgets, as far from investigative work as you could get without leaving the force altogether.

Turganbayev shared the results of his aborted investigation with Sadyrkulov, the man who had dragged him into it in the first place. The chief of staff thanked the colonel and said, enigmatically, that "we've already sorted it out." There were indications that Sadyrkulov had already concluded that Janysh was behind the gift and that he confronted the president with the gruesome tale involving his powerful younger brother. And now Sadyrkulov too wanted the matter closed.

With a short goatee giving him a nonthreatening professorial demeanor, Vadim Nochevkin is one of Kyrgyzstan's top investigative reporters. For years, he followed the country's wild gyrations for a small newspaper called *Delo nomer* ("Case Number"), a name that evokes the numbering of criminal files, the paper's bread and butter. Under an irreverent motto, "The Sun Shines on Everyone Equally," printed across the top of the front page, the newspaper dives into crime stories, both mundane and high profile. To make itself appear better staffed and to avoid boring readers with the same few bylines, the paper instructs its handful of reporters to alternate their real names with pennames in print. For a paper called "Case Number," the ear-and-finger tale was the equivalent of Watergate, and Nochevkin dug in.

He had already established a journalistic relationship with Sadyrkulov, and now the chief of staff summoned him for a chat that followed their usual routine. Sadyrkulov and his driver would pick up Nochevkin somewhere in town, drive around for a bit, and park in a quiet place. Then the driver would go for a walk, and the chief of staff and the reporter would talk in the backseat. During this chat, Sadyrkulov told Nochevkin that the people behind the New Year's gift were motivated by "jealousy, by the desire to avenge their impotence, by failures of their own projects. In other words, they couldn't handle the competition."

Nochevkin asked if the president knew.

"The president knows everything," Sadyrkulov replied. "And he drew his own conclusions, without making excuses for some of the people involved." Sadyrkulov then decided to compliment his boss's wisdom. In hindsight it appears that it wasn't so much praise as wishful thinking, the final hope that he could pull the president away from his family's influence.

"Bakiyev doesn't repeat Akayev's mistakes," Sadyrkulov told Nochevkin during their backseat chat. "He strives to be objective and independent in his actions. And this guarantees that our country will develop completely differently from the way things have been going for the past fifteen years. And I can't say more right now, so stop torturing me." But the digger in Nochevkin kept pressing the chief of staff about the identity of the finger-and-ear mastermind; he wanted names. Finally, and strictly off-the-record, Sadyrkulov leaned close to the reporter's ear and whispered a single name: "Janysh."

Leaping out of the chief of staff's car, Nochevkin knew he had a blockbuster on his hands. Although he wouldn't be printing Janysh's name, he still had reams of explosive stuff about the behind-the-scenes machinations in the White House. At the newspaper's small office, Nochevkin wrote up his burst of journalistic sunshine that would dominate the front page. Following the ground rules of the interview, Nochevkin showed the draft to Sadyrkulov, who signed off on it. But just hours before taking the page proofs to the printing plant, Nochevkin got a phone call from the chief of staff with an urgent plea: "Kill the story." When the reporter protested that the issue had already been laid out, ads and all, and was set for publication that very evening, Sadyrkulov assured the newspaper's management that he'd "compensate" it for the trouble. Angry at his temperamental source, Nochevkin pulled the story and replaced it with one of those random and humdrum criminal tales supplied in abundance by Bishkek's police blotter.

When I met Nochevkin in his small office in central Bishkek, it was already late in the evening, and he sat alone among stacks of old newspapers, notebooks, and full ashtrays, a wintry breeze hustling in some fresh air through an open window. Nochevkin speculated that Sadyrkulov, true to his insatiable appetite for palace intrigue, showed the story draft to the president as a way to increase pressure on Janysh. Nochevkin said he heard that the president got angry and even yelled at his younger brother. So even without being published, the story served its purpose in Sadyrkulov's eyes, and now he wanted it dead, maybe because the president asked him not to air his family's dirty laundry publicly. "Sadyrkulov thought that he won that round," Nochevkin said.

Aijan, Sadyrkulov's oldest daughter who was very close to him, had a similar recollection of how the finger-and-ear matter ended. "The president apologized to my dad, told him he was sorry about Janysh's behavior, and asked my dad to let the matter slide."

For Turganbayev, the police colonel who traced the body parts up the chain of command, payback for diligent digging came swiftly. On a warm evening in July, Turganbayev was invited to a boozy party organized by his colleagues. A few tables away, there was a gaggle of young women whom Turganbayev did not know. What happened next ended Turganbayev's career. He was accused of beating up two of the women and attempting to rape them. Someone snapped photos that purported to show the colonel in action.

Turganbayev said it was all a setup from beginning to end: the invitation, the party, the girls, the drinks, the doctored photos. "The saddest thing is I was framed by my own colleagues." Those were dark, "horrible" days for Turganbayev, a married father of four. While he awaited trial, newspapers turned over every lurid detail of the disgraced colonel's alleged partying. He was unemployed. He feared that someone might kill the women and pin the murders on him as an attempt to silence the witnesses. So Turganbayev took them to a safe house in the mountains. "I was hiding them; they cried all the time, they were being intimidated," he recalled.

Turganbayev told me that he confronted Janysh. The bullheaded wrestler claimed that he told the president's brother: "I'm so sick and tired of all this. I don't want my police job back. But you've pushed me into a corner, so I have to fight back." He didn't tell me how Janysh reacted to this outburst.

Many months later, a court would acquit Turganbayev of all charges.

Sadyrkulov, of course, knew what was happening. He must have suspected that the smear campaign was connected to Turganbayev's finger-

and-ear probe—the probe that Sadyrkulov had dragged him into in the first place. But the chief of staff couldn't save his old police buddy. "Sadyrkulov always said that he is a cop in the absolute best sense of the word 'cop,'" recalled Erik Arsaliyev, a mutual friend of the two men. "So it weighed very heavily on Sadyrkulov that he couldn't protect him now."

Sadyrkulov may have won the finger-and-ear battle, but he was quickly losing the broader war. In 2008, Sadyrkulov's powerful bureaucratic fiefdom within the government came under assault. A new political blueprint—drafted by a consultant who went by the nickname Africanych because of his unconventional patronymic—set out an entirely new executive structure, in effect a parallel bureaucracy that would give the president's family direct control over everything. Though Sadyrkulov would keep his job as the chief of staff, his role would be severely circumscribed. The man who reveled in being the power behind the throne, the big-picture guy, the gray cardinal of the White House would now become a mere errand boy carrying out tasks dreamed up by the newly created Secretariat. This shadowy outfit with an Orwellian-sounding name would in turn take orders from no one except the president's family.

Sadyrkulov was furious. He printed out and showed to close friends an e-mail describing the Africanych plan. "I simply cannot work in conditions of such concentration of power," he told Ibraimova. Valentin Bogatyrev, a well-connected political consultant who knew him, described Sadyrkulov's situation in even starker terms. "He was cast aside in a very insulting, unceremonious way." There was a personal twist too. For some time now, Sadyrkulov had been conducting an affair with a woman named Oksana Malevannaya, a former television executive with close-cropped blonde hair. They had a son together, though Sadyrkulov never divorced or left his wife. Such dalliances are common among the Kyrgyz business and political elite. President Bakiyev, also married, had taken on a concubine himself, and there were persistent rumors of frequent liaisons with other women too. Now, Sadyrkulov's lover was tapped to run the Secretariat.

The looming, humiliating end of his personal power was the final straw that pushed Sadyrkulov toward the exit. Some of his allies within the government and the Parliament were feeling restive too, as the power in Kyrgyzstan was quickly flowing into the mercurial circle of the president's relatives. Elmira Ibraimova, the deputy prime minister and a close friend of Sadyrkulov, considered resigning in the fall of 2008. But she shelved that plan to deal with a devastating airplane crash that killed Kyrgyzstan's entire junior basketball team en route to a tournament in Iran. Throughout the year, the chief of staff was counseling his allies against rash, emotional resignations. If Sadyrkulov was going to jump, he wanted to have a game plan for what to do next.

Sometime in late December, Sadyrkulov met with the president for a frank late-night chat greased by vodka. In his own later account of the meeting, Sadyrkulov said he made a final, fruitless plea for the president to distance himself from the cesspool of corruption and nepotism festering around him. Around that time, he also rejected an offer to become foreign minister.[14] Sadyrkulov handed his resignation letter to Bakiyev in early January of 2009, and the president accepted it on the spot. Hours later, Ibraimova, the deputy prime minister, stepped down too. Sadyrkulov was his own man now.

His first reaction was a huge sense of relief. All the tension and gloom of the past few months seemed to lift. To mark his newfound freedom, Sadyrkulov threw a small party for his close friends and allies. As a band played onstage, Sadyrkulov danced and cracked jokes. "It's as if a hump on my back has suddenly fallen off, and I can feel the wings growing underneath," he told Galina Kulikova, a longtime friend who now served in Parliament as a member of Sadyrkulov's puppet political party.

"But what should we do now? Should we also quit?" Kulikova asked him.

"The time for that hasn't come yet, but it may well come soon," Sadyrkulov replied. "For now, your task is to manage our people in Parliament."

And here was the crux of Sadyrkulov's plan. Having personally witnessed—and quashed—the opposition's heartfelt but futile haranguing against the regime, the former chief of staff wasn't going to become just another angry guy shouting himself hoarse at political rallies. He was planning something much more ambitious and effective: he was going to use the vast bureaucratic machinery of the state against the president and his inner circle.

One leg of that plan involved Ak-Jol, the puppet political party whose deputies owed their jobs in large part to Sadyrkulov's evil political genius. At some point those deputies were to take up publicly the issues of government corruption and ineptitude and perhaps engineer a vote of no-confidence in the president, and then quit en masse. Once that symbolic slap in the face was delivered, Sadyrkulov was planning to activate his informal network of influential regional officials, and key police and military officers. In the two months between his resignation and his death, Sadyrkulov worked frantically to implement that plan and find money and diplomatic backing to make it happen. In private meetings with officials in Kazakhstan, Sadyrkulov enjoyed spinning the finger-and-ear tale as an example of the Bakiyev regime's depravity.

In all his grand plans, Sadyrkulov didn't seem to envision himself as president. One reason was that as an ethnic Kazakh he stood little chance of winning the top job in an honest election: in Kyrgyzstan, you have to be a Kyrgyz to be a player at that level. This wasn't like running to be chairman of an obscure college Communist Party committee, his only direct electoral experience. Another reason was that his own political past was too blemished to allow him to become a unifying figure in any kind of a popular revolt. But one can't help thinking that a deeper reason was that after all the years of behind-the-scenes machinations, Sadyrkulov simply grew to love the thrill of plotting. So in the next government, he preferred to be a gray cardinal again.

One day in February, Sadyrkulov showed up at the bunkerlike U.S. embassy on the outskirts of Bishkek and pitched his revolution to Washington. Back in his gray-cardinal days, Sadyrkulov had already established rapport with key U.S. diplomats, at one point treating the U.S. ambassador to a lavish, wine-soaked dinner at 12 Chimneys. By coincidence, it was the same countryside retreat where the man whose Audi rammed into Sadyrkulov's Lexus a year later would claim to have spent the night before the crash.

At his dinner with the American ambassador at 12 Chimneys, the president's chief of staff was a boisterous host, showing up with his hair "wet and disheveled," according to a U.S. diplomatic account. It turned out that right before dinner, Sadyrkulov had dunked his head into a mountain spring, his favorite way of decompressing after a hard day. During the meal, the chief of staff was "not shy about sharing stories about those who have double-crossed him, and how he has settled the score," the dispatch notes. After polishing off the French wine he kept ordering, Sadyrkulov led the American ambassador toward the mountain spring so that she too "could partake of this 'magical' Kyrgyz ritual."[15]

Now, having become a coup plotter, Sadyrkulov came to the U.S. embassy to persuade the Americans to double-cross President Bakiyev. A skillful salesman, Sadyrkulov pitched his revolution by emphasizing the one thing that America really cared about in Kyrgyzstan: the Manas military base supporting the war in Afghanistan. Ever since President Akayev had allowed the Americans to set up shop at Manas International Airport, the base had sprouted multiple layers of geopolitical intrigue and local tensions. Moscow was always lukewarm about the idea of permanent American outposts in the old imperial backyard. Beijing, too, worried about being encircled by American military bases. Through a regional security group dominated by them, Russia and China put their concerns on paper and urged Central Asia to kick the Americans out.

In Kyrgyzstan, the ruling elites always viewed the American base with ambivalence. In a land with few stable sources of revenue, the base was a natural resource of sorts, a reservoir filled not with oil or gas but with American greenbacks. It was an open-pit mine that disgorged easy money. Every year, the base provided hundreds of millions of dollars in rent, along with lucrative side deals for the supply of fuel and other goods. Also on the positive side of the ledger was the fact that the base elevated the international image of Kyrgyzstan. It was no longer just a remote mountainous republic with too many consonants in its name. It was the only place on Earth to host both American and Russian military bases, a strategic fulcrum of a turbulent region.

But alongside the obvious benefits, the U.S. military presence came with hidden costs: namely, the deteriorating relationship with Moscow and all that could mean for the Kyrgyz economy. With tacit Russian encouragement, President Bakiyev started making threatening noises about the future of the Manas military base. Around that time, an incident took place at the gate of the base that turned the Kyrgyz public opinion sharply against the Americans and gave Bakiyev an easy talking point.

In the early afternoon of December 6, 2006, Alexander Ivanov slowly maneuvered his heavy truck, laden with aviation fuel, up a narrow side road near the airport. Rounding a grove of trees and an icy snowdrift, Ivanov joined the line of other trucks idling at the security checkpoint leading to the U.S. military base. After four years of delivering fuel for the bulky American aircraft parked just behind the wire, Ivanov knew the routine by heart, and could practically do it all blindfolded. Soon enough, his truck would rumble to the front of the line, he'd turn off the engine, and an American serviceman would come to inspect the vehicle while Ivanov waited in the special tent for the all-clear signal. Then, after a thorough pat down and a document check, Ivanov would get behind the wheel again, drive through the gates, dump the fuel into the holding tanks, and go back to the depot for another round.

Drivers like Ivanov were crucial cogs in the American war in nearby Afghanistan. Almost every soldier coming in or out of the country flew on airplanes that stopped at Manas to refuel. And many of the fighter jets and bombers roaming the Afghan airspace were topped up midair by tanker aircraft taking off from Manas. All that fuel was brought to the base one truck at a time by people like Ivanov. Many pay grades above them, a complex, murky, and highly lucrative chain of fuel supply contracts stretched from the Pentagon to a secretive and well-connected firm operating out of an office suite at Bishkek's Hyatt Hotel. The firm's dealings on the international fuel market, and its possible links to the Bakiyev family, would eventually cause a scandal and prompt a flurry of investigations. But we'll get to that later.

For now, let's return to the military tent where Alexander Ivanov sat down on a chair that December afternoon to wait for a U.S. soldier to give him a thumbs-up to return to the truck. What happened next may never be fully known. The U.S. soldier, Zachary Hatfield, later said that Ivanov acted aggressively and threatened him with a knife. At that point, Hatfield shot him twice in the chest with his service pistol, killing him on the spot. Ivanov had no criminal record and no history of violence or alcohol abuse. He lived in a small apartment with his wife of many years. They'd met in college on a double date. Now Alexander and Marina had two kids, and he valued his job, which provided a solid income.

"When his colleagues came to me in the evening and said he'd been shot by an American soldier, I couldn't believe it," Marina told me one afternoon in Bishkek. Hatfield was quickly whisked out of Kyrgyzstan. When I spoke to her nearly five years after her husband's death, Marina said, "I wish they'd reach some kind of a decision, maybe find him guilty. It's sad, they came and killed my husband, and we'll never know anything." U.S. officials apologized to Marina and paid her $50,000 in compensation. Hatfield was discharged from the air force. A grand jury found evidence against him insufficient for prosecution, and there was never a trial.

After Ivanov's death, Marina's private grief became a public spectacle and a PR disaster for the Americans. A small crowd of protesters burned the American flag in front of the embassy, and pressure to evict the base mounted steadily. Alexander Ivanov was an ethnic Russian—in fact, his name sounds almost like John Doe in English, the everyman. A documentary soon aired on Russian state-owned television accusing the base, without a shred of evidence, of a variety of sins, including smuggling Afghan heroin aboard U.S. aircraft. President Bakiyev spoke forcefully against the base, a line of invective fueled by Ivanov's death. Behind the scenes, his killing was being used as an element in the wider strategy "to increase pressure on the U.S. to raise the rent for the base," recalled Zamyra Sydykova, the Kyrgyz ambassador to Washington at the time.

In early 2009, President Bakiyev traveled to Moscow and announced his decision to expel the U.S. base within six months. At the same press conference, Russian officials promised Kyrgyzstan more than $2 billion in grants and loans. Though Moscow denied any quid pro quo, the coincidence seemed too delicious to ignore. In Washington, Ambassador Sydykova advised Secretary of State Hillary Clinton to refrain from making strong retaliatory statements so as not to kill off chances of saving the base. It was all in fact a big poker game, and the Americans understood the motivations of Kyrgyz leaders well. "Their sense of desperation and entitlement has ballooned, and they wish to cut a better deal—with us if we increase compensation, or with Russia if we do not," the American ambassador to Kyrgyzstan wrote to Washington at the time.[16]

It was in this environment that Sadyrkulov, the rogue former chief of staff, came to the U.S. embassy to make his pitch. He asked the American diplomats in Bishkek not to negotiate with Bakiyev but instead to support a Sadyrkulov-led revolt, after which the base's future would no longer be in doubt. It was a smart pitch, but American officials didn't believe Sadyrkulov could pull off a repeat of the Tulip Revolution. They were worried too what President Bakiyev's reaction would be once he found out—as he inevitably would—that the U.S. ambassador was meeting with the man who wanted to overthrow him. It was far safer at the time to play ball with the regime than to plot against it and risk losing the base for good. "We held our nose and dealt with the government that was in power," a U.S. official told me later. Within months, Washington agreed to nearly quadruple its monthly rent for the base to $60 million. And just like that, Bakiyev flip-flopped again and allowed the base to stay. Shortly afterward, a persistent anti-Bakiyev campaign began on Russian state television, a staple in Kyrgyz homes.

In the two months he had left to live, Sadyrkulov dismissed all concerns for his personal safety despite signs that he was being watched. A car was often parked in the shade of gnarly trees right by the entrance to the small museum where the former chief of staff used an office as his revolution headquarters. The car shadowed Sadyrkulov's comings and goings, its occupants not even bothering to disguise the surveillance. Melis Turganbayev, the unemployed finger-and-ear investigator with extensive connections in law enforcement, warned Sadyrkulov to be careful: "There's bad talk out there, you have to watch your back." Sadyrkulov laughed off the matter: "They don't have the guts to do anything to me." To many friends and allies raising similar concerns, he kept repeating variations on the same theme: "They won't dare touch me" or "They don't have the guts."

His close ally Elmira Ibraimova pleaded with him to throw away the Vertu mobile phone that Maxim Bakiyev had given him as a present just days before he resigned. Ibraimova worried that the expensive gift may have been stuffed with bugs and other surveillance gear. "Are you crazy? Do you know how much it costs?" Sadyrkulov protested, twirling the shiny device in his hand. For her peace of mind, he promised to have the phone checked out, and debugged if needed, by friends in the security services. Like a little kid, Sadyrkulov was in love with his new toy and was eager to show it off. "You see the body of this phone?" he asked Ibraimova, tapping the slick silvery surface. "It's made of a titanium alloy. It doesn't burn, it will never burn!" Those words came back to Ibraimova when Sadyrkulov's own body was turned into a roadside pile of coals a few weeks later. "It's as if he had a premonition about his own fate," she said.

A demure woman in her fifties, Ibraimova had reasons to be paranoid about Sadyrkulov's safety. Many years ago, her own father, Sultan, was an up-and-coming Soviet functionary who rose to the post of prime minister of Soviet Kyrgyzstan, just one notch below the top executive job. In the 1980s, just as Sultan's influence and reputation were at their peak, his colleagues prevailed on him to take a short break from his hectic schedule at a government-owned country residence on the shores of Kyrgyzstan's Lake Issyk-Kul. Sultan told his family that he didn't really need a vacation, but all the arrangements had already been made, so in a way he felt "forced" to go. When he and his wife arrived at the lake house, the place seemed deserted: for some reason, the two housekeepers had been sent home that evening; the chief of the security detail was on vacation; and there didn't seem to be any police around. That night, a man snuck into the residence and killed Sultan with a single gunshot. The killer was soon caught, but he hanged himself on a train journey while being transported under armed guard. Word was that the man was crazy and unhinged. Sultan's family never fully believed the lone-gunman story, which remains the only official version given for Sultan's mysterious lakeside murder.[17]

Now, nearly thirty years later, his daughter Elmira was beseeching her political mentor and friend Sadyrkulov to stop acting like a child and take his security seriously. Kyrgyzstan is a very small country, so rumors and news have a way of traveling fast in the overlapping circles of the country's movers and shakers who booze, gossip, and do business together. Out of that cauldron, Ibraimova fished out a troubling morsel of scuttlebutt: a contract to kill Sadyrkulov had already been placed with a notorious mobster named Kamchi Kolbayev, a baby-faced, thirty-seven-year-old Don Corleone of Kyrgyzstan.

Following a long Soviet criminal tradition, Kolbayev was the so-called respected thief, a crowned prince of jailhouse aristocracy now entrusted by his colleagues to rule a vast criminal empire according to an informal code of "understandings" that are ruthless but noble, as any bleeding-heart mobster will tell you. Respected thieves require official protection, or at least acquiescence, and Kolbayev's rise up the criminal food chain coincided with the entrenchment of the Bakiyev regime and the elevation of Janysh. Kamchi benefited greatly from the murder of a major competitor: Ryspek Akhmatbayev, the Robin Hood who once dominated the country's criminal underworld, won a parliamentary seat, and died in a flurry of gunfire outside a mosque.

Kamchi fared much better. One November evening in 2008, crime bosses from across the former Soviet Union gathered in a fancy Moscow restaurant to discuss pressing business matters and anoint new respected thieves. According to a Russian newspaper account of the meeting, the guests included such colorfully nicknamed individuals as Basil the Resurrected, Hamlet, Railcar, the Ogre, the Little Japanese Man, and Granpa Hassan. Kamchi was there too, and his peers crowned the Kyrgyz as a "respected thief," elevating him to the rarefied top rung of organized crime. The title, peculiar to the Soviet criminal underworld, denotes an eventful life lived according to a rigorous criminal code that prohibits any normal employment, prescribes utter disdain for law enforcement, and usually involves significant prison stints and elaborately coded tattoos. Very few criminals rise to the rank of respected thief, whose closest international equivalent might be the Italian mafia's *capo di tutti cappi*. (The original Russian term, *Vor v Zakone*, is often translated as Thief-in-Law, which is confusing as it conjures a meddlesome mother-in-law.)

A couple of years after attaining the respected-thief status, Kamchi became big enough to land on the U.S. Treasury Department's list of major transnational crime figures whose assets are subject to a freeze. The

U.S. government identified Kamchi as a key member of the Brothers' Circle (formerly known as Family of Eleven, and the Twenty), a multi-ethnic criminal group spread across the former Soviet Union and active in Europe, the Middle East, Africa, and Latin America. "The Brothers' Circle serves as a coordinating body for several criminal networks, mediating disputes between the individual criminal networks and directing member criminal activity globally," the Treasury Department says.[18] Tagged by President Obama as "a significant narcotics trafficker" under the Foreign Narcotics Kingpin Designation Act, Kamchi serves as the Brothers' Circle's overseer for Central Asia, a principal staging ground for global trafficking of Afghan heroin.

If this was the man gunning for the former chief of staff, then things really were bad. Ibraimova shared the rumor with Sadyrkulov and urged him to leave the country immediately. But again, Sadyrkulov dismissed her concerns. "Calm down, Elmira, I already heard about Kamchi. He's not going to lift a finger against me, we have already settled everything," he said.

"How can you be so sure?" Ibraimova asked.

"Well, I have people who talked to Kamchi, they explained everything, and he promised not to get involved."

"And you believe him?"

"Elmira, he is a respected thief," Sadyrkulov said invoking the mobsters' vaunted code of ethics. "If he promised something, he's bound to stick to that promise."

Why was Sadyrkulov so cavalier about his safety, even after receiving human body parts as a New Year's gift? Having managed over the years to outsmart many powerful opponents, and to convert enemies into allies, Sadyrkulov had so much faith in his own survival talents that no warning about impending doom carried quite enough weight to frighten him.

Sadyrkulov's longtime driver, Kubat, was scared. When Sadyrkulov left the White House and gave up his official car, he continued employing Kubat, who now chauffeured his boss around in a white Lexus. The Lexus was on loan from one of Sadyrkulov's many powerful and wealthy friends. Erik Arsaliyev had made his money in retailing and real-estate investments and now served in Parliament as part of Sadyrkulov's puppet political party. He seemed to spend much of his time breeding horses at his country estate and hunting wild yaks in the mountains. He had a brand-new Lexus to spare.

Initially happy to keep his job, Kubat the chauffeur soon started having panic attacks and went AWOL for ten days. One night, his driver buddies spotted him in a bar, drunk and crying. "They'll kill my boss and me," he slurred though tears. But a few days later, Kubat reported back for duty, blaming his sudden disappearance on family troubles. He didn't speak a word about safety concerns to Sadyrkulov and resumed driving him. While it is possible that Kubat simply suppressed his fears to keep his job, another possibility is that someone threatened him and then told him to go back to work for Sadyrkulov, perhaps as a way to keep track of the rebellious chief of staff. Ibraimova thinks that some elements in the sequence of Kubat's disappearance, his drunk confession, and then his quick return to Sadyrkulov don't quite add up. With Kubat dead, "you can only guess now," she said.

Sadyrkulov's final drive to Kazakhstan came together on a short notice. In the morning of March 12, 2009, in his museum office off a tree-lined boulevard, Sadyrkulov held his usual round of chats with opposition leaders and colleagues, including a phone call about a potential legal problem: some politicians were calling for the reopening of the criminal probe into the "financiers' case," Sadyrkulov's murky hunt for half a million dollars a decade earlier. Then Sadyrkulov took out his cell phone and speed-dialed an old acquaintance, a Moscow-based journalist and well-known Central Asia pundit, Arkady Dubnov. He was attending a conference in Almaty. Dubnov's articles, commentary, and television appearances are read and watched closely both by the region's political classes and by Moscow's foreign-policy crowd, so he was an important opinion leader for a coup plotter like Sadyrkulov to cultivate.

"Where are you? Oh, it looks like I woke you up, I'm sorry," Sadyrkulov said. His longtime executive assistant, Elena Jalgasova, was sitting next to him at the time, but she could hear only her boss's side of the conversation.

"Well, we planned to get together and chat whenever you are in Almaty," Sadyrkulov continued. Dubnov said something on the other end.

"Great, I'll get over there now," Sadyrkulov told the pundit, and hung up. Turning to Jalgasova, the former chief of staff said, "I'll run down to Almaty for half an hour or so, have this chat, and come back."

Although the Russian journalist was the only known appointment he had in Kazakhstan that day, Sadyrkulov had been reaching out to a range of officials and businessmen in Kazakhstan. One of them was an Almaty-based tycoon who controlled an important Kyrgyz television channel. Its backing would be crucial if Sadyrkulov's coup were to succeed. It is also likely that Sadyrkulov used his fund-raising skills to approach other potential wealthy donors based in Almaty. Such fund-raising was much harder in Kyrgyzstan because those who had money were afraid to lose it by backing the opposition, or were in cahoots with the regime anyway.

Azimbek Beknazarov, the bull-necked former prosecutor whose brash style earned him the monikers bulldozer of the revolution and Beknosaur, recalled meeting with Sadyrkulov a few days before his death. The two discussed plans to overthrow Bakiyev. "He said that he'll help financially," Beknazarov later testified in court. "He said there are folks over there [in Kazakhstan] who can help get the money." Like a fisherman bragging about the size of the fish he just caught, Sadyrkulov drew his hands apart to indicate a large amount of money. "Would that be enough to get rid of Bakiyev?"

Pulling together a crew for his unplanned dash to Almaty, Sadyrkulov wanted to bring his bodyguard, a young man named Sasha. But Sasha didn't have his passport on him, and fetching it from his remote apartment would take too long. So Sadyrkulov told him to stay behind, sparing his life. The chief of staff invited a close friend to join him and his chauffeur on the drive to Almaty. Thus, he inadvertently marked for death Sergei Slepchenko, an iconoclastic political scientist with a bearlike stature, an intense demeanor, and a scruffy beard—as well as a sharp mind and a warm heart. Never content to waste time, Sadyrkulov knew he had a long drive ahead of him. So he figured he should occupy those hours by talking to someone smart, and he immediately thought of Slepchenko, whom he sometimes jokingly called "the Beard."

The Beard's recent insight about Kyrgyzstan was that revolutions were likely to keep repeating themselves, as elites competing for scarce economic resources and power never figured out how to do it within the existing system. On March 12, Slepchenko was at work in his think tank. When Sadyrkulov invited him for a long drive, the political scientist called his wife to warn her he'd be home late.

Before setting off on the road, Sadyrkulov fussed over a small detail: whether to wear a suit and tie or something more comfortable for the long drive. On the advice of his executive assistant, he settled on a suit. "He gave me a hug and walked me out of the office," Jalgasova recalled. "I never saw him again."

The next morning, news of the discovery of the burned Lexus spread quickly through Kyrgyzstan. Erik Arsaliyev, the thoroughbred aficionado who owned the car, was woken up early that morning by a policeman ringing his doorbell. "Your car has been involved in a crash," the cop told him as he drove him to the site overlooking a steep gorge. There, Arsaliyev noticed that the Lexus, despite being thoroughly incinerated on the inside and blackened on the outside, had no body damage except for a small dent under the driver's door. That's where the Audi with a dozing driver behind the wheel slammed into the Lexus. The Audi, also burned but not as badly, was sitting nearby. Later that morning, an ambulance delivered three small piles of coals, the remains of the passengers, to a Bishkek morgue, where Sadyrkulov's friends and allies began to gather.

Hearing the news, Vadim Nochevkin, the investigative reporter, couldn't help but entertain this momentary thought: could this be the mother of all plots dreamed up by Sadyrkulov, the grandmaster of intrigue? Perhaps, Nochevkin thought, Sadyrkulov staged his own apparent death to throw his enemies off balance and to prepare in secret for some diabolical grand finale that only he was privy to. Knowing Sadyrkulov, "I could fully believe something like that," Nochevkin said. But the truth of course was much simpler. Sadyrkulov did perish in that car, which was quickly established by his dental records and by the presence of gallstones among the remains—and later confirmed by extensive DNA testing.

With the confession of Osmonov, the Audi driver, the police said they saw no reason to investigate foul play. The young man was a small-time trader from southern Kyrgyzstan with a previous conviction for a brawl and extortion. He seemed genuinely sorry for the morning car crash, which he blamed on lack of sleep the night before. When skeptics wondered why a brand-new Lexus would light up like a Chinese firecracker from a mild hit, the minister of the interior went on national television to say that it wasn't that unusual for cars to catch fire in low-speed collisions. He cited specific cases, ten of them. When an opposition leader suggested Sadyrkulov had been murdered, police forced him to testify and either back up his allegations with evidence or face charges of obstruction of justice. Such tactics dampened the enthusiasm of truth seekers. President Bakiyev warned the opposition to stop insinuating political murder. "You must not manipulate people's feelings and their grief and turn a tragedy into politics." He added that he was personally supervising the investigation.

Sadyrkulov's elderly parents were still alive, living in a village outside Bishkek where their son was born. To spare them the heartbreak and the gory newsreels, Sadyrkulov's friends kept them in the dark for months about their son's death and took away their television set, on the pretext that it needed to be fixed.

To anyone with a brain, the traffic-accident theory made no sense from the start. The spot where the Audi hit the Lexus is at the bottom of a U-shaped curve in the road. The Lexus was parked on the shoulder at the time of the crash. So to hit it, the Audi would have needed to round the curve slowly and carefully or else it would have simply crashed into the safety parapet at the lip of the cliff or rolled off the mountain. "I was screaming and foaming at the mouth at the police, 'Why don't you try to fall asleep and make that turn?!'" recalled Aijan, Sadyrkulov's oldest daughter. The investigators looked at her with sympathy, she said, but didn't engage her on the substance of her questioning.

Then there was the mystery of Kubat, the driver who only weeks earlier cried over a drink in fear for his life. Kubat's body, or what was left of it, was found on the front passenger seat; the bodies of Sadyrkulov and Slepchenko were in the backseat. The driver's seat was empty. Confronted with this riddle, the police explained it away by theorizing that Kubat's door on the driver's side got jammed in the collision, so he climbed over to the passenger seat to try to get out of the burning car that way. But for whatever reason neither he nor his two companions managed to get out.

Neither Sadyrkulov's expensive, indestructible phone nor his ubiquitous leather briefcase (whose metal corners wouldn't have burned) were ever found. What could he have carried in that briefcase that was so valuable? There were many other questions. Why was the Lexus parked in the middle of the night on the shoulder of a mountain road? To get to that spot from the Kazakh border checkpoint (his last known location), Sadyrkulov would have needed to pass through Bishkek first, and then—instead of going home as he intended—travel an additional thirty minutes in the opposite direction. Why would he do that? The police said he was going to his country house in the area, which didn't sound convincing. But the cops swatted down every doubt as insignificant and told people to stop looking for conspiracy theories. "The fact that this was a traffic accident is obvious and indisputable," a high-ranking police official pronounced a mere three days after the fact.

Shortly after Sadyrkulov's death, Melis Turganbayev made a quiet visit to the crash site, where a couple of active-duty police buddies showed him around. "It was so obvious to me that the whole thing was staged," he said. It was also obvious that Osmonov held the key to unlocking the mystery. Turganbayev took an active interest in the case, and it just so happened that an old police friend of his was now a prosecutor involved in the inquiry. Turganbayev got in touch with him. "You know Osmonov is waffling in his testimony," the prosecutor said. "He's saying some inconsistent things." For instance, Osmonov claimed that he'd spent the night before the crash at 12 Chimneys, the club just up the road from the crash site. He was there to visit a woman named Aigerim who worked at the club. But when the cops went to check out Osmonov's story, no one remembered him at 12 Chimneys. What's more, the club had no employee by the name Aigerim. Before Turganbayev could arrange a discreet chat with Osmonov and urge his allies in the law enforcement to protect him, the prisoner was moved out of the jurisdiction of the friendly prosecutor.

In the meantime, the country's opposition leaders, weakened and demoralized by Sadyrkulov's death, kept looking for a way to shed some light on the murky story. Having been in and out of government and business for years, these opposition figures had their own connections within the Kyrgyz political establishment and law enforcement, and were collecting scraps of information and rumor about Sadyrkulov's death. All their digging and guessing found an unusual outlet: a potboiler political novella about the final days of a character modeled on Sadyrkulov. The book's goal was to embarrass the regime and provide the public with a competing storyline to all the traffic-accident drivel offered by the government. And so what if it was fiction.

The author, writing under a penname, was Emil Kaptagayev, a physicist and mathematician long active in the country's political circles. In writing the novella, Kaptagayev wasn't pursuing a secret literary ambition. Billing the work as fiction was the only way to string together bits and pieces of information, rumor, educated guesswork, and imagined scenes into a coherent narrative, scathing and prescient in its descriptions of the regime. Called *The Bloody Path,* the book is peopled by a cast of instantly recognizable characters whose names are only a few letters or transliterations away from their real-life counterparts. Janysh Bakiyev, the president's fearsome brother, is Jaken; Medet Sadyrkulov is Meder. In the novella's most chilling pages, Jaken has Meder kidnapped and thrown into a basement. There, Jaken sticks needles under Meder's fingernails, shoots him in the knee, scalds him with a hot iron, cuts off an ear, and finally tells his underlings to kill him and make it look like a traffic accident.

Shortly after the novella was serialized in a local newspaper, masked men snatched the author on the street and took him to a wheat field outside the city. There they beat him for a few hours, checked his laptop and phone, and finally left him slumped on the ground. "You know what this is for," one of his kidnappers told him. Surprised to be alive, Kaptagayev went into hiding.

As months dragged on, Erik Arsaliyev, the owner of the Lexus, grew despondent and grumbled publicly about what he thought was a hushed-up assassination of his friend and mentor. Arsaliyev was walking along the edge of a Bishkek park one day when a car drew up alongside him.

Someone stepped out to tell Arsaliyev to shut up. "Otherwise, you'll repeat your friend's fate. It was your car that burned, but who knows, maybe the next time it will be your turn to burn. And when you burn, you won't burn alone." With that, the messenger hopped back into the car and sped off, leaving Arsaliyev dazed on the sidewalk. He had a big family. The entrepreneur once had a full head of hair, but in the weeks after the encounter it fell out in thick strands. Scared and depressed, he left town to be closer to his horses and to ski. The hair never grew back. When I met him for a coffee long after these events, he removed a black baseball hat with a small alligator stitched on the front and drew his hand over a perfectly bald pate.

There were of course those who believed the regime was blameless in Sadyrkulov's death, or at least pretended to believe that. In that group, there was no voice stranger than that of Oksana Malevannaya, Sadyrku-lov's former lover who had borne him a son and then went on to head up the Secretariat that crimped the chief of staff's power. During lunch at the U.S. ambassador's residence in Bishkek in early 2010, Malevannaya described Sadyrkulov as "her husband, soul-mate and the father of her youngest child." Trembling and tearful, she told the ambassador she could have never continued working for the government had she believed it was in any way connected to Sadyrkulov's death. And besides, the country's security services were "too stupid" to carry out an assassination like that. So it was a traffic accident, Malevannaya concluded, and finished her lunch.[19]

At the trial of Osmonov, the judge concurred and sentenced him to twelve years for manslaughter. Sitting in a metal cage in the courtroom, Osmonov took the guilty verdict in stride. He would do his time at a minimum-security prison where he would soon be eligible for parole.

A dapper man in his early seventies, Leonid Luzhansky was a lawyer hired by the Sadyrkulov family to keep tabs on the investigation. Before going into private practice, Luzhansky spent decades as a police officer and prosecutor, specializing in serious crimes. Like many others, he never believed the traffic-accident story. Osmonov struck him as unusual in his quiet resolve to accept the charges, but at the same time that quality was familiar to Luzhansky from his dealings with the criminal underworld.

Luzhansky referred to that world of respected thieves, gangsters, and tacit understandings as the "Dark World." Though it sounds like a fantastical reference, something out of *The Lord of the Rings,* the label is in fact a common way to describe the world of organized crime in Kyrgyzstan. Luzhansky seemed to have a grudging respect for Osmonov, for whatever set of principles he carried with him in that dark world of his. "He was not a petty criminal. From what I could tell, he was a real, blue-blood dark man," Luzhansky recalled. And now Osmonov stoically accepted the long jail sentence for manslaughter.

The truth about Sadyrkulov's death would remain hidden for another two years.

A few months later, another mysterious tragedy hit the battered and intimidated ranks of Kyrgyzstan's opposition activists. This time, the target was Gennady Pavlyuk, a fifty-one-year-old journalist who wrote under the penname Ibrahim Rustanbek. Pavlyuk, a lanky amateur musician who had grown up in a historically Russian district of single-story wooden homes on the edge of Bishkek, wore his hair clipped short and combed forward. He was a gregarious, talkative man with boundless energy. In his long journalistic career, he had worked for most major Russian-language publications in Kyrgyzstan and had also contributed to Russian and Kazakh news media. More recently, Pavlyuk had founded his own Internet portal called The White Steamship, a name borrowed from one of Chingiz Aitmatov's novellas.

In the thick of the Bakiyev era, Pavlyuk allied himself with one of the country's top opposition leaders: a suave, charismatic lawyer named Omurbek Tekebayev. Tekebayev had begun his career as a physics teacher in a village high school. He rose to national prominence during the Tulip Revolution, after which he became speaker of the Parliament. Like most of his fellow revolutionaries, Tekebayev fell out with President Bakiyev, and at one point in 2006 publicly called the president "a dog." He elaborated on the insult: "If he's a man, he should go hang himself." Tekebayev resigned and focused on building up his political party, called Ata-Meken.

A few months after the canine slur, Tekebayev headed to a conference in Warsaw to deliver a speech on the prospects of democracy in Central Asia, a perennial favorite of the Western think-tank crowd. At the Warsaw airport, customs officials opened his suitcase and pulled out a Russian-style *matreshka* nesting doll, one of those standby souvenirs the former Soviet Union bequeathed to the world. The customs officials opened the doll, and out fell a clear plastic bag filled with white powder. Upon further testing, the powder turned out to be heroin, about twenty ounces of it, with a street price of more than $50,000. Had Kyrgyzstan's leading opposition figure and constitutional lawyer really used his speaking gig in Warsaw to smuggle dope to Europe?

The scandal was quickly dubbed Matreshkagate, but Tekebayev denied knowing where the damn doll had come from, claiming it had been planted in his luggage. Polish police believed him and set him free. In Kyrgyzstan, veteran police colonel Melis Turganbayev, whom we have already met through the president's chief of staff, later investigated Matreshkagate. He identified a Bishkek airport employee and a cop who slipped the doll into the politician's bag, on orders from a high-ranking government official.

This wasn't the last setup Tekebayev would face. A couple of years later, when Bakiyev was already gone, a man looking very much like Tekebayev was filmed having kinky sex with a much younger woman—a belt was involved. The black-and-white video, apparently shot inside the Parliament building, aired on Russian television ahead of a key Kyrgyz election. The video killed the electoral chances of Tekebayev, a married father of a teenage daughter.

This was the man who during the Bakiyev era enlisted Pavlyuk, the veteran journalist, to spread his antigovernment message. On November 15, 2009, Pavlyuk published a long interview with Tekebayev, quoting him as saying, "The Bakiyev regime is in agony, it is politically, historically and morally doomed." The rest of the two-thousand-word article continued in that spirit. Five days later, Pavlyuk penned an unflattering profile of Maxim, headlined "Max Bakiyev as a Tough Macho of Kyrgyz Politics."

In private correspondence with Tekebayev, Pavlyuk wasn't shy about his plans. "The overriding goal I've set for myself is working toward

POLITICAL VICTORY, toward your ascent to power," Pavlyuk wrote to Tekebayev in a pitch for a media project. (The capital letters are his, not mine.) The opposition leader liked what he heard and put Pavlyuk on a retainer. As is common for anyone who ever freelanced, the journalist nagged his employer for money. "Please send my salary today, in full, if you can," Pavlyuk e-mailed Tekebayev.

Olga Kolosova, the journalist's girlfriend, shared several of his e-mail exchanges with me. Pavlyuk remained close to his ex-wife, Elena, with whom he fathered two sons. His older son had been hit by a car in 2005 and died on the spot, a tragedy that haunted Pavlyuk for the rest of his life. Pavlyuk and his ex-wife remained friends, bonding anew after their son's death. But for the past decade, Pavlyuk had been living with Kolosova in a small apartment in downtown Bishkek. Though they never formally wed, they considered themselves husband and wife.

Alongside his political work for Tekebayev, Pavlyuk was busy raising money for another media project. He had big plans for a magazine, a newspaper, and a website, but couldn't find backers. The media landscape is bleak everywhere, but even more so in Kyrgyzstan, where political pressure silenced many journalists. "Everyone he saw turned down his proposal," Kolosova told me. His ex-wife, Elena, later told a court that Pavlyuk had complained to her about being blacklisted by the Secretariat, the omnipresent political superstructure created by the president's family. Pavlyuk also grumbled to Elena about having upset Maxim Bakiyev, which wouldn't be surprising given the general tone of his writings.

During the fall of 2009, Elena recalled, Pavlyuk appeared gloomy and brooding, in a state of constant pressure that seemed to age him rapidly. Then one day, a ray of sunshine entered his life. It concerned that media project for which he had trouble finding money. Suddenly, an intriguing e-mail materialized in his inbox from an outfit with a strangely long name: the Foundation for the Development of International Relations between the Countries of the Commonwealth of Independent States and the European Community. The e-mail said the foundation's board of directors was planning to award a $105,000 grant "aimed at the support of independent print publications in Kyrgyzstan." The e-mail's author, a woman named Marina, informed Pavlyuk that his colleagues had nominated him as a candidate for the grant.

"When he came home he was so happy, he said, 'Finally . . . ,'" Kolosova told me. He dashed off a response thanking Marina for the "hopeful letter." Yet the initial joy was quickly tinged with suspicions. Pavlyuk and his girlfriend couldn't find any trace of this foundation on the Internet. "We scoured so many websites," she recalled. Pavlyuk wrote back to the mysterious Marina. "Could you please tell me what your foundation's website is, its phone numbers, addresses? I'd like to learn a bit more about the foundation's work, about the project, etc." Instead, Marina wrote back to say that the pool of candidates for the grant was shrinking, from the initial two hundred to about three or five people. Pavlyuk, she told him, was still in the running. He was invited for an in-person interview in Almaty, Kazakhstan, where the final decision would be made.

The seasoned journalist kept trying to pin down Marina and her associates on details about the foundation. "Dear Marina, yesterday I got a phone call from a young man who introduced himself as Abay, and we discussed my possible trip on December 16," Pavlyuk wrote. He asked the caller about the foundation's mission and history. "But the line suddenly went dead so he didn't give me any information about the location of the office, the phone number, etc. And I asked you, if you recall, to give me the foundation's website. For now, I view our correspondence (my apologies) as a friendly practical joke." Here Pavlyuk used a Russian expression for a wild-goose chase. "Where I am supposed to go—to look for an old man in the village?"

Kolosova recalled that Pavlyuk was told to just come to Almaty, where he would learn everything he needed to know about the foundation. A room in his name had already been booked at the Hotel Kazakhstan, an Almaty high-rise. "This is strange—nobody knows anything about this foundation, I wonder if I might be getting myself into a scam," Pavlyuk wondered. He called the Almaty hotel and discovered that there was a fully paid reservation in his name for one night. Desperate for money, he suspended disbelief one more time. "Some of our doubts were dispelled, and he decided to go," Kolosova said. Early in the morning on December 16, he kissed her good-bye and took a cab to Almaty. He checked into the Hotel Kazakhstan, where a prepaid reservation was indeed awaiting him, courtesy of his benefactors at the mysterious foundation. Later that day, a young man picked him up in the lobby, and they drove off in the man's car, probably for the long-promised final interview about the $105,000 grant.

The next day, Kolosova got a phone call telling her that a man resembling Pavlyuk had fallen out of a sixth-floor window of a residential building in Almaty, a dreary Soviet-era apartment block. The man landed on the concrete canopy over the entrance, his legs and arms bound with tape. In the rental apartment, police found his jacket, laptop bag, and a roll of duct tape. Kolosova traveled to Almaty, hoping it was all some awful mistake, that the victim wasn't Pavlyuk. But it was him—he was in a deep coma. He clung to life for five days, then died without regaining consciousness. The killing of one of their well-known peers stunned Kyrgyzstan's journalists. Rumors swirled about the possibility of state involvement in his murder. But just like the suspicious death of the president's chief of staff, Pavlyuk's murder would have to wait a while to be solved.

When I visited her in 2010, Kolosova, Pavlyuk's widow, lived in a tiny apartment she shared with a feisty white cat. A photo of Pavlyuk, smiling and strumming a guitar, stood propped on a dresser in her tiny living room, next to an Orthodox icon. Over tea and chocolates, Kolosova told me she feared for her safety and wanted to leave the country. She was hopeful that authorities would eventually bring her husband's killers to justice. In the meantime, Kolosova had a more immediate concern: finding money to build a proper tombstone over Pavlyuk's grave.

CHAPTER 5 *The Land of Perpetual Revolution*

The reign of President Bakiyev ended the same way it began, with a revolution and an exile. He fled, first to a large ceremonial tent in his home village in southern Kyrgyzstan, and then out of the country. Facing an irate populace, his brothers, sons, and cronies ran for the exits too, not all of them successfully. Bakiyev eventually settled in Belarus, at the personal invitation of the local dictator. The only two presidents Kyrgyzstan had known in its twenty years of independence ended up as outcasts and fugitives: one in Moscow teaching physics, the other in Minsk living in a forced retirement. Bakiyev, the hopeful product of the optimistically named Tulip Revolution, mutated into a villain so quickly that his allies didn't know what hit them. "We got tricked like little kids," Roza Otunbayeva, the perennial opposition leader who helped bring Bakiyev to power, told me shortly after she helped overthrow him. "He made all the right speeches back then." During his five-year reign, nepotism and graft surpassed the excesses of the previous regime, while government opponents began to suffer suspicious deaths. In the words of Russia's Vladimir Putin, the master of the one-liner, Bakiyev "stepped on the same rake" that had whacked his predecessor on the head.

Downtown Bishkek is a careful grid of streets, many lined with stately 1930s Soviet architecture. Sidewalks are shaded by trees, and concrete-lined irrigation ditches run along the edge of the roads. On a clear day, you can see the jagged white peaks of the Ala-Too range just outside the city. The presidential palace, a big boxy building known here as the White House, though it's closer to gray, sits on the edge of the main square.

The square and the adjacent avenue merge into a vast expanse of open space flanked on one side by the history museum. The horse-bound Manas statue sits in front of the museum, next to a tall pole topped with an oversized red and gold Kyrgyz national flag. In the fluid spirit of Kyrgyz statehood, there are sporadic discussions about tearing up the old, Soviet-influenced flag design and replacing it with something new, more authentically Kyrgyz, perhaps less red. But for now, it is the red and gold banner that flaps in the wind, and pairs of honor guards take turns standing motionless in a glass booth underneath.

A big cube of a building, the history museum is devoted almost exclusively to the 1917 Russian Revolution, which brought the Communists to power. Its darkened rooms are filled with shiny statues of workers, soldiers, and peasants, the deified trinity of Communist mythology. They are forever charging at something. Plaques exhort them onward and praise their achievements. This, from Karl Marx: "The liberation of the working class must be attained by the working class itself." Or this, from Lenin: "The revolution was accomplished by the proletariat. They showed heroism; they shed blood." Soviet rulers force-fed these hoary Communist clichés from a century ago to their Kyrgyz subjects and packed the kitschy collection into the custom-built museum resembling in shape a giant Apple Store.

The slogans acquired an odd new resonance amid Kyrgyzstan's recent history of uprisings, which took place literally in front of the museum. And a new exhibit appeared alongside the Communist kitsch. Laid out in glass display cases are personal items that once belonged to those who were killed during the anti-Bakiyev revolution in April of 2010. One case holds a suit, shirt, and tie, arranged as if their owner had vanished from under his clothes. Another case contains an old Nokia mobile phone, a shaving brush, and a bottle of cologne, three quarters full. It has a maroon label that misspells "Tet-a-Tet" in golden letters. Yet another display holds a police riot shield and a helmet, because cops also lost their lives here. A life-size statue of Lenin towers incongruously over it all, finger pointed down.

It's a jarring collection of mundane accouterments of life that were scrounged from wardrobes, bathroom closets, desks, and family photo albums, displayed to remind the world that their owners had once been alive. That they shaved every morning and put cologne on; went to work or to school; wore suits and ties or police uniforms; won medals and academic honors, carried IDs; had kids and wives and mothers. And then, on the rainy afternoon of April 7, 2010, their lives ended not far from this dark, wretched museum as President Bakiyev clung to power until he no longer could.

That day, Azat Tolegunov, a twenty-one-year-old security guard at a Bishkek café, became curious about protesters gathering downtown. "So I decided to go join the people. You see, life has become harder for everyone," he told me. By then, Kyrgyzstan was already convulsed by a chaotic protest movement. One of the sparks that set it ablaze was the government decision to hike tariffs for electricity, gas, and water. In places like Naryn, a Kyrgyz town where winter temperatures routinely drop to minus forty, higher tariffs meant people had to choose whether to buy bread or heat. All of this was happening against the backdrop of a regime that seemed aloof and corrupt. Not long before the revolution, the government announced plans to sell a major state-owned electricity utility to a well-connected firm for a song. "The people of Kyrgyzstan don't have the words to describe their feelings when one of the giants of the national economy is being handed over to a heretofore unknown little firm," Roza Otunbayeva, then one of a handful of opposition members of Parliament, wrote to Bakiyev's prime minister.

In Central Asia and elsewhere, people are prepared to put up with authoritarian, corrupt rule provided it delivers economic benefits or, at the very least, doesn't rip them off too blatantly. By early 2010, the worsening poverty across Kyrgyzstan collided with the ostentatiously screw-you attitude of the ruling clan. In its waning months, the clan's support base wobbled on the point of a needle. His domestic political allies had long ago turned on Bakiyev, some out of principle, others because they were cut off from the trough of money and influence; the country's business elites grumbled about being held hostage to the whims of the president's son; key foreign players—Moscow and Washington—viewed the regime as erratic, greedy, and unreliable, and Moscow took that message straight to Kyrgyz living rooms, where Russian state television is widely watched. Washington mostly kept mum, eager to preserve its military base.

Though weakened and demoralized by years of harassment, opposition activists managed to hold sporadic rallies across the country, drawing increasing numbers of people and whipping up passions against the regime's many excesses. In March, the country's opposition parties joined forces in the newly created National Movement of Kyrgyzstan. Otunbayeva became one of its leaders.

The various strands of the protest movement exploded in Talas, a remote town locked between two mountain ranges. It happens to be the mythical birthplace of Manas and the site of his mausoleum. Some would invoke the proud, rebellious spirit of Manas as one reason the Kyrgyz are so quick to rise up. Another reason often cited is the nomadic history of the Kyrgyz. Nomads are used to picking up and leaving for greener pastures. They don't own land, so their livelihood isn't tied to a piece of ground, and by extension to the ruler of the domain. Historically speaking, nomads are much freer to speak up against their rulers than sedentary peasants, who have too much to lose.

On April 6, crowds swiftly captured the building of the Talas provincial administration. (Kyrgyz protesters are adept at this tactic, honed during the Tulip Revolution.) When the interior minister showed up to take charge of the situation, he too was captured and beaten to a bloody pulp. In Bishkek, the Bakiyev government panicked and started snatching opposition leaders ahead of yet another rally planned for April 7 in downtown Bishkek. One leading activist was arrested in his office; another was taken into custody after a small detachment of police stormed his house. Versed in the arts of clandestine plotting from the earlier uprising, Otunbayeva went to stay with a relative. But she kept using her mobile phones to gather details of the burgeoning revolt, and security forces eventually homed in on the signal and swarmed the large apartment building where she was hiding. Otunbayeva turned off her cell phones before the security forces could locate the apartment, and used only her relative's landline, thus evading capture.

Exactly what role she and her colleagues played in steering the revolt is a matter of some dispute. Unlike the Tulip Revolution, which flowed from a rigged election and took months to reach a crescendo, the April Revolution exploded in a flash of fury and violence that appeared to have a spontaneous quality.

When Azat Tolegunov, the café guard, arrived on Bishkek's central square on April 7, a planned opposition gathering had been dispersed by the police, and things were quickly getting out of hand. Security forces wheeled out a water cannon to cool down the protesters, but it seemed to have little effect. "The cannon watered the protesters the same way a gardener waters his plants," a police cadet who was there recalled later.

At some point that day, protesters charged at the White House. Snipers perched on rooftops started shooting, taking advantage of the big open spaces around the government headquarters. Tolegunov saw a man go down by the ornate fence in front of the White House. "I ran toward him, I wanted to help," he told me. The man was bleeding from his stomach. When Tolegunov leaned down to grab him, he heard a loud bang, felt pain, and fell down next to the wounded man. "He was looking at me, and I was looking at him. I wanted to help but I couldn't move," Tolegunov said. I met him in a cramped ward at the National Hospital in Bishkek. A grenade had ripped out chunks of flesh and ligament from one of his legs. He was lying in bed, wearing a blue T-shirt with the word *Kyrgyzstan* stitched in red letters across his chest. His father fussed over him.

The protesters' willingness to walk into bullets spawned an array of conspiracy theories. I heard rumors of alcohol and of mysterious psychotropic drugs that removed fear from protesters' minds and propelled them, zombielike, toward the White House. Mars Sariyev, a respected political analyst, told me he thought "psychotropic substances had been added to vodka." I asked Tolegunov whether he felt fear at any point, and he said yes, of course he was scared. "They thought they'd shoot two, three people, and everyone else will run away. But quite the opposite—it makes you more aggressive."

Other witnesses described similar scenes. "At first, the snipers were hiding, but then they walked openly on the roof [of the White House]; at first they fired selectively at those who approached the gates. I saw a boy of about thirteen get shot in the head. . . . I was standing by the columns [of a building across the road from the White House]. I was shot in the throat, and the bullet exited between my ribs," a protester named Maksan Moldobayev, a twenty-seven-year-old junior government employee told Kyrgyz interviewers from his hospital bed.[1] The overwhelming majority of the protesters did not carry weapons, and did not expect to get caught up in a violent uprising. But a small group did have weapons, which they seemed to have taken from the riot police deployed against the demonstrators.

In the morning of April 7, cadets at Bishkek's police academy were ordered to have a quick breakfast, dress in camouflage and riot-control gear, and deploy to the central square to disperse the crowds. A police cadet writing under the penname Chingiz later recounted his experiences in a fifteen-page essay striking in its descriptions of what it's like to be a junior cop sent into the middle of a revolution.[2] "Reaching the flagpole [in front of the history museum], I saw a horrible picture. A mob was savagely beating up my comrades, as if they were their blood enemies. The picture of the mob reminded me of an avalanche in the mountains that crushes everything in its path," Chingiz wrote. His fellow cadets did not carry firearms, and their officers had shotguns loaded only with rubber bullets. That description is consistent with other accounts of the shootings that day.

Much of the death was delivered from afar, by snipers picking off their victims from the safety of the White House roof. The protesters couldn't retaliate against those snipers, so they directed their wrath at whoever happened to be wearing a uniform. "I saw how a group of people were beating up soldiers in a military truck. After that, they seized two trucks and a blue police bus," another wounded protester later told the Kyrgyz NGO from his hospital bed. Protesters used heavy vehicles like this to ram through the fence surrounding the White House. Many were shot through the windshield.

Around that time, an off-duty Bishkek taxi driver managed to steal an armored-personnel carrier with a roof-mounted machine gun. Looking for a vehicle better equipped for an armed assault than a regular truck, the cab driver walked up to the headquarters of the State Security Service. An armored personnel carrier sat in the courtyard, its hatch flung open. While armed guards looked away, distracted by other attackers, the cabbie hopped through the hatch and drove off. Cruising the streets in his new ride, he recruited a veteran of the Soviet war in Afghanistan to man the machine gun. They parked across the street from the White House and began shooting at the rooftop sniper positions, inviting a barrage of return fire.[3]

Not far from that spot, Chingiz and his fellow police cadets were being surrounded by a large crowd. Chingiz took off running. "The surface on which I ran was wet and slippery [it was raining that day], and if I took a careless step, I could fall, and that fall could be fateful. So I ran with great care. The equipment that I wore weighed twenty pounds, but in that situation I couldn't feel the weight. I ran as if I was wearing shorts and a T-shirt. This is what fear does to a man," Chingiz wrote. After some wandering and feverish smoking, and attempts to reach family and friends on his cell phone, Chingiz reconnected with his fellow cadets, and they were redeployed to the White House.

Thoughts of saying, "To hell with it" and deserting entered his mind, and he wrestled to shoo them away. "Sitting down on the curb, I saw how our officers were discussing the political situation in the country. Cadets too were talking about it. I could see anxiety and fear on their faces. That's understandable. We have things to lose. And for whom? For the people in power we don't particularly like? For those who are thinking only about how to save their skin? But we must follow orders without discussing them. Of course we could take off our uniforms right this minute and go face the people with the words '*biz el menen*,'" Chingiz wrote, using the Kyrgyz phrase for "We are with the people." Scrawled as graffiti on the facades of shops and homes, the phrase first surfaced during the Tulip Revolution and became a plea not to loot or attack, a quick expression of solidarity with the revolutionaries, whether heartfelt or purely expedient. Sometimes it worked; sometime it didn't.

But doing this, Chingiz continued, would be treason. He reminded himself of a story about Genghis Khan, the great Mongol conqueror. When he defeated the armies of rival khans in battle, the bodyguards of the vanquished khans often delivered the now-powerless rulers to Genghis Khan, angling for favors. Genghis Khan ordered brutal executions of those bodyguards on the spot. "If you betrayed your master, you'll betray me too," he told them. So Chingiz stayed in uniform and smoked nervously.

Suddenly he felt the vibration of his cell phone in his pocket. It was Dinara, a girl he knew (and, one senses, had a crush on). Like anyone who ever tried to impress a girl, Chingiz played up the drama of the moment and the risks he was facing. "I lifted up the phone so she could hear the gunshots," he wrote.

Dinara took the bait. "I'm afraid for you."

"Don't be afraid, it's all going to be fine. Oh, by the way, if something does happen, will you come visit me in the hospital?" he asked.

"Are you an idiot? How can you say things like that in this kind of situation!" Dinara yelled into the phone.

Chingiz laughed, and asked her to bring him his favorite food to the hospital. She laughed too.

Meanwhile, a real battle was unfolding in front of the fence ringing the White House. The protesters focused their efforts on breaching the main gate, using heavy trucks to ram the fence. The White House snipers killed some drivers, but new ones took the steering wheels and kept pressing. The protesters got hold of an armored personnel carrier, and Chingiz realized it was just a matter of time before the gate was breached. Cops were tossing tear-gas grenades at people behind the fence, and the protesters were picking them up and tossing them back. As a result, everyone was crying. It was already dark outside. Plumes of smoke were rising above the White House. And gunfire crackled.

It was a good time to revisit the idea of deserting. A fellow cadet tossed Chingiz a set of civilian clothes and advised him to change quickly, hop over the fence, and get the hell out.

"Was there an order?" Chingiz asked.

"Yes, there was, you see everyone else is changing."

Pulling on a random pair of jeans, Chingiz looked around and saw a police officer he knew, a corpulent man, gingerly scale the fence and escape. "I was impressed by what acts of heroism a man—even a fat man—can pull off to save his life," Chingiz wrote.

Of course there had been no orders to change into civilian clothes and desert. Chastised by his commander, Chingiz changed back into the riot gear and milled about the interior courtyard of the White House, smoking, chatting with fellow cadets. They eventually were ordered to retreat quietly, assemble by the old bus depot, and await a ride back to the academy.

The next morning, Chingiz learned that two of his friends, Edil and Nikita, had been killed in the clashes near the White House. Dazed, Chingiz and other cadets silently drank a couple of vodka shots to commemorate the dead. Then Chingiz went to a local morgue to collect Edil's body. A crowd of people had already gathered there to look for the bodies of their loved ones. Eighty-five people were killed during the revolution, most of them unarmed civilians. Some of their clothes and shaving kits would eventually find their way to the history museum.

Wounded in the lower part of his body and bleeding profusely, Edil had been alive when he was brought to the hospital. Someone placed tourniquets on his legs. But in the commotion of that night, he bled to death. Chingiz couldn't bear to attend Edil's and Nikita's funerals. "I didn't want to acknowledge that they were no longer alive. Getting drunk, I remembered the days when we all lived in the cadets' barracks; when we patrolled the city together; when we cordoned off concert venues. I studied with them for several years, but it seemed like I had known them all my life."

On the evening of April 7, President Bakiyev and his entourage dashed from the White House to the Manas airport and boarded his official airplane. They flew south, and we'll catch up with them soon. That night, protesters broke through the White House defenses and, in a spasm of righteous fury, trashed the building and many shops downtown. Wags would later refer to it as the Day of the Looter.

A couple of days later, on a glorious April afternoon, I went to Bishkek's main hospital to talk the wounded, the "heroes of the revolution," as they were quickly becoming known. I wanted to understand what exactly motivated them to wake up one morning, drop whatever else was going on in their lives, and go storm the White House. In the case of Aftandil Khadyrkulov, not many good things were happening in his life, which is why he took a taxi downtown on April 7 and joined the protesters.

A burly man with a buzz cut and a bandage around his neck, Khadyrkulov worked as a police major in the counter-narcotics squad in Jalalabad, a town in southern Kyrgyzstan that sits along the heroin-smuggling route running from Afghanistan to Europe. In 2006, he told me, he was fired because of collusion between drug barons and corrupt cops. He went after someone he was supposed to leave alone, and paid for it with his job. I had no way of verifying his account, but it fits into the general pattern of police corruption. Khadyrkulov appealed the dismissal as unfair, and in 2008 a court agreed with him. But even with the court order he couldn't get his job back, and he remained unemployed and seething at the government. Khadyrkulov has four kids and a wife who works as a teacher.

Propped on his hospital bed, he said that in the months before the revolution he was feeling desperate, enslaved by the regime. "If we remain like ostriches with heads hidden in the sand, then they'll keep humiliating us," he said. So on April 7, he took a shared taxi to the central square. "They just started shooting at us, they showed no respect, I saw so many people get shot around me," he said. He felt lucky to survive. The next day, he put on a white armband of a people's militia and accompanied a large crowd meandering through Bishkek. The militiamen, he said, tried to prevent the more unruly elements from breaking windows and starting fights. At some point the mob stumbled upon a police precinct, where the terrified cops fired a few warning rounds into the air. Khadyrkulov went to have a word with the police. He told them the mob was looking for Maxim Bakiyev and wanted no trouble with the cops. Then, as Khadyrkulov stepped ahead of the crowd to move past the precinct, the police fired. A bullet hit him in the neck, bored down, and wedged itself in his shoulder. "The bullet that missed me on April 7th finally caught up with me on the 8th," he told me.

Imels Baitikov stitches arteries for a living. Kyrgyzstan's top vascular surgeon, Baitikov, fifty-five, is an intense man—when I dropped in on him at the hospital he was yelling at an underling. His mustache droops down past the corners of his mouth, imprinting a perpetually sad expression on his face. When the wounded began arriving on the 7th, his staff were so shorthanded that recovering patients were enlisted to prepare wound dressings. Baitikov told me he encountered no signs of alcohol or drugs among those he treated. Video footage from April 7 shows there were some armed plainclothes men among the protesters. But Baitikov told me that no one he treated looked like a fighter. "These are just regular people dying, not military. This is hard." Baitikov paused to fight back tears, lighting a cigarette with a huge plastic lighter. "They are very young—it leaves a deep trace, especially for my younger surgeons."

By nature of his profession, Baitikov had seen the bloody episodes of Kyrgyzstan's recent history from up close. In 1990, a messy land dispute between the Kyrgyz and Uzbeks in ethnically mixed southern Kyrgyzstan mushroomed into full-blown slaughter. Baitikov ran the field hospital. "For a year after that, I had nightmares," he said.

The April 7th carnage left him searching for a meaning to the deaths, and his speech turned into a stream-of-consciousness dialogue with himself. "This is genocide, or apartheid. Eighty-four corpses. What did they die for? That's not how it should be. Of course, these poor souls, now we can say that maybe they didn't die in vain, that maybe because of them we'll have a better life. But it's a high price, a very high price. What did they achieve? I still don't know. They liberated the White House, but what's around it? I don't know what's going to happen next." He told me his surgeons all needed psychological counseling, and a vacation. "And I'm also human just like everyone else. The only difference is I can stitch arteries a little bit. That's it."

Mao Tse-tung, China's Great Helmsman with a high tolerance for bloodshed, had this to say on the subjects of revolts: "A revolution is not a dinner party, or writing an essay, or painting a picture, or doing embroidery; it cannot be so refined, so leisurely and gentle, so temperate, kind, courteous, restrained, and magnanimous. A revolution is an insurrection, an act of violence."[4]

A few days after the latest Kyrgyz uprising, I walked over to the White House. An incinerated truck, its cab perforated by bullets, stood

In the days after the revolution, the wrought-iron fence around the White House became a makeshift shrine to the protesters who were killed during the storming of the presidential palace. (© Philip Shishkin)

wheel-less behind the perimeter fence. The protesters had driven it through the fence and left it there to burn. One section of the fence was now a makeshift memorial, strewn with flowers and little candles burning in plastic cups. Clumps of flowers also lay on a few spots on the sidewalk where people had been shot. Photos of some protesters who died here were taped to the bars of the fence. One showed Nursultan Tabaldiyev, a first-year college student, born in 1992. While I stood there looking at the photos, a few people around me broke into a spontaneous collective prayer, their palms turned upward. On the fence, someone pinned up this poem.

We only have ourselves to blame
For blindly following the czar.
We act as though we've been enslaved;
How plentiful deceptions are.
From our corpses, you built yourself a stairway
And stepping on our heads, you climbed up to your throne.

Life went on, as it always does. Across the street, Fatboy's was serving eggs, pancakes, and lukewarm coffee. A movie theater on the other side of the main square greeted passersby with three big posters that advertised the following, from left to right:

- *Battle of the Titans,* in 3D. A toothy maw of something unidentifiable stared from the movie poster.
- *Our Condolences to the Fallen. April 7th.* Three red carnations were painted underneath.
- *How to Train Your Dragon,* in 3D.

A little farther down the street, a camouflaged soldier in wraparound shades stared down from another large poster. Assault rifle in his hands, he invited downtown shoppers to take part in "paintball combat." A phone number was provided.

After the revolution, an interim government pronounced itself in charge, and President Bakiyev fled Bishkek. He holed up in his ancestral village outside Jalalabad in southern Kyrgyzstan. One afternoon a few days later, I caught a flight from Bishkek's Manas International Airport down south. A small turboprop plane greeted passengers with a yellow note stenciled on the fuselage: "Chop Here with Crash Axe." For most of the one-hour flight, the plane glided over an undulating expanse of mountaintops, the range that roughly bisects Kyrgyzstan into north and south.

This is more than a geographical division. One view of Kyrgyz politics is that it's never been a contest between democracy and dictatorship, right and wrong, morality and corruption—but a power struggle among rival clans. The north-south division is important in this clan war. Akayev, Kyrgyzstan's first president, is a northerner. Bakiyev is a southerner. What the West calls nepotism is nothing more that the obligation to provide for the clan. This unsentimental take gained currency after the dashed hopes of the Tulip Revolution.

Flowers and rocks mark the spot where a protester was shot to death, most likely by snipers firing from the roof of the White House. (© Philip Shishkin)

On the day I visited Bakiyev's ancestral village of Teyit, the approach road to it was guarded by huddles of young men with wooden sticks of varying shapes and sizes. Jittery, they searched cars and asked questions. In the middle of the village, down Bakiyev Street (named after the clan patriarch, not the president), guards and visitors hovered next to a blue metal gate, behind which the local boy who made good and then lost it all was temporarily stationed. Things were not going well for Bakiyev that day.

In the morning, he set off in a motorcade for Osh, a big southern city where he intended to give a speech to a rally of supporters. Ever since the coup, Bakiyev promoted the notion that he was popular in his native south. He even suggested he could run a southern statelet from here, while the interim government fumbled along in the north. But when Bakiyev arrived in Osh, he was greeted with rocks, and when he tried to speak, electricity was cut off and he couldn't use the microphone. His guards fired warning shots into the air, and his motorcade sped back to the village.

Behind the blue gate, a man from Bakiyev's coterie of supporters and hangers-on walked around the courtyard showing a gash above his right eyebrow. Someone had attacked him with a stick in Osh, he said. Bakiyev himself emerged from a ceremonial yurt with a turquoise roof. Dressed in a pinstriped suit and a blue shirt, his hair neatly combed, Bakiyev paced back and forth with a cell phone glued to his ear. Puffy pouches under his eyes suggested lack of sleep. Bakiyev hung up the phone and stepped forward to face a crowd of supporters, mostly women, who had just been ushered through a side entrance. He was angry that his planned Osh rally had been derailed. "Today's government is a government of bandits, and they call themselves democrats," he said.

Bakiyev is one of seven brothers, and some of them were on hand nearby. Away from the crowd, I spotted Janysh, the president's younger brother and his feared head of security. He wore camouflage military fatigues with his name stitched on the flap of the breast pocket, and chain-smoked Marlboro cigarettes. Many in Kyrgyzstan blamed Janysh for the deaths of the protesters storming the White House. Many wanted to see him on trial, or simply lynched.

"Yes, I gave the order to shoot at people who were armed, at the cars that were being used to ram through [the perimeter fence around the presidential palace]," he told me. He disputed the notion that his soldiers killed unarmed protesters and said fire had been directed at the palace from the crowd. He also said that some protesters were shot from such an angle that it suggested they were shot by their own colleagues. "Bullets don't fly that way," he told me, making a circular motion with his finger in the air. He said the protesters were moving like "zombies" toward the palace. Janysh wanted an "independent investigation" and until then he had no plans to give himself up because he was "not stupid."

Another Bakiyev brother, Kanybek, darted in and out of the house and told me he was "very tired" and couldn't talk. Ahmat Bakiyev, a farmer and businessman, was sitting on a bench in the courtyard. "I'm in a foul mood," he told me. He vowed the Bakiyevs would "defend themselves" if attacked by the interim government. In the months to come, his mood would get worse, for he would become the only Bakiyev sibling to end up behind bars, though not for long.

Bakiyev's presence in southern Kyrgyzstan posed problems for the self-proclaimed interim leaders in Bishkek. They appeared adrift as they tried to consolidate power, while he snubbed his nose at them, called them bandits, and refused to resign. Bakiyev's sojourn in Jalalabad also added a particularly jumpy quality to local politics. With neither side fully in charge, all sorts of curious characters stepped out of the wood-work to fill the void. One day shortly after the revolution, Asylbek Tash-tanbekov, a squat former running champion without a job, was pro-claimed mayor of Jalalabad. This sudden career twist came as a surprise to Tashtanbekov, not to mention many Jalalabad residents who'd never heard of the guy.

After the revolution, the town's old mayor resigned, part of the domino effect of Bakiyev's fall. His replacement, "the people's mayor," was a couple of days into his job when a rally addressed the question of his suitability for the position. There were a lot of women in that rally, and some alleged that the people's mayor was slow in meeting the needs of the people. One case cited was that of a woman who needed money for medical treatment but apparently couldn't get it. "So we said, let's appoint our own mayor," said Zulfia Abdrazakova, an elderly woman in a floral-print headscarf. She kept her eyes closed when she spoke. I learned later that she was blind and ran a local charity for the blind and the deaf.

This is how Tashtanbekov entered the picture. A Jalalabad native, Tashtanbekov, fifty-two, had worked in the town administration before, and had been known to some of the protesters since he was a boy. When he was younger he'd scored big victories in the eight-hundred-meter and fifteen-hundred-meter races, he told me proudly in the mayor's office. A huddle of white telephones sat silently on his desk, while his mobile phone kept erupting in a raucous folk-song ring tone. He'd worked as a coach and as an official in the mayor's office, but for the last two years he'd been mostly without work.

He was initially reluctant to become mayor and felt it was impolite to push out the guy who'd just been given that very job. But he overcame that reluctance partly because the old mayor seemed exhausted and not all that excited about being mayor anymore. When I asked him whether he supported the interim government or Bakiyev, he seemed unwilling to pick sides because no one really knew how things were going to shake out, and it would have been unwise to pledge allegiance to the losing side. The mayor fidgeted in his chair and said he was on the side of "peace and conciliation." Pressed on the issue, he finally said he backed the new leaders in Bishkek.

We spoke in his crowded office not far from Jalalabad's Freedom Square, where authorities had erected a slender statue to commemorate the 2005 Tulip Revolution. The latest uprising lacked any of that romanticism, or even a catchy name, both because of the déjà vu quality of events and because of the bloodshed. Walking around Jalalabad, where mayors rose and fell based on the whims of the crowds, I thought of Kyrgyzstan as a bizarre case of direct democracy taken to its most absurd extreme in a society where institutions and laws are weak or nonexistent, where clans are strong, and where poverty makes people edgy, easily manipulated, and ready to attempt risky things.

The presence of loudly disposed women at rallies became a fixture of political life in Kyrgyzstan. Describing a recent rally where a heckling argument occurred between two rival camps, a local journalist mentioned something called OBON. The word sounded like the ubiquitous Russian acronym for Police Special Forces, and I assumed he was talking about riot police. It turned out the acronym stood for Heckling Women Special Forces. These histrionic commandos have been effective in Kyrgyzstan's modern political history. They scream and drown out their opponents; they can land a punch if need be, or fall on the ground in a theatrical show of sorrow; security forces don't quite know how to deal with them, they are just a bunch of middle-aged and elderly women. Waiting in a Defense Ministry reception area a few days later, I overheard two senior security operatives, both tough-looking men, discussing the challenges of OBON. "You know, in Jalalabad fifty women were able to seize the governor's office—what the hell do you do in a situation like that?"

With the mayor's job in play, a similar round of musical chairs occurred in the provincial governor's office. After the music stopped, the man who ended up sitting down was Bakiyev's former ambassador to Pakistan. A few days later, in a flurry of new decrees, the interim government announced the appointment of a new Jalalabad mayor. His name was not Asylbek Tashtanbekov, the OBON-backed running champion.

A few miles away in the Bakiyev family compound, the ousted president was grasping at straws. With the Russians and Americans turning away from him, he was desperate for any sign of support. His dreams of digging in and ruling a diminished patch of loyal ground in the south also seemed to be melting away. Reality began to set in: his political base had shrunk to the size of his ancestral village here, nothing more. A plan B was needed.

At one point his aides printed out a news report saying that Belorussian president Alexander Lukashenko had called the revolution an unconstitutional coup and offered asylum to Bakiyev. Pacing in front of his ceremonial tent, Bakiyev perked up and praised him for his "courage." It was the only public expression of support from a foreign leader, and it couldn't have come from a nicer guy. Alongside Uzbekistan, Belarus is the last unabashedly Soviet dictatorship. Lukashenko, nicknamed Batka, or Daddy, in Belarus, is a former collective-farm boss with a buffoonish, populist demeanor and zero tolerance for criticism. Germany's foreign minister, an openly gay man, recently called Lukashenko "Europe's last dictator," an old Western slur that Daddy had grown tired of hearing. So, after competing at a cross-country skiing event (where he finished first because he's "in a great shape," according to the Belorussian state television), Lukashenko took a moment to respond to the impertinent German. "I'd rather be a dictator than a queer," he said.

On April 15, Bakiyev scrawled a resignation letter in jumpy handwriting, handed it to international intermediaries, and flew out of Kyrgyzstan, probably never to set foot in his homeland again. After a brief stop in Kazakhstan, Bakiyev and his entourage continued to Belarus, as guests of the proudly straight dictator. After landing in the safety of Minsk (great hockey and tractors), Bakiyev declared that his resignation letter was not valid and he still considered himself president. Good, because no one else did.

A few weeks later, a curious recording surfaced in Kyrgyzstan. It purported to be a phone conversation between Maxim Bakiyev and his uncle Janysh, secretly recorded by Kyrgyzstan's intelligence services.[5] Although there was no independent verification of its authenticity, those who had heard both men speak before said the voices on the tape sounded remarkably like Maxim and Janysh. On the tape, Maxim spoke quickly, bubbling over with ideas and enthusiasm, his speech laced with profanities. Janysh grunted a lot, elongated the endings of words, and mostly listened. The subject of the call was how to put together a quick counterrevolution and topple the interim government, which appeared very wobbly in those early days. A few excerpts:

> *Maxim:* So what I thought would be technically realistic is to find about five hundred guys — hello, can you hear me? — so I was saying, find some crazy fuckers, among whom you'd have about ten people who can actually string a few words together. So they would all enter the White House, and say, "Now we are the interim government" and start fucking churning out decrees.
>
> *Janysh:* Yes, aha, hmmmmm.
>
> *Maxim:* They wouldn't need to dig in for a long siege and sit there for twenty-five days. All they have to do is enter the White House, issue a couple of decrees, and that's it. This interim government is more legitimate than the old interim government.
>
> *Janysh:* Yes, but you see, all those [interim government members] are scattered all over the place. That bitch [Roza Otunbayeva] is sitting in the Ministry of Defense.
>
> *Maxim:* We only need to do two things now. First, we have to delegitimize the interim government. And second, we have to maintain the unrest, so that someone somewhere is always stirring things up. And their [forthcoming] elections, that's complete bullshit. Fuck their elections.

The two spoke for a while, with Maxim suggesting that he bankroll one or two figureheads who could lead the new uprising. "I'm the only one who can spring some serious cash in the country, and they know it," Maxim said. The "Chief," as he referred to his father, seemed reluctant to embrace a countercoup, so Maxim told Janysh they'd have to find someone else, and rattled off some names. Maxim left little doubt of who'd really be in charge. "I'll set very strict conditions. I'll say do this, this, and that, fucking free Angela Davis, ha ha," Maxim told Janysh.

> *Maxim:* Ideally, this would be the Chief, he's legal, he's legitimate, he'll say, "Go fuck yourselves!" But I spoke to the Chief about this yesterday. And he told me this would probably involve, you know . . . the same stuff that happened back in April. I told him it would probably be worse than that. Because we'll have to be very ruthless, right?
>
> *Janysh:* Yeah.
>
> *Maxim:* So he said, "That's it. I don't want to do this."
>
> *Janysh:* Yeah, he won't do it.
>
> *Maxim:* I told him, "We can't seize the White House peacefully." . . . Those [five hundred fighters] must be very well equipped. We should give each of them two or three thousand bucks and tell 'em, "Go do this, and you'll get the same amount afterward." Cops won't fight back.
>
> *Janysh:* Of course they won't, they've seen it all before.
>
> *Maxim:* This whole operation will take two hours—they'll shit their pants and fall on their asses. Our guys enter the White House, go on TV, and say, "Go fuck yourselves!" But it must be done with speed and secrecy. We obviously won't announce it ahead of time.
>
> *Janysh:* Lightning fast!
>
> *Maxim:* But if we do this, you or I must be on the ground to lead the operation, because I don't quite see another person who can take charge here. Someone who can identify all the systemic targets that need to be attacked, to be blocked.
>
> *Janysh:* Like Lenin did it in 1917. [Here Janysh was referring to the Communist revolution when Lenin's foot soldiers seized the telegraph, a story taught to every Soviet schoolchild.]
>
> *Maxim:* Why I'm saying you or me? Because we need a person with nothing to lose.
>
> *Janysh:* Yes-yes-yes. So who will be the overall leader?

Maxim: No, you see, the person who will lead the operation must not show his face publicly. He must only be the on-the-ground commander. The person with the flag, the person addressing the public on TV, that will be someone else. It's obvious that if you lead this thing and then pop up on television, it will be a fucking mess, it's better not to even try this.

Janysh: Yeah, ha-ha-ha.

Maxim: Ha-ha-ha-ha.

Janysh: Okay, let's think this over.

Maxim: You see, [the interim government] is like a house of cards now, they are weak, and the people don't fucking support them. Neither do the police nor the army. All we need to do is find a person who won't irritate people even more, that's it.

Toward the end of the conversation, after discussing logistics of the operation, Maxim asked his uncle about the possibility of reaching out to his contacts in Russia.

Maxim: You should get in touch with them. For the Russians, you are the ideal person. They love guys like you with military epaulettes, guys who can drink vodka with them, guys who have a certain fuck-it-all quality.

The plotting between the nephew and the uncle didn't result in a countercoup. But two months later, when vicious interethnic fighting broke out in the south of Kyrgyzstan, people remembered Maxim's plan to make sure that "someone somewhere is always stirring things up."

All this intrigue was aimed at the same woman who had appeared at so many other critical junctures of Kyrgyzstan's history: Roza Otunbayeva, former diplomat and perennial opposition leader. She was now the interim president.

Otunbayeva was trying to hold Kyrgyzstan together from a temporary warren of offices inside the Defense Ministry. The Russian, American, and Chinese ambassadors were waiting for a meeting with her, eager to reconnect with the woman they had met before but who now, unexpectedly, was running the country, or at least trying to. The Russian ambassador, Valentin Vlasov, was a plainspoken former Kremlin envoy to

Chechnya, famous because at one point he had been abducted by Chechen rebels and held hostage for six months. Now, Vlasov presided over the expansion of Russian economic and political influence in Kyrgyzstan.

The American ambassador, a career diplomat named Tatiana Gfoeller, had reasons to be anxious before meeting with Otunbayeva. The interim president didn't hide her contempt for American diplomats in Bishkek, accusing them of coddling the Bakiyev regime in order to save the Manas military base. Washington would soon replace Gfoeller with a new envoy, although in fairness it wasn't Gfoeller's fault. She was merely following orders.

The American military buildup in Central Asia, though for now aimed at Afghanistan, spooked the Chinese, who suspected those military bases might one day be used against China. Not surprisingly, the Chinese government has publicly urged Central Asian leaders to send the American troops home as soon as possible.

After the ambassadors had their separate chats with the new president, I went in to find Otunbayeva slumped behind her desk. For someone who'd helped bring about the downfall of two consecutive regimes, Otunbayeva didn't look menacing. She just looked tired. Her pitch black hair sat helmetlike over a round face that often broke into a smile. To unwind, she sometimes did yoga, though lately she hadn't had much time for it. "These days, I sleep while walking, so if I lose my train of thought, maybe you could give me a nudge," she told me. She was drinking strong tea to keep herself from nodding off at her desk, a red and gold Kyrgyzstan flag behind her. She was still settling into her new quarters. While we spoke, a soldier wheeled in a large safe and put it in the corner of her office.

Otunbayeva stood out in a political culture dominated by men, usually men with huge egos. Kyrgyz history did produce female leaders every now and again, and Otunbayeva wanted to be seen as one of them: "A woman jumps on a horse and can fly ahead of any man. A woman as a fighter, a woman as a messenger, a woman as a polemicist—all of these things are real." The most famous woman in the country's history is Kurmajan Datka, who died in 1907. She bucked tradition by refusing an arranged marriage and wed an ambitious local chieftain instead. The man ruled over the Kyrgyz tribes within the Khokand Khanate. After Kurmajan's husband was killed in a palace coup, she punished the plotters and assumed his mantle as the ruler of the Kyrgyz. She was awarded the high military rank of Datka (which loosely translates as "general"). She fought the Russian encroachments, but eventually pledged allegiance to Saint Petersburg. Then, two of her sons and two grandsons were accused of running a smuggling operation and killing customs officers. Despite her entreaties, the Russians publicly hanged one son and sentenced the rest of the accused to hard labor in Siberia. Crushed, Kurmajan gave away her cattle and settled into a solitary life in her home village. There are statues to Kurmajan Datka in Kyrgyzstan, and her face decorates the 50-som banknote. In the sheer number of monuments, museums, and place-names dedicated to her around the country, Kurmanjan is second only to Manas.

There were questions about Otunbayeva's own political longevity. Politicians with more money, a stronger clan base, and infinite ambition lurked around her. They thrust her forward as a consensus interim leader they could all rally around without suspicion she would turn on them the same way Bakiyev did. The experience of two ousted presidents taught Kyrgyzstan's elites that no single person can be trusted with too much power. So their plan was to change the form of government from presidential to parliamentary in the hope of limiting the authority of any one leader. Under the new constitution, the president's time in office would be limited to a single term. Of course, none of this would be enough to prevent the rise of a truly ambitious dictator. But it would slow the process down a little, lay trip wires for the aspiring autocrat to set off.

Like many small countries, Kyrgyzstan is often defined in relation to bigger countries, as if its existence only matters because it's of some use to others. "We are not a puppet, we want to succeed as a country," Otunbayeva said when we spoke a few days after the revolution. "We don't want to be manipulated: one person opens a military base, another says I also want a base; one says, 'I'll give you money,' the other says, 'I'll give you more money.' Yes, a destitute person may follow such logic. But we should be smart; we shouldn't sell ourselves."

The revolution inspired many conflicting emotions in Otunbayeva. There was shame over looting and destruction; there was sorrow for those who were killed; there was a certain pride that her people can rise up and shake off a bad regime, unlike their neighbors who are too cowed to protest dictatorships; there was fear that things might fall apart; and there was hope that a better government might emerge out of this mess. "Just recently when the situation was escalating here, things were also happening in Thailand. And I was reading that there had been eighteen coups d'état in Thailand's history, and I got so scared."

Otunbayeva seemed both intimidated and impressed by mobs—intimidated because of their destructive unruly power, impressed because they represent the people's right to rise up against injustice when all else fails.

One hot afternoon in Bishkek, I accompanied Otunbayeva on a visit to a hospital. She was driven in a black Mercedes down a traffic-choked street and ushered into the ward of Almazbek Akchekeyev, thirty-one. A gaunt man, he lay under a blanket printed with yellow flowers. "Please hold on, don't lose your spirit," Otunbayeva told him. "We'll give you housing, I promise." Akchekeyev's wife, Mahabat, later told me he was a police officer who lost both legs in a grenade blast during the revolt. "The worst is behind us," Mahabat said. I wondered if that was really true in a country where even able-bodied men had a hard time finding work.

One morning, ten days after the revolution that brought Otunbayeva to power, a crowd gathered in the overheated basement of the history museum in downtown Bishkek. It was an "emergency forum" of Kyrgyzstan's civil-society groups, a loud gathering of activists of all stripes who'd spent years campaigning against the many excesses of the country's successive rulers. Now they peppered the interim president's chief of staff with annoying questions about the new government's legitimacy or lack thereof.

The newly minted chief of staff was Edil Baisalov, who had flown into Bishkek from his Swedish exile the day after the uprising. A former duty-free negotiator and opposition activist who caught a pipe to the head while crossing a Bishkek street, Baisalov now found himself in an unusual role. All of a sudden, he wasn't on the outside criticizing the government. He *was* the government.

"Edil wasn't even in the country during the revolution," someone said.

"But he's a fighter!" someone else shouted.

"I saw how all of you were divvying up government jobs," another activist admonished Baisalov.

"I didn't divvy up anything," Baisalov protested.

"Do you have any moral right to come in here and take advantage of the fruits of the revolution?" yet another activist asked the newly repatriated chief of staff.

"I don't have any moral right," Baisalov, a little flustered, said quietly.

"What exactly is the mandate of the interim government?" another voice chimed in.

Amid all the ferment, a man stood up and offered this analogy. "The interim government is our common baby—without us it can't sleep, it can't eat, it can't pee, it can't poop." Many in the audience snickered, but I thought it was an apt comparison. The interim government was weak, disorganized, and in many ways incompetent. In the coming months, the true scope of its weakness would manifest itself with tragic consequences. But at the moment, the Kyrgyz had nothing better going on. The Bakiyev regime, rotten and corrupt, was gone, and not even the biggest skeptics of the current leadership wanted its return.

Another forum attendee sprang up from his seat and addressed the interim government in verse, stifling tears and mixing metaphors. "Let your galloping horse not stumble and cry / Let the flame in your heart not flicker and die."

Indeed, the revolution ignited a minor poetic renaissance. Roza Otunbayeva, whose first name means "rose" in Russian, provided an irresistible target for poets and metaphor cobblers. The Rose who had led the Tulip Revolution and was now back for round two was too juicy a poetic hook to pass up. Bakiyev had also acquired a catchy nickname that captured the spirit of his rapacious, dollar-driven presidency. He was known simply as the Buck. A couple of days after the uprising, a Bishkek professor wrote a poem whose title he borrowed from Umberto Eco's novel *The Name of the Rose*. It was published in a local newspaper. An excerpt is below:

> Happiness, brother, and tears . . .
> The Buck has crashed, good riddance!
> The Rose is in full bloom
> But there are so many fears.
>
> The list of demands on you grows
> Every day, a new leader appears
> I believe in the strength of the Rose
> But there are so many fears.

Leaving the basement of the history museum, Baisalov was in a grumpy mood, his two mobile phones ringing nonstop. The chief of staff conjured up his own metaphor of the political situation, one bereft of excessive romanticism. "It's like a massive pile of shit, on top of which they planted a rose," he said, climbed into the back of a black chauffeur-driven sedan, and sped off to the Defense Ministry, Roza's temporary quarters.

Baisalov wasn't even supposed to be here, helping run the new government. He was supposed to be getting ready to go to Harvard to study government at the highbrow Kennedy School. Having fled Kyrgyzstan on a freezing night in 2007, his wife and baby daughter in tow, Baisalov had lived in Sweden for more than two years. He maintained regular contact with the Kyrgyz opposition and spoke publicly and frequently against the Bakiyev regime. He was particularly close to Roza, whom he'd gotten to know well in the run-up to the earlier Tulip Revolution. Baisalov, incidentally, helped come up with the name "Tulip" to attach to that uprising.

Along with keeping tabs on the fluid situation in Kyrgyzstan from the comforts of Sweden, Baisalov was also looking for an apartment in Cambridge and studying the pros and cons of various dining-hall plans. He'd just won a full scholarship from George Soros to attend Harvard. It was far from obvious that the Bakiyev regime was about to collapse, and Baisalov thought a year at Harvard might do him some good. On

April 8, the day after the revolution, he flew to Kyrgyzstan, where his elderly parents still lived. Roza named him her chief of staff on the spot. His wife and daughter still in Sweden, Baisalov shelved his Harvard plans and embraced a task that would cause him to burn out within a few months. He was Roza's assistant, spokesman, advisor, and all-purpose fireman. It was he who publicized Bakiyev's handwritten resignation note.

In the first jittery days after the revolution, I met Baktybek Saip-bayev, a big, jovial man who owns an ice-cream business together with his wife. In a concrete bunkerlike building on the outskirts of Bishkek, they make several flavors of Snow Leopard ice cream and sell it mostly through modern supermarket chains, which began appearing in Bishkek a few years ago. In 2005, during the Tulip Revolution, Saipbayev lost a few thousand dollars in ruined ice cream and stolen equipment during the looting of Beta Stores, a Turkish-built shop downtown.

The April Revolution cost him much more. The Narodnii chain of some forty stores was so thoroughly looted that Saipbayev estimated he lost about $20,000. He hoped to get some of it back through insurance. "We lost a lot of ice cream. They either destroyed it or ate it," Saipbayev said. Then he smiled, as only the true connoisseur of his own product can: "At least I hope they ate it." As he walked through his small factory, strewn with stacks of plastic containers and suffused with a milky smell, Saipbayev managed to remain philosophical about the motivations of looters who flocked to Bishkek from the countryside. "A lot of them have never tasted bananas, oranges. They don't have this stuff in their villages, so they saw an opportunity." Giddy at encountering such plenty, these village guys swiped packs of cigarettes, bottles of booze, food, and clothes as they toured Bishkek's Disneyland of consumption. They were scavenging and snacking.

There was another group of looters for whom Saipbayev had no sympathy at all. That group approached the task like professionals. They backed trucks into store loading bays and packed them with refrigerators, television sets, with anything that was worth taking. After the Tulip Revolution, Saipbayev and many other businessmen began looking for broader insurance coverage, a Kyrgyz premium of sorts. Alongside the usual calamities, they wanted protection from revolts and looters, from socioeconomic upheavals that "can clean out a store much more efficiently than a hurricane," Saipbayev told me.

On a rainy Sunday afternoon, after the forced hiatus of the revolution, Saipbayev was preparing to make ice cream again. While we spoke, he was unloading heavy sacks of powdered milk from the back of his minivan. It took him a couple of days to find the milk because supplies from a factory in Talas, where he usually got it, had been disrupted by the uprising. Talas, the birthplace of Manas, is where the revolution began. A former manager at an international pharmaceutical company, Saipbayev had worked in Russia and Kazakhstan but he always wanted to live where he was born, and he wanted to run his own business. After several false starts, including a project that fell apart when a relative made off with $5,000 of the seed capital, Saipbayev settled on ice cream. It's wholesome and happy, and everyone likes it. The business took off. Saipbayev had two kids in college: a son in Germany and a daughter in France. "They don't want to live under a khan, and there's a whole generation of people like that," he said. As for Saipbayev himself, he simply wanted to be left alone to make ice cream and not have to worry about rapacious bureaucrats demanding bribes or revolutionaries destroying his product.

Even with all the hassles and business losses, Saipbayev seemed sympathetic to the revolution. A doctor by training, he likened a corrupt regime to an infected wound. "If there's pus in the wound, you have to let it out, otherwise it will lead to sepsis — you have to clean the wound out," he said. "People here started to understand that you can get rid of these assholes in power. And the politicians are beginning to be scared."

The impulse to send the "assholes in power" packing is a commendable one. But alongside the obvious benefits, it acquired a farcical dimension as one revolt led to another, and different groups of assholes took turns occupying the White House (with yet more assholes banging on the gates). One rally, for instance, had as its central demand the removal of the ornate cast-iron fence around the presidential palace — so that protesters could protest more effectively and spare themselves the inconvenience of having to climb over the fence. Wisely, this demand was not met.

In October of 2012, a determined mob of unsmiling men walked briskly toward the White House, shouting slogans. Leading them was Kamchibek Tashiyev, a square-jawed former boxer and a prominent nationalist politician with a short temper and a nose bent slightly to the right. The mob shoved past a sheepish-looking scrum of police and began scaling the fence. "Once upon a time, Genghis Khan seized power with just seventeen people; who will come with me?" Tashiyev thundered at a rally earlier that day. Jumping off the fence onto the interior courtyard of the White House, protesters jogged toward the entrance. A handful of skinny cops confronted them meekly. They shot rubber bullets from long-barreled rifles, but the protesters quickly overwhelmed them and chased them away. The whole scene had the distinct feel of a playground brawl, except the protesters weren't playing games. A jerky video of the day's events could easily be mistaken for the opening frames of the two earlier uprisings that ended in coups d'état. Was this the beginning of Revolution 3.0? Turns out the by-now-ritual scaling of the presidential fence was driven by gold, lots of it.

For months in the run-up to the mission, Tashiyev and his comrades had been pressing the government to nationalize a major gold mine operated by a Canadian company. Each year, more than a tenth of Kyrgyzstan's national income comes from scattered particles of gold buried under a glacier, high up on a mountain plateau close to the Chinese border. The Tien Shan peaks here rise tall and majestic, almost skewering the sky. The name means "celestial mountains" in Mandarin, and by the time you climb up here, short of breath and with a splitting headache because of the thin air, the name seems a perfect fit. Whoever decides these things made sure this gold wouldn't be easy to find. And, once it was found, it would be even harder to extract.

Soviet geologists discovered the Kumtor gold deposit in 1978 but deemed further exploration prohibitively expensive. So the gold remained buried until the 1990s, when Central Asia opened up to the world after more than seventy years of Soviet rule. The region's plentiful natural resources began attracting foreign dealmakers and carpetbaggers, oilmen and gold prospectors, in a grand Wild East race to snag lucrative concessions from fledgling local governments desperate for new sources of revenue.

Kyrgyz gold has been dogged by controversy from the start. In Bishkek, the foreign dealmaker to watch in the 1990s was Boris Birshtein, a supremely connected Soviet émigré to Canada whose firm traded gold and other commodities across the former Soviet empire. Birshtein became an informal advisor to the Kyrgyz government, maintaining an office not far from the president's. Birshtein gained notoriety in the mid-1990s when the Kyrgyz Parliament objected to a suspicious airlift of state-owned gold out of the country and into a Swiss bank vault. The official story was that the gold had been whisked out of Kyrgyzstan as a collateral for a loan, but the secrecy surrounding the deal raised eyebrows and eventually prompted several high-ranking officials to resign. It was Birshtein's local connections in Kyrgyzstan that helped open the door to the Canadian company that would win the right to develop the Kumtor mine.[6]

Gold doesn't come naturally in gold bars. For every four grams of Kumtor gold, workers must dig through one ton of ore. After gigantic trucks haul the ore from the vertiginous open pit, the raw material is ground, sifted, separated, spun in large blue centrifuges, and leached in vats, where a cyanide solution teases out the microscopic particles of gold. At the end of the process, after a few more alchemic permutations, a technician in a heavily guarded room pours the molten gold into bars. Even that isn't pure gold but an alloy containing impurities of silver and other metals. Given the monumental windup to this final step—cutting through a millennial glacier and setting off explosions to move the reluctant mountain—these impure bars feel underwhelming, almost like a nature's way of mocking humanity's pursuit of wealth.

The drive to the mine site is long and monotonous, requiring a slow climb along a series of switchbacks beginning on the shores of Lake Issyk-Kul. Cliffs of barren rock rise on either side of the road as the terrain slopes steeply upward. Pine groves and hills of shrubbery cover the austere landscape. A shallow river flows over a rocky bed nearby, snaking through a handful of hamlets. Vegetation becomes sparser the higher you climb. Eventually it vanishes altogether and gives way to blinding vistas of snow and ice surrounding an azure lake formed by a melting glacier. It is so clean you can drink from it.

In 1998, a Kumtor truck carrying cyanide tumbled into a river, releasing the hazardous chemical downstream and harming local residents and livestock. The spill became the mine's original sin, turning public opinion against the Canadians. No conversation about the mine's impact on Kyrgyzstan—and there would be plenty in the years to come—could unfold without revisiting the spill, or the clumsy handling of its aftermath. A related line of attack portrayed the mine's operators as wily foreigners who, abetted by corrupt local officials and shrewd intermediaries, had managed to hoodwink the Kyrgyz into an unfair deal.

With each revolution, a new crop of Kyrgyz leaders came under public pressure to right the perceived wrong, renegotiate the profit-sharing agreement with the Canadians, and delve deeper into the mine's environmental and labor practices. The Canadians' sensible rejoinder that Kumtor provides thousands of well-paid jobs, abides by all existing laws, and contributes mightily to the Kyrgyz economy gets drowned out in the fury fed by publications with titles like *Gold Mafia at Kumtor.* The pamphlet was written by a man who says he saw fish floating belly up in the river after the cyanide truck fell into it.

The Canadians' occasional missteps only contribute to the tensions. In 2009, a Kyrgyz laborer at Kumtor was unloading a barrel from a truck. A large chunk of ice slid off the top of the barrel and hit him on the head, causing a severe injury. A father of five, he could no longer work and suffered from near-constant headaches, seizures, and blackouts. He had violent episodes too, but he couldn't remember them afterward, his brother told me. Two years after the head injury, the Kumtor laborer died of a heart attack. He was forty-eight. Kumtor, which had covered his medical care, balked at his widow's request for compensation, arguing that the heart attack had nothing to do with the head trauma. The mine's lawyers continued to fight the widow in the courts even after she produced medical evidence that seemed to suggest a link. The company relented only after Kumtor's Kyrgyz miners went on strike, forcing Kumtor to halt gold production for the first time in years. Paying the widow was among the miners' demands. Perhaps Kumtor lawyers initially resisted because they wanted to avoid a precedent of settling potentially spurious claims. But in focusing on the legal trees, Kumtor missed the forest of public opinion. Its battle against the widow smacked of cruelty and small-mindedness, particularly as the global price of gold soared and gave the company plenty of cash to spare.

A calmer discussion about the mine's environmental and labor practices and about the size of its contributions to the Kyrgyz economy needs to take place, but the issue often gets hijacked by the indomitable spirit of Kyrgyz populism.

It is in that spirit that Kamchibek Tashiyev, the former boxer who leads a major opposition political party, climbed the White House fence, wearing a black suit more fitting for office work. "Kumtor belongs to the people, and it is the people who should be managing it," Tashiyev said, in an appeal that would be music to the ears of the Lenin statues populating the history museum nearby. After darting around the White House front yard and confusing the ill-prepared police, Tashiyev and his supporters were eventually restrained by arriving reinforcements. As a member of Parliament, he had immunity from arrest, an obstacle authorities would soon override, ordering him detained for two months on charges of attempting a violent coup. Tashiyev, who denied plotting a revolution, promptly went on a hunger strike behind bars. The government said it had no intention of nationalizing the gold mine, though it vowed to press ahead with official inquiries into the Canadian company's practices.

On his day of glory, Tashiyev didn't need to scale any fences because Kyrgyz parliamentarians all have offices in the White House anyway. (The presidential administration occupies only the top floors.) All he needed to do to get in was show his ID, but he wanted a more cinematic entry. The day after his acrobatics, someone attached a hand-drawn cardboard sign to the White House fence: "No need to climb this fence. A normal entrance is nearby. We want peace."

The Kyrgyz are used to nationalizing, carving up, and reselling companies and other assets pried away from their ousted rulers and their families and friends. It's a messy and at times comical process. After President Bakiyev and his retinue fled abroad, authorities auctioned off mementos of his regime, including a yacht that apparently served as a sort of a luxury baton passed by the Akayevs to the Bakiyevs. Fitted with two bedrooms and mahogany furniture, the single-masted Bavaria-38 Cruiser plied the waters of Lake Issyk-Kul, first for the primary enjoyment of Akayev's son, and then, when things changed, for the enjoyment of a Maxim Bakiyev associate. In October of 2011, a government auctioneer in a dark suit set the starting price at $64,000, raised a wooden gavel . . . and there were no bids. He announced the price two more times, and still received no bids.

"What's going on?" the auctioneer asked.

One prospective buyer volunteered that whatever luxury the yacht may have possessed had worn off, perhaps because the managers of an Issyk-Kul resort, where the yacht was temporarily moored pending the auction, took advantage of the pleasure boat and took it on joyrides. The mileage was far higher than declared on the auction bill, and there were dents in the hull.

"Were you riding it all summer?" the auctioneer asked a resort manager sitting nearby.

"No, no, we didn't touch it," the manager hurried to say.

Citing the wear and tear, the prospective buyer haggled the price down by a quarter and bought the boat. He turned out to be the owner of another Issyk-Kul resort, colorfully named Dolphin Deluxe. A Kyrgyz reporter inquired whether the yacht's new proprietor was perhaps scared by its "sad history."

"Nothing scares me," the Dolphin Deluxe man shot back.[7]

Such vivid reminders of the transitory nature of the Kyrgyz presidency and its many perks hovered over the revolutionary leaders and scared them straight, at least for a while. "Do you really think that in the end we want to be dealt with the same way that Bakiyev was dealt with?" Roza Otunbayeva, the woman who succeeded Bakiyev as president, told me a few days after the revolution. In fact, Otunbayeva would become the first president in Kyrgyzstan's history to peacefully cede power and avoid exile.

The ferment of Kyrgyzstan's recent history gave rise to a new derogatory expression, "to Kyrgyz around," which means, roughly, "to raise hell in the streets for no good reason." After unloading the powdered milk for a new batch of ice cream, Baktybek Saipbayev, the Bishkek entrepreneur whose merchandise got looted and eaten in both revolutions, told me a new joke was making the rounds in Bishkek: "Don't wake my inner Kyrgyz." The ice-cream maker meant it lightly, but in the months following Bakiyev's ouster, that inner Kyrgyz turned out to be an ugly guy.

In a village on the edge of Bishkek a week after the revolution, black-helmeted riot police were holding off a crowd of protesters. An armored infantry vehicle sat at an intersection, a gunner lounging on its roof. Snow-covered mountains rose in the distance. They were tall and craggy, dazzlingly white against an azure sky unblemished by a single cloud.

The protesters were demanding the release of 120 people detained the day earlier. That day, a mob flooded onto a field and started parceling out land for themselves, according to a master list someone had drawn up. There was one problem: that land already had owners. But the land grabbers, most of them destitute laborers, saw an opportunity in the chaos of the revolution. Their logic was simple. In the capital, a group of politicians had seized power. So why can't we seize land?

Behind the line of riot police, I met Bahyt, a short man with the creased and tanned face of someone who spends a lot of time outdoors. A forty-one-year-old father of five, Bahyt spoke with a lot of emotion, his voice skidding into a high pitch when he wanted to emphasize a point. "I'm penniless," he told me with a shriek. All six of his family members live in a small rented room. "I just wanted a plot of land to build a house."

Like many of his countrymen seeking refuge from Kyrgyzstan's dismal economy, Bahyt used to work in Russia. These labor migrants man construction sites, work at outdoor markets, and do other menial jobs, often facing contempt or indifference from local officials and residents. Sometimes they fall prey to gangs of skinheads. A Kyrgyz friend of mine told me his brother worked as a waiter at a Japanese-themed café in Moscow. The manager ordered him to keep his mouth shut around clients to bolster the illusion he was Japanese. The Kyrgyz have Asian features.

In Moscow, Bahyt handled interior-finishing jobs in new office buildings. He shared a small trailer with four other workers, sending most of his earnings back home to his family. Then the financial crisis hit Moscow's seemingly bottomless construction market, and Bahyt lost his job.

Looking for work, he moved to Tomsk, a town in Siberia where it gets so cold that "even a tomato can't ripen," he said. Bahyt took a job guarding a gas compressor. One day, he had to fix something at the site. As he was swinging a heavy hammer, his hold slipped, and the hammer shattered his foot. He couldn't work anymore, and the Siberian cold gnawed at the fracture, causing a dull pain. So he took a long train ride home to Kyrgyzstan, where he recovered and found occasional construction jobs. His latest employer was locked in a dispute with a contractor, and as a result Bahyt hadn't been paid in months. Desperate, he went to plant watermelons near the Kazakhstan border. Then the revolution happened, and Bahyt saw a chance to finally score some land he couldn't otherwise afford.

Faced with the mob of land grabbers, the interim government fumbled for a response. The mayor of Bishkek addressed the protesters and told them they should have land. The protesters took that as an invitation to grab it. Aida Kemelova, an epileptic single mother of three, showed me a piece of paper with a signature, which she said was permission to get land. A bread seller at a bazaar, she told me she was on the verge of eviction from her rental apartment. Bahyt showed me a similar squiggle scrawled on the photocopy of his passport. The mayor left, and the protesters got down to business with measuring tapes. This didn't sit well with the local landowners, and an argument ensued. Though what happened next isn't entirely clear, word spread through the crowd that a man with a double-barreled shotgun had opened fire. That man, Bahyt told me, was a Turk. The Turks, with their European facial features, are easily distinguishable from the Kyrgyz.

The Turks of Central Asia have a bitter history. They used to live in southern Georgia, near the Turkish border. In 1944, Soviet dictator Joseph Stalin decreed that they be resettled to Central Asia. Stalin was paranoid about the emergence of a fifth column among some ethnicities of the Soviet Union. One way to punish them and stifle their national spirit was to toss them around in the massive Soviet salad bowl. This is how one survivor described the ordeal: "At 4:00 a.m., four soldiers came into our house and said we had one hour to pack. We were not told where we would be sent. About 120 families were loaded into one freight car. We traveled eighteen days and nights to Central Asia. Many died of typhoid. At each stop they would unload the dead."[8]

In the village of Mayevka, outside Bishkek, the descendants of these refugees settled on a big collective farm, alongside the Kyrgyz and the Russians. When the land grabbing and the unrest began, the Turks sent their women and children away and waited, said Alik Aliyev, a Turk in his fifties with a scruffy, unshaven face. "Then we saw a crowd approaching from the direction of the fields. They had clubs and rocks and they were screaming wildly," Aliyev said. He was giving sworn testimony to a group of investigators from the State Security Service, and I was allowed to listen in. "We weren't evenly matched, so we retreated deep into the village." Eventually, the Turks grouped together and were able to hold the Kyrgyz mob at a distance for about two hours. "We were calling every emergency number we could find, asking for help. Our phones were getting overheated from all the use. The cops were waiting for an order, I heard."

No help was forthcoming, and the Kyrgyz crowd, having swollen in numbers, finally charged at the Turks. They were specifically looking for Turkish homes, Aliyev testified. They would run up to the fence of a house, and if a Kyrgyz or a Russian face popped up, they would move on. On the gate to one house, I saw a line, scrawled in chalk, identifying it as Kyrgyz, probably to warn off the rioters.

There was bone-chilling screaming, Aliyev recalled. "I don't even know how it is possible for humans to scream like this." The Turks scattered. Aliyev climbed over a fence and ran toward the next street. Behind him, smoke was rising from houses and haystacks that were set on fire. He hid in some bushes and waited. Then, when the cops finally arrived, Aliyev emerged from hiding and went to help his friends and relatives put out the fires. It was already dark, and a neighbor asked Aliyev to help identify a body, lying on its back in the street.

With the help of a flashlight, Aliyev recognized a good friend of his, Kaptan Karipov. Karipov, forty, was married to Aliyev's cousin and they had two kids. "His head was bashed in with rocks. There was a hole between his eyes, and there were stab wounds on his neck." Aliyev was speaking inside a smoldering wreck that had once been Karipov's house.

Days after the revolution, clashes over land broke out on the outskirts of Bishkek, and the interim government couldn't stop the violence. A Kyrgyz mob murdered the owner of this house, an ethnic Turk, and vandalized his house. (© Philip Shishkin)

On the tiled floor I saw broken jars of tomato preserves, the tomatoes squished and bright red, trailing seeds; shattered tea bowls spilling out of wrapping paper; a high-heeled boot, its black leather crumpled and dirty. In a burned shed, the charred corpse of a young bull was still smoking. "What were the security forces waiting for? If they'd come in time, this wouldn't have happened."

Later, I posed that question to Keneshbek Dushebayev, the new director of the State Security Service. We already met him, back in 2005 when he served as Akayev's chief of police for a single day before the Tulip Revolution and then negotiated by phone with Bakiyev from atop a children's slide. Now Dushebayev said the minister of the interior, who supervises the police, was replaced after the events in Mayevka, and assured me that the new leadership is "more decisive." In the evening after the murders—there were five that day—Otunbayeva authorized a shoot-to-kill policy against those attacking the property or lives of others. The police rounded up 120 people who participated in the riots. The next day, protesters demanded their release, and they were all set free. The government later said six people were under criminal investigation for their role in the violence. One afternoon, I got a phone call from Bahyt. He still had no land. When I asked him about the crowd's attack on the local Turks, he told me it was the Turks who started the fight.

In the corner of Mayevka, Aliyev's house survived the riots, but his car, an aging Mazda, had been stolen and was later found banged up beyond repair. As he gave testimony in the destroyed house of his dead friend, a big chunk of corrugated roofing material crashed down onto a blackened stove in Karipov's kitchen, a couple of feet from where Aliyev was sitting. Aliyev looked at it blankly. He didn't move from his bench. "I'm going to leave the village now," he said. "There's nothing here for me."

CHAPTER 6 *The Financier Vanishes,*
and Other Riddles

*O*f all the days he could get sick, this was the worst possible day.
Eugene Gourevitch, once Kyrgyzstan's premier financier and confidant
of the ruling family, was now a wanted man. In the days after the revolution, he needed to stay alert and think quickly to evade capture. Instead,
on this warm April afternoon, Gourevitch was delirious with a fever that
seemed to come out of nowhere. His head swayed from side to side as
he struggled to stay awake in the backseat of a car smuggling him out of
Kyrgyzstan. Gourevitch was so ill that he didn't even notice when the
car rattled across the border into neighboring Kazakhstan.

At least, that's where he hoped he was headed. He had to trust his
escorts, a pair of shadowy Chechen operatives, to honor their side of the
bargain. When they'd found Gourevitch in his Bishkek hideout a few
days earlier, the Chechens made him a simple offer. They'd smuggle him
out of the country, but it was going to cost him. Exactly how much would
be determined later. All he was told was, "Look, don't worry about it, it
will be affordable, it's not a huge deal." Gourevitch wasn't in a position
to haggle or demand guarantees. He wasn't even sure exactly who these
guys were, or how they had found him. But he had no other ideas of how
to save himself from the anti-Bakiyev revolutionaries who were on the
prowl for the former regime's associates, particularly those with knowl-

edge of the Bakiyevs' financial operations. And Gourevitch was at the top of that list. If the new government arrested him, the best he could hope for would be a lengthy prison term. So Gourevitch got into the Chechens' car. It was as much a kidnapping as it was a rescue. And now that damn fever was spiking again.

Barely two months earlier, Gourevitch had been living a very nice life. For a time, he rented a large luxury apartment in downtown Bishkek, the ultimate bachelor pad. For the first year of Gourevitch's stint in Kyrgyzstan, his wife and baby daughter stayed back in New York. Rolling in cash and connections, Gourevitch was the very picture of a high-flying investment banker. A fawning television interview from those days showed a confident Gourevitch dressed in a dark blue suit, a radiant yellow tie, and matching cufflinks. On camera, he dismissed rumblings about the nature of his Kyrgyz breakout as "envy of our success." His wife and daughter eventually joined Gourevitch in Bishkek. He moved out of the bachelor pad and rented a large house in a scenic resort area outside of town. His wife brought their nanny from the United States. A personal driver chauffeured him around town.

The first crack in the facade of the successful entrepreneur appeared in March, a month before the revolution. After years of sifting through complex financial transactions, Italian prosecutors brought criminal charges against dozens of suspects in the audacious "merry-go-round" scheme that had allegedly bilked the Italian Treasury out of hundreds of millions of dollars in fraudulent tax refunds. Eugene Gourevitch, now the custodian of hundreds of millions of dollars of Kyrgyz state money, was among those charged in the Italian case. When news of this reached Kyrgyzstan, opposition leaders reacted with understandable fury. It was a PR godsend. For years now, there had been unconfirmed rumors about the financial shenanigans of the Bakiyev regime. And now, for the first time, you could pin them on a concrete man. And what a convenient man it was: a young Jew from America by way of Moscow, a confidant of the president's son, and now an indicted associate of the Italian mafia! The opposition had a field day with this.

"If all the national treasures of Kyrgyzstan have been thrust by the current regime into the hands of international *Mafiosi*, then how can the people of Kyrgyzstan continue to believe the regime?" Edil Baisalov, exiled in Sweden, thundered to an influential website covering Central Asia. Gourevitch's standing in Kyrgyzstan took a big hit. Mikhail Nadel, the super-banker who'd invited him to the country, told me he felt "utter shock" upon learning of the Italian charges against the bright young man he'd championed. The Bakiyev administration didn't say a whole lot on the subject, but tried to distance itself from Gourevitch personally. All of this became moot when the government was overthrown a month later. All of a sudden, Gourevitch had a big target painted on his back.

His former protectors and associates were conveniently out of the country. In an amazing stroke of luck, Maxim Bakiyev happened to be in Washington on a previously scheduled visit during the revolution. Zamyra Sydykova, Kyrgyzstan's ambassador to the United States at the time, went to pick him up at Dulles Airport. Maxim emerged gloomy and preoccupied, speaking nonstop on two mobile phones as news of the revolt back home caught up with him in America. Maxim later told Gourevitch that had he stayed in Bishkek, he "would have stopped the revolution, but there wouldn't be eighty casualties, but eight hundred casualties. My hands would have been covered in blood." And that, Maxim told him, "wouldn't be worth my relationship with God."

During the revolution, Nadel the jet-setting banker happened to be in Israel for knee surgery. "Otherwise I would have been hanged from the first lamppost," he told me later. "You are aware of the anti-Semitic sentiment in Kyrgyzstan. I wouldn't have stood a chance." Nadel had a point. Just days after the revolution, someone affixed a large hand-drawn banner to the White House fence. "There's no place in Kyrgyzstan for dirty Jews and for people like Maxim," it read. While the man on the street vented against Jews, Kyrgyz investigators drilled into safety-deposit boxes belonging to Nadel and his associates, extracting millions of dollars in cash.

Kyrgyz officials later alleged that on the night of the uprising, as Nadel's financial empire was crumbling, millions of dollars were transferred from AUB to bank accounts abroad. In his office one afternoon, Temir Sariyev, the interim government's finance chief, showed me a schematic printout of the path of a single multimillion-dollar money transfer.

The money left AUB, split itself into batches, dribbled through dozens of countries and offshore companies, and finally landed somewhere. The printout I was shown had a lot of lines, circles, and squares. Sariyev said more than $270 million left the country this way between April 1 and 8, apparently as the regime smelled trouble. In the waning days and hours of the previous government, he said, financial whizzes used a mobile server to send money abroad. Nadel denied all of it. "Nothing of the sort ever happened," he told me. "When the shooting started, everyone went home, and that's it." He was sentenced in absentia to sixteen years in prison in connection with these alleged transfers, a conviction he vowed to appeal.

With both Maxim and Nadel out of the country, Gourevitch was the most visible, and notorious, member of the former regime's financial elite to remain on the ground in Kyrgyzstan. Gourevitch took his wife and daughter and fled from their large suburban house. The gated community was a target for vigilantes looking for the associates of the former regime. Through his guards, Gourevitch arranged to rent an apartment in Bishkek where his family was now hiding. When Gourevitch and his wife made a quick trip to their old rented house to pick up some clothes, family albums, and other personal effects, they were greeted by the owner with a shotgun in his hands. The owner told them to get lost and never come back. "It's funny today to even talk about these things, but someone out there in Bishkek is wearing my suits and ties," Gourevitch told me. A similar fate apparently befell even more famous wardrobes. Maxim later told Gourevitch that he was watching television one day and saw a member of the interim government wear a tie that looked suspiciously like one of Maxim's missing ties. After I heard this, my mind drifted back to the distant Tulip Revolution when protesters grabbed ties out of the ousted president's closet and wore them proudly.

For the moment, Gourevitch had bigger things to worry about than his suits and ties. He needed to get the hell out of Kyrgyzstan. It would be far easier for his wife and daughter to sneak out because their names were unlikely to be on any major international black lists. So Gourevitch paid someone $20,000 to chaperone them through the official Kyrgyz-Kazakh border crossing, where their American passports were stamped and they were safely on their way to Almaty. Once there, they caught a flight to New York. Gourevitch couldn't travel with them. On top of the Kyrgyz manhunt, Gourevitch was also the subject of an Interpol "red notice" seeking his arrest and extradition on the Italian charges. So the minute Gourevitch showed up at an official border crossing anywhere, he'd be handcuffed. Having gotten his family out, Gourevitch spent four days pacing around his rented Bishkek apartment pondering how to escape from the country where he'd been a chauffeured princeling only two months earlier. He still hoped his business associates would come and bail him out, but that wasn't happening. His old guards, from a private security firm hired by his investment bank, eventually told him they were being followed and had to cut him off. "Any minute now, someone's going to knock on this door," one of the guards told Gourevitch. The cornered financier then arranged to go stay with his old driver, figuring no one would think to look there and he could gain a few more days to plot his escape.

This is where the mysterious Chechens found him. Gourevitch suspects they were tipped off by his old security detail. The good thing about the Chechens was they had no ulterior motives, no political vendettas, and no righteous fury about Gourevitch's shady past. They were only interested in Gourevitch's money. And that, of course, was also the bad thing about the Chechens. How much exactly would they demand for their services? Gourevitch told them that whatever reports they'd heard of his spectacular wealth amassed from plundering the state coffers were grossly exaggerated. "If we are talking millions, then forget it," Gourevitch told the Chechens.

"We'll make it work," one of the Chechens answered.

And off to Kazakhstan they went, using smugglers' trails that avoided any official checkpoints. Once they reached Almaty, Gourevitch was presented with the bill: $20 million. Still running a high fever, Gourevitch thought he was hearing things. But the Chechens weren't kidding. "They wanted $20 million, otherwise they would kill me," Gourevitch said. It took all his powers of persuasion to get the Chechens to settle for less. Despite claims about his fantastical wealth, Gourevitch claimed that he was not that rich. His real payoff, he told me, would have come with the initial public offering of Asia Universal Bank, something that was off the table now that the bank was being dismantled and nationalized by the new government. Gourevitch told the Chechens that all he had was $600,000 in an AUB bank account, of which half belonged to his mother. All of it was worthless now. Gourevitch also had a brokerage account in another bank with $400,000 in it. The Chechens made him call his banker to confirm that figure while they listened in on the call. They took all of it and let Gourevitch go, keeping his passport.

Stranded in Almaty without documents or money, Gourevitch went where traveling Americans in trouble have gone before: the U.S. consulate. In consultation with his American lawyer, Gourevitch concocted a complicated plan. He wanted to surrender to U.S. law enforcement on the Italian arrest warrant and be extradited to America so he could deal with his legal issues from there. In effect, Gourevitch wanted to use his Italian legal problems as a ticket out of his Kyrgyz legal problems, wisely judging the latter to be far graver for his health and safety. In Almaty and Washington, Gourevitch and his lawyer started talking to U.S. officials about a surrender followed by an extradition to the United States. "I wasn't expecting them to send a helicopter or a plane for me, but I was expecting something." Gourevitch said. "If a wanted criminal comes to surrender to his home country, I thought they would make arrangements to take me to the States." But the Americans, he told me, weren't interested in taking Gourevitch into custody. They issued him a new passport and told him he was on his own. "I felt betrayed." (Citing privacy reasons, the U.S. embassy in Kazakhstan declined to comment on his case other than to say that Gourevitch had paid a single very brief visit to the consulate.)

Now what was he supposed to do? He couldn't catch a plane out of Almaty because he had entered the country illegally and because his name was double-flagged for arrest by the Kyrgyz and by the Italians. Should he be captured, it was highly likely that the Kazakhs would send him back to Kyrgyzstan instead of Italy, as a gesture of goodwill to the new leaders in Bishkek. Becoming a sacrificial lamb for the sins of the Bakiyev regime wasn't a risk Gourevitch was willing to take by showing up at the Almaty airport. Desperation and fear began to set in as Gourevitch walked the streets of Almaty, with no clear plan of how to get to New York to see his wife and daughter. He worried that the Chechens, disappointed by not snagging the expected millions from Gourevitch, might come after his family.

Money was also an issue. The Chechens had cleaned him out, and even though I suspect he probably had cash stashed away in some distant bank account or a safety-deposit box, he couldn't get to it now. So for the moment, Gourevitch was broke, an unusual condition for him. Help materialized from an old friend. Maxim Bakiyev, now also a fugitive, reached out to his former financial advisor and offered to spirit him out of Kazakhstan. After his brief sojourn in the United States and other international travels, Maxim had flown into Britain and applied for political asylum there. He was granted permission to stay while British authorities evaluated his application. Through a law firm, he issued a single public statement that accused Kyrgyzstan's new leaders of trying "to make me a scapegoat for the chaos in the country." Then, Maxim faded from public view.

As ruthless as he was toward his enemies, Maxim could be loyal to those he deemed useful, and Gourevitch assumed he fell into that category. "He had his own sense of loyalty which very conveniently fit with his own commercial interests," Gourevitch told me. "He knew that I could still be useful to him in the business world while others have served out their business purpose." As will soon become clear, Maxim did have very lucrative reasons to keep Gourevitch safe and free, so he spirited him out of Kazakhstan. One night, the fugitive banker boarded a chartered aircraft that was spared any border formalities or document checks. The plane's primary passengers were Marat Bakiyev and his family. Marat is Maxim's older brother and the former head of Kyrgyzstan's National Intelligence Service. Alongside his uncle Janysh, Marat oversaw the regime's extensive surveillance and repression apparatus. And now Marat arrived on an Almaty airfield for a clandestine flight out of Central Asia. His destination was Belarus, the same reclusive European dictatorship where his father had already settled.

Why was Belorussian strongman Alexander Lukashenko so welcoming to the Bakiyev clan? One reason was dictatorial solidarity. For years, the oddball ruler of Belarus faced a disorganized but persistent opposition movement at home. He jailed a few opponents, sent others packing for exile, and mocked all as foreign puppets. Like many dictators, Lukashenko viewed himself as a victim of plots and as the only force standing between order and chaos. To ensure continuity, Lukashenko anointed his eight-year-old son as his successor and dragged the boy to view military parades and meet foreign leaders. The boy often wore military fatigues or tailored civilian suits and carried a gilded pistol concealed in a holster under his jacket. Tongue-in-cheek, some Belorussians suggested that Lukashenko had devised a contingency plan in case his subjects finally lost patience and forced him to flee in a hurry. A few years ago, he ordered the construction of a monstrous, glass-encased structure rising high above the drab landscape of eastern Minsk. Shaped like a multifaceted cut diamond (its official geometric designation is "rhombicuboctahedron"), the structure glows in the dark with a shifting pattern of lights. It houses the national library. But wags joked that in reality it is a spaceship ready to blast off in an emergency and take Lukashenko and his armed miniature sidekick back home to whichever alien universe spawned them.

While still stranded on Earth, Lukashenko reveled in being the enfant terrible of Europe and couldn't miss a chance to snub his nose at his foreign critics. Inviting an ousted foreign dictator resented elsewhere to come stay in Belarus must have felt great for the mercurial Lukashenko. Maxim also told Gourevitch that Lukashenko was returning a favor. "There was some kind of a business deal between them in the past that Bakiyev had honored, and Lukashenko felt strongly about the events in Kyrgyzstan," Gourevitch said. Besides, he added, "Lukashenko understood that the Bakiyevs wouldn't just live there but would make investments there." Local media reported that Bakiyev purchased an opulent house for $2 million on the outskirts of Minsk, where he lived with a young Kyrgyz woman, his unofficial second wife.

Landing in Minsk, Gourevitch fell off the international law-enforcement grid and occasionally partied with the Bakiyevs. He attended the ousted president's birthday celebration held at a Minsk restaurant. Kurmanbek Bakiyev appeared "at peace with himself," Gourevitch recalled. "I didn't see any signs that he was eating away at himself." Gourevitch also ran into Janysh Bakiyev, the fugitive former security chief wanted for an array of charges in Kyrgyzstan. "They are really hiding him," Gourevitch said of Janysh. Recuperating in Belarus, Gourevitch was also busy laying the groundwork for his next business venture, which would earn Maxim a few million dollars.

The exiled financier used his Belorussian hideaway to negotiate safe passage to New York. Gourevitch didn't want to be a fugitive for the rest of his life. He wanted to deal with the Italian charges, perhaps enter a plea bargain, and even do time if absolutely necessary. It was the Kyrgyz prosecution that he wished to avoid. Eventually, Gourevitch told me, he and his lawyer succeeded in persuading the Italians to allow the disgraced financier to return to New York and resume negotiating the eventual terms of his Italian punishment. "It's difficult to plan ahead because I don't know if my plea bargain will involve a jail term," Gourevitch told me in February of 2012 over coffee a couple of blocks away from his apartment in the tony Central Park South neighborhood. By then, a Kyrgyz court had already sentenced him in absentia to fifteen years in a maximum-security prison for his role in the suspicious sale of a jet-fuel firm at the Manas International Airport. Kyrgyz prosecutors alleged that as a board member of the state-controlled airport authority Gourevitch signed off on the deal to sell the firm below market value to an "international criminal organization." Even though there were four other board members who all rubber-stamped the transaction, Gourevitch was the only one to be convicted. He told me it was a setup, and that he planned to appeal the conviction to the UN Commission on Human Rights.

"I love waking up to the smell of fresh 15 in the morning," Gourevitch wrote on Twitter after the Kyrgyz announced his fifteen-year sentence. For a while, his Twitter profile photo featured the logo of the U.S. Interstate-15 highway.

As he awaited the resolution of the Italian case, Gourevitch drifted through life without fixed employment. "I'm not going to be able to go out and get a job with my track record, but thankfully there are other things I can do. I'm trading a bit for pocket money," he told me. Occasional photos he posted on Twitter, showing palm trees and the ocean, suggested he wasn't starving. He retained an appetite for risk, tweeting once: "Gotta love stocks that move 20%. In a day. In each direction." In fact, there was quite a bit more to his investment strategy than keeping up with volatile stocks.

Gourevitch also engaged in online spats with his many Kyrgyz critics. In one exchange, Gourevitch, who doesn't meet the conventional criteria of male beauty or fitness, joked that he'd undergone plastic surgery and now looked like Brad Pitt.

I asked Gourevitch if he had any regrets about what he'd done in Kyrgyzstan, and the question made him think for a moment before answering. "The opportunities I saw there were beyond anything I'd imagined in my life," he finally said. "And I think I lost perspective in certain ways in certain things that I've done that I shouldn't have done." He paused to defend his track record, suggesting that when all the bad was subtracted from all the good, there would still be a "net positive" for Kyrgyzstan. "I was not the enabler of Max or the idea generator, that was not my role," Gourevitch said. "I'm not this Jewish mastermind person that I've been made out to be who came to Max and whispered in his ear and said, 'This is how you fuck this country.'"

At the time, I had no way of knowing that this man in a furry sweater sipping a cappuccino was spinning yet another conspiracy that was impressive even by the high standards one has come to expect of a Gourevitch venture. In early September of 2011, investigators at the Securities and Exchange Commission noticed that something strange was happening to the shares of Global Industries, Ltd., a small Louisiana company building offshore oilrigs and pipelines in the Gulf of Mexico. One day that month, someone working through a brokerage account at an Austrian bank scooped up $1.5 million worth of Global's shares, accounting for about one-tenth of Global's entire trading volume on the Nasdaq exchange that day. The same buyer came back for more the next morning, purchasing another $2 million of Global's stock, again about one-tenth of the daily volume.

The mystery buyer clearly knew something that the rest of the market did not, a piece of intelligence that was poised to lift Global's shares out of small-cap obscurity and make them much more valuable. The suspense lasted for three days until a French firm announced its acquisition of Global Industries at a steep premium to its share price. The mystery buyer promptly sold Global stock at a profit of $1.7 million. The trades carried the fingerprints of a classic insider-trading scheme, but the SEC sleuths couldn't identify the ultimate beneficiary. They did manage to freeze the proceeds of the final stock dump, rendering the profit illusory.[1]

In London, Maxim Bakiyev was furious, for it was his money. And it was Gourevitch placing the bets, based on insider tips purchased from a British broker with good connections but with apparent financial difficulties. It would be good to "get some dough because I'm pissing in the wind again," the broker, Tayyib Ali Munir, once told Gourevitch on the phone. The reason we know all this is that Gourevitch was secretly recording the conversation for the benefit of the FBI. Starting in late 2011, the besieged financier became a confidential FBI informant, helping the U.S. government build a criminal case against Maxim and the hapless broker.

How did the FBI get Gourevitch to become a snitch? To use a term of art, the feds appear to have gotten him by the balls. While Gourevitch was lying low in Belarus, decompressing after his escape from Kyrgyzstan and holding his first exploratory meetings with Munir, who traveled to meet him there, a U.S. judge issued a warrant for his arrest. That made Gourevitch a wanted man in three countries: in Italy on charges of money laundering; in Kyrgyzstan on charges of fraud and embezzlement; and now in the United States on charges of extortion. U.S. investigators alleged that sometime during his illustrious stint in Kyrgyzstan's world of high finance, Gourevitch had conducted an "extortion conspiracy." Its target wasn't specified in the court document I saw, but given U.S. law enforcement's interest in the matter, it probably involved a U.S.-linked company or an individual.[2] The charges appeared serious enough for Gourevitch to seek leniency by offering to give up Maxim Bakiyev. So when the indefatigable financier flew from Belarus to New York in late 2011, he laid bare to the FBI a brazen insider-trading scheme played out with Maxim's money.

Cooling his heels in London after the revolution that ended his family's grip on Kyrgyzstan, Maxim didn't waste any time in trying to multiply his fortune. Through a shell company registered in New Zealand,

Maxim set up an account at a Latvian bank stuffed with $45 million worth of securities. With Maxim's blessing, Gourevitch used the account for insider trading, using "edge" information furnished by Munir, the London broker. The shell-company camouflage on that account explains why the SEC couldn't identify the ultimate beneficiary of the trades in the Global stock. For his troubles, Munir often insisted on keeping 40 percent of whatever profits Gourevitch made with Maxim's money. Munir, in turn, gleaned his investing tips from a network of well-connected sources, including a former director on the New York Stock Exchange.

The tips weren't always solid. In 2011, Gourevitch and Maxim plowed $9 million into the shares of Intermune, Inc., a small U.S. biotechnology firm, following Munir's tip that it would soon be acquired by a large pharmaceutical company interested in its patents. As months dragged on and no merger took place, Gourevitch and Maxim found themselves sitting on a pile of shares rapidly losing value. Munir urged Gourevitch to convince Maxim to double down and buy yet more Intermune stock, after which Munir and his associates would generate favorable publicity about the company and drive up its share price. That would allow Gourevitch and Maxim to sell the stock and cut their losses. In industry lingo, the move is known as a pump-and-dump scheme. But there's no evidence Maxim was prepared to trust Munir's sources again and throw good money after bad.

By contrast, the tip-off about the forthcoming takeover of Global Industries proved accurate. But Gourevitch and Maxim botched a perfect insider trade by letting greed cloud their judgment and buying so many shares that the SEC took notice and froze the transactions. Munir pleaded with Gourevitch to convince Maxim to pay $122,000 to the sources of the Global tip-off. Those sources felt they had earned the money, and it wasn't their fault the SEC blocked the trade and deprived Maxim of his profits.

If Maxim paid up, Munir continued, those sources would give him a sneak peak at eight corporate earnings reports forty-eight hours ahead of their public release. Munir also told Gourevitch he could provide inside information about as-yet-unannounced initial public offerings. But it appears Maxim was growing exasperated with Munir and his sources.

The FBI affidavit notes that Maxim "refused to make any further payments as a result of, among other things, the unsuccessful Intermune investment and the SEC's freezing of the proceeds of the Global trade." Despite these setbacks, the FBI says Maxim "realized several million dollars in profit" from insider trades based on Munir's tip-offs.

Since Gourevitch was broadcasting the whole scheme in real time straight to the FBI, Munir was arrested and charged with insider trading. He pleaded guilty in October of 2012. Not much is publicly known about Munir. His lawyer told me he's "just a little guy," although he appears to have gold-plated social connections. The woman who posted his $1.2 million bond and identified herself in court papers as his girlfriend bears the same name as the London-based scion of one of Saudi Arabia's wealthiest families. "She has a little more notoriety than he does," the lawyer told me. Munir's girlfriend declined to speak with me.

That same October, Maxim was arrested in London on a U.S. warrant seeking his extradition to the United States on charges of conspiracy to commit securities fraud. His lawyer didn't respond to my request for comment.

Around the same time, Gourevitch flew to Rome to deal with the much older Italian money-laundering case. The multiple conspiracies he spent years constructing were finally crashing down on top of him. As of October 2012, he remained in Italian custody. When I reached him by e-mail to ask if we could talk again, he wrote back to say, "The timing is terrible."

While members and associates of the old regime scattered abroad, Kyrgyz authorities turned their attention to the unexplained, high-profile deaths during the Bakiyev era. At the top of that list was the death of Medet Sadyrkulov, the former presidential chief of staff, whose life provides a dramatic thread running through the country's modern history. A close ally and enabler of President Bakiyev, Sadyrkulov eventually turned on his boss, resigned, and started plotting his overthrow. Two months after his resignation, Sadyrkulov's thoroughly incinerated remains were found inside a Lexus SUV parked on the edge of a precipice outside Bishkek.

At the time, investigators quickly concluded that Sadyrkulov died in a freak traffic accident and swatted away any suggestions of foul play. The driver of another car confessed that he'd fallen asleep behind the wheel, lost control of his Audi and rammed into the Lexus, setting both vehicles on fire. A Bishkek court sentenced the young driver, Omurbek Osmonov, to twelve years in prison for manslaughter. After the verdict was read out, Leonid Luzhansky, the Sadyrkulov family lawyer, walked up to a dispassionate Osmonov, still sitting in his courtroom cage, and told him, "You realize you just signed your own death sentence? They will never let you live." To which Osmonov replied, "There's God's will for everything." Next, Luzhansky asked the prosecutors to protect Osmonov. "If something changes, he could be a very valuable witness," he said.

Something did change in April of 2010. At the time of the revolution, the gentle terms of Osmonov's sentence allowed him to live at home and work regular jobs while checking in with his parole officer. By some accounts, Osmonov wasn't hurting financially. Instead of the Audi burned in the crash, he was now driving a Mercedes. But he grumbled to his wife that he'd been shortchanged on the compensation agreed upon for staging the car crash. "They promised him money and an apartment. But they didn't keep their promises. My husband told me he was deceived and the money went to someone else," the wife later told investigators.[3] Barely a week after the revolution, Osmonov was murdered. His corpse was found among the gray apartment blocks on the edge of Bishkek. There were eleven stab wounds and signs of strangulation. Someone really wanted to make sure he was dead.

The interim government reopened the criminal investigation into Sadyrkulov's death. President Otunbayeva, an opposition member of Parliament at the time of his death, called it a murder right after it happened. And one of her closest advisors and eventually her chief of staff was Emil Kaptagayev, the beaten-up author of the crime novella about Sadyrkulov's final days.

The case made its way to the desk of Melis Turganbayev, the same man who had investigated the provenance of the severed body parts delivered to Sadyrkulov on New Year's Eve, an inquiry that cost the officer his job and nearly landed him in jail on rape charges. But now, having solved his legal problems, Turganbayev was back on the police force, and the Sadyrkulov matter caught up with him again. There was no escaping it. Turganbayev was eager to get back to work. Over the previous decade, he'd been whiplashed in the highly politicized ebb and flow of criminal inquiries that proceeded to a preordained result—or mysteriously faltered, depending on the latest tilt of political machinations in the White House. Turganbayev had lost his job twice when he proved too obstinate and pressed ahead with lines of questioning that were best dropped. He'd been framed for rape by his own colleagues. In 2003, a star witness of his was found hanged in his prison cell before he could testify about a murky attempt on the life of a government security chief. Now Osmonov, the Audi driver, was dead too. And it could have been predicted. Turganbayev liked Sadyrkulov, knew him reasonably well, and felt like he owed it to him to dig deep. To solve Sadyrkulov's murder, Turganbayev first needed to solve Osmonov's. "That's where the thread started," he told me.

Turganbayev plunged into the murder inquiry with a zeal and urgency intensified by a subliminal fear that things could change again, that he wouldn't be allowed to proceed. "I hope they have enough political will to clean up the country," Turganbayev said of the new government. We were sitting in his office, a wrestling trophy of two men joined in a grapple perched on a nearby bookshelf. The cop hoped that by exposing depravity at the very top of Kyrgyzstan's fickle governments, he could produce "maybe a lesson to those in power of how low we've fallen": fingers and ears in the mail, crooks everywhere. And what if no one cared to hear that lesson, and he got slapped and shown the door again? "I don't particularly care, I'm used to this." He sounded a bit self-righteous, an avenger of the country's sins. But I thought his outburst was heartfelt; years of bottled-up frustrations had finally found a productive outlet, and Turganbayev wanted to seize the moment.

Last time, before he got fired, Turganbayev had copied all materials related to Sadyrkulov onto a thumb drive, a long-standing habit in case evidence was later destroyed, and it often was. Right after the 2010 revolution, for instance, a raging fire consumed the prosecutor general's sprawling headquarters in downtown Bishkek, a repository of the nation's criminal files. No other government buildings were burned.

From extensive interviews, Turganbayev's team determined that most logistics preceding the murder of Sadyrkulov—including the murder itself—had been handled by people employed directly by the government: border guards, cops, and members of Janysh Bakiyev's State Protection Service, who conducted the actual killings. Folks from the criminal underworld, the so-called Dark World, were recruited to handle not the murder itself, but only the cleanup, which is where Osmonov came in. According to Turganbayev's year-long investigation, this is how it was done.

After Sadyrkulov's Lexus crossed into Kazakhstan, Kyrgyz border guards at the Korday checkpoint were told to watch for his return and report it up the chain of command. When the Lexus appeared at the border again, word went all the way up to the general in charge of Kyrgyzstan's Border Protection Service. The general placed a call directly to Janysh Bakiyev, and that's where the role of the border guards ended. In the time it took Sadyrkulov to clear border formalities and customs, the State Protection Service mobilized a team, which assembled just down the road from the border checkpoint. Dressed as traffic policemen, State Protection troopers flagged down the Lexus for what must have looked like a routine traffic stop. When Kubat, the driver, pulled over, he was moved to another car, and a State Protection operative took the wheel of the Lexus. Two more operatives crowded into the backseat on either side of Sadyrkulov and Sergei Slepchenko, a political scientist and a friend of the former chief of staff.

The motorcade then headed toward Bishkek, zoomed through the dark, empty streets of the capital, and continued on a highway toward the mountain resort area on the other side of town. After about thirty minutes, the cars turned off the main road and onto a potholed mud track winding through a village where old rickety cottages stood next to new country homes built by the well-off and the politically connected. Land in this resort area was expensive because of its proximity to Bishkek. After a few turns, the cars pulled up to a tall brick fence, behind which stood the imposing house of a former high-ranking government official. Sadyrkulov and his two traveling companions were led inside, down a tiled garden path and under a corrugated iron canopy.

Not far from this spot, Sadyrkulov had his own country place where he often spent summer weekends with visiting grandchildren, a happy place where he came to escape the high stress of the White House. That was perhaps the reason this location was chosen for the final conversation the former chief of staff was about to have. Afterward it would be easy to suggest, as the police in fact did, that Sadyrkulov was on his way to his country home when his car crashed. In fact, Turganbayev's investigators determined there had been a plan to kill Sadyrkulov a few days earlier, on the eve of the International Women's Day, a national holiday in Kyrgyzstan. But the organizers abandoned the idea because the resort area was too crowded around the holiday. Sadyrkulov's nighttime return from Kazakhstan a couple of days later presented a perfect opportunity to snatch him and try again.

Janysh Bakiyev arrived at the country house about ten minutes after Sadyrkulov was brought there. Surrounded by goons and security operatives, the two enemies had a talk.

"You don't understand normal language, bitch? What is it that you want? Ask for forgiveness!" Janysh yelled, according to witnesses who later testified to the police. It appears that Sadyrkulov didn't cower or apologize even as security operatives kept punching and kicking him. The former chief of staff had always been stubborn and proud. After a while, Janysh ordered his operatives to "finish it." Sadyrkulov asked him to spare the lives of Slepchenko and Kubat the driver. With that, two men grabbed Sadyrkulov's arms to hold him still. Another man garroted him with a piece of rope. Slepchenko and Kubat were strangled afterward. Janysh left the scene.

It was now the turn of Osmonov and his Dark World buddies to make it look like a traffic accident. The three corpses were placed in the Lexus, Kubat's in the front passenger seat, the other two in the back. A dark man—it's not clear if it was Osmonov or someone else—drove the Lexus to the edge of the mountain road, about five minutes from the murder scene. The car was thoroughly doused in gasoline and, investigators suspect, another highly flammable liquid, perhaps napalm. It was set on fire.

Now Osmonov had to take care of the final detail. He was supposed to ram the Lexus with his Audi and push it over the edge of the cliff. The burning Lexus would have rolled down a steep gravelly mountainside and hit the boulders in a shallow creek at the bottom. The corpses would have been tossed around inside the car, and it wouldn't have mattered that Kubat's body had been placed in the passenger seat. It would have been so much easier for investigators to call it a traffic accident with a straight face. But Osmonov failed in that final mission. He did hit the Lexus, but the Audi didn't have enough speed to push the heavy SUV off the road. The Lexus was a fireball by then, so Osmonov didn't have the time or the guts to try again. The state of panic in which the police found him later that morning may well have been genuine. It was a big screwup that nearly exposed the whole traffic-accident ruse. It took the best of logic-bending genuflections by the police and the state bureaucracy to maintain the cover-up.

At 3:00 a.m. one September morning, nearly a year into the probe, Turganbayev's organized-crime investigators swooped down on thirteen suspects, including State Security operatives and border guards, many of whom were still on active duty. They were roused from their beds and delivered bleary-eyed for questioning. Over the next few days, police rounded up more people, including the former chief of the national Border Guard Service, a decorated general who allegedly called Janysh Bakiyev with news of Sadyrkulov's arrival at the border crossing—and, perhaps unwittingly, sealed the former chief of staff's fate. Kyrgyzstan issued international arrest warrants for Janysh and for the two organized-crime bosses of interest to the investigation.

One of them we've already met: Kamchi Kolbayev, Central Asia's kingpin whose alleged involvement in the international heroin trade got him noticed in Washington. The other is Almanbet Anapiyaev, a squareheaded enforcer and Kolbayev's sidekick, who climbed Kyrgyzstan's criminal ladder the old-fashioned way, through martial arts. Alongside many other shady ventures, Anapiyaev owned a gym in Bishkek where strapping young men loyal to him honed their skills in a wrestling style called *Alysh,* a traditional Kyrgyz martial art similar to judo. Remember Manas, the Kyrgyz Superman? The Manas opus tells of two knights grappling in a bout of *Alysh,* giving the sport the ultimate Kyrgyz endorsement. Among modern-day knights wrestling in Anapiyaev's gym was none other than Omurbek Osmonov. Osmonov's widow later told investigators Osmonov had staged the car crash "together with some guys he trained with. Their leader was Almanbet Anapiyaev."[4] The man who confessed to killing Osmonov had also trained in Anapiyaev's gym.

Ensconced in the comforts of Dubai, Anapiyaev insisted that neither he nor his patron, the "respected thief" Kamchi Kolbayev, had anything to do with Sadyrkulov's murder. "It's just nonsense that someone as immensely powerful as Janysh Bakiyev, with a loyal staff of special-forces professionals, would require my services to eliminate Medet Sadyrkulov," Anapiyaev told a Kyrgyz interviewer. "Why would Janysh recruit regular athletes and increase the number of unnecessary witnesses?"[5] At the time, Anapiyaev focused on a long-cherished ambition: as president of the International Alysh Federation (yes, such a thing really exists), the enforcer organized big wrestling tournaments and lobbied for the Manas-endorsed martial art to become an Olympic sport.

Meanwhile, Janysh Bakiyev lived incognito in Minsk, Belarus, the final refuge of the Bakiyev clan. Belorussian authorities of course knew he was in the country, but Janysh kept a low profile for everyone else, perhaps because his hosts asked the deeply vilified figure to keep it that way to avoid international complications. The ploy worked until a Belorussian blogger spotted Janysh leaving a café in downtown Minsk, snapped a photo, and posted it online. The photo went viral in Kyrgyzstan, where authorities demanded his extradition. Belarus refused. Shortly afterward, the blogger was sitting in a café when a waiter approached him with a folded paper napkin, a message from a gentleman on the terrace. The blogger, whose first name is Mikhail, opened the napkin and read the following: "Mikhail, Mr. Bakiyev sends his regards." The blogger ran out to the terrace, but the gentleman was already gone.

According to Kyrgyz investigators, Janysh had played a central role in Sadyrkulov's murder. Many of the suspects detained in Turganbayev's dawn raids said they saw and heard him in the courtyard of the house where the former chief of staff was strangled. For such a high-profile assassination, it was a fairly crowded scene, allowing Turganbayev's sleuths to reconstruct the final hours of Sadyrkulov's life in granular detail. "To tell you the truth, I was very surprised, I didn't expect honest testimony," Turganbayev said. "It's as if the suspects were ready to either get killed or get interrogated. And so they started talking, who saw what, who stood where, the different roles . . . And all the testimony was consistent," Turganbayev told me. "You know Janysh was personally involved in carrying out all his sins. If we ever catch him, I don't think he will even deny this."

Inevitably, perhaps, Turganbayev's storyline faced some skepticism. It seemed to fit all too neatly into the narrative of the evil former regime, with Janysh cast as the devil incarnate. It didn't help that the general outline of Turganbayev's story, minus imagined scenes and overdramatized detail, matched to a surprising degree the roman à clef written by the prominent opposition activist Emil Kaptagayev two years earlier. Kaptagayev now held the same influential position long monopolized by Sadyrkulov: presidential chief of staff. Kaptagayev pointed out that he didn't pull that novella strictly out of his head, but relied on interviews, scuttlebutt, and educated guesses from people not entirely out of the loop. Still, the similarities between the novella and the results of Turganbayev's criminal investigation puzzled many, including Turganbayev himself, who told me he'd like to know more about Kaptagayev's sources and methods.

Turganbayev's career, nearly destroyed by accusations of assault and attempted rape, blossomed after the revolution, partly because of the high-profile Sadyrkulov case. The colonel who had been unemployed and facing jail time not that long ago now carried the rank of police general, wore an expensive golden wristwatch, occupied a spacious corner office, and served as deputy interior minister of Kyrgyzstan. Adjacent to his office was a small, overheated waiting room crowded with supplicants and underlings trying to see the important man. From inside his plush office, Turganbayev could observe the room's occupants via a small fish-eye camera mounted on the ceiling. Once untouchable, the Sadyrkulov case was now an undeniably savvy thing to pursue, and it rankled Turganbayev to no end that he was damned if he did and damned if he didn't. Years earlier, his pursuit of the case had cost him his job; now it invited speculation that he was merely carrying out a politically motivated script written elsewhere. Supporters of the detained Border Guard general took to the streets demanding his release from custody. Parliament dragged Turganbayev to hearings on the matter, where the newly minted general kept insisting that there was "no politics" in his investigation.

Still, as cold-blooded and dramatic as the plot to kill Sadyrkulov sounds, many in Kyrgyzstan found Turganbayev's version far more believable than the traffic-accident story. Even Vadim Nochevkin, the investigative reporter instinctively inclined to question everything, found no good reasons to mistrust him. "There are more reasons to believe than to disbelieve," he said.

More than two years after Sadyrkulov's death, you could still see faint black stains burned into the pebble-strewn ground on the spot where his crazy journey through modern Kyrgyz history came to an end. Down below in the gorge, a line of trees meandered along a creek, small houses peeking out through the treetops here and there. On a concrete parapet a few yards away, a teenager had spray-painted a love message: "I love you, Katyusha! Your Rashid." At the house where Sadyrkulov had been strangled, a dog frolicked in the sun-dappled front yard. The house itself seemed empty but well kept.

Sadyrkulov's daughter Aijan and I met for coffee one afternoon in Bishkek. A statuesque brunette, she looks like her father. The preliminary results of Turganbayev's investigation had just come out, and I asked her about them. She went silent for a moment. "I suspected all along that's pretty much how it happened," she finally said. I asked her if she felt any relief or closure. She paused again, this time for longer. The café was dimly lit, so I didn't notice her quiet tears right away. She spoke of her wedding, and of how her father seemed to hesitate in sadness before passing her hand to her fiancé. "It's as if he didn't want to let go of me," she said. "So no, there's no relief. It feels like old wounds in my soul got reopened again."

Aijan had particular scorn for Oksana Malevannaya, the influential former head of the presidential Secretariat. Although Sadyrkulov never divorced his wife (Aijan's mother), he conducted a long, public affair with Malevannaya, who bore him a son. Aijan told me her father never admitted paternity of the boy, and she was inclined to believe him. After Sadyrkulov died, Malevannaya told anyone who'd listen that it was impossible that he'd been murdered by the government. It was hard to tell whether she genuinely believed in what she was saying. "I wish she'd just die somewhere," Aijan told me.

Malevannaya didn't die. She remained head of the Secretariat right up until the April Revolution, when she was arrested and charged with abuse of office. Alongside several other former officials, Malevannaya faced an irate courtroom packed with relatives of those who had died storming the presidential palace. In an essay dripping with sarcasm and rage, Malevannaya described the scene. "One after another, the 'April heroes' approached the microphone and cursed us out, wishing death upon our relatives and children. They demanded that we be deprived of defense attorneys because 'murderers aren't entitled to lawyers.' They demanded that the sentence be announced immediately: 'either life imprisonment or a firing squad.' And if the judge procrastinated they pronounced themselves ready to 'pass our own sentence.'"[6] After a while, the spectators started throwing things at the cage in front of the courtroom where the defendants were sitting. Finally, the spectators worked up sufficient fury to charge at the cage. The defendants scampered out and ran across the interior courtyard toward a gate, which some of them tried to scale.

The trial resumed the next day. Malevannaya, who likes to wear her blonde hair in a stylish tomboy haircut, brought a long black wig in case she needed to run away and hide from the crowd again. Sometime in the next few weeks, as the trial ground on, Malevannaya did manage to run away from Kyrgyzstan. How exactly she pulled it off is unclear, but she surfaced in Almaty, a fugitive from Kyrgyz justice, or what passed for it in the aftermath of the revolution. In early 2012, she flew into Kiev, Ukraine, intending to apply for political asylum. She was traveling with a four-year-old boy, apparently Sadyrkulov's son. The Ukrainians turned her away at the airport, and she flew to Georgia to try her luck there.

Kyrgyzstan's leaders fumed at her asylum shopping and wanted her extradited. As of this writing, she remains in Tbilisi, her future uncertain.

Meanwhile, investigators in Kazakhstan were pulling at threads from another mysterious death of the Bakiyev era. In 2009, a prominent opposition journalist named Gennady Pavlyuk, his legs and arms bound with duct tape, fell out of a sixth-floor window in Almaty and died five days later. Pavlyuk had been lured to Almaty with promises of a $105,000 media grant e-mailed to him by a woman named Marina. Investigators determined that behind the urbane, civic-minded, and entirely fictional Marina stood a very different creature: a short, fat man with childlike hands and a face of exceptional ugliness. Topped by a buzz cut, it featured small, cold eyes, a pug nose with flared nostrils, and a hyphen of a mouth framed by enormous sagging jowls. The face belonged to Aldayar Ismankulov, a veteran operative employed by the National Security Service of Kyrgyzstan.

By the time he sat down in front of his computer to pose as the grant-giving Marina and entrap Pavlyuk, Ismankulov had already developed a reputation as a sort of a Kyrgyz Jason Bourne—albeit less fit—who was often tasked with dirty but necessary assignments. For a time he served as head of the Security Service's organized-crime branch, a position that put him in close contact with the country's most powerful mobsters, including the Robin Hood character whom we've already met. At one point, Bishkek police arrested Ismankulov with a handgun whose serial number had been sanded off, a red flag for weapons used in contract hits. He often traveled on a fraudulent passport identifying him as one Leonid Pak. Sometime in 2009, Ismankulov got an order to find out exactly what Pavlyuk was up to in his antigovernment campaign, and what sorts of documents that could embarrass the government he'd stashed away in his safe. Ismankulov was also told to get rid of Pavlyuk, according to the Kazakh inquiry.

Known as *kompromat* in Russian, such documents are a common feature of political and business disputes in the former Soviet Union. They can run the gamut from simple blackmail involving photos of, say, a rival politician cavorting with prostitutes to legitimate investigative journalism, such as documents detailing government corruption. It is unclear what kind of *kompromat* Pavlyuk had dug up, or whether he had any at all, but his kidnappers believed that he did have something, and tortured him to reveal the password to his safe. Then they tossed him out of the window to his death. According to Kazakh investigators, Ismankulov hired two men to handle the logistics, like booking a hotel room for Pavlyuk and renting the apartment where he was eventually taken.

When Pavlyuk checked into the hotel, one of those men met him in the lobby and introduced himself as Abay, an employee of the generous foundation that had invited Pavlyuk to Almaty for the final grant interview. Pavlyuk had already spoken to this "Abay" on the phone a few days earlier, when Abay called the skeptical journalist in Bishkek and asked him to suspend disbelief about the miraculous grant and come to Almaty, where all his questions would be answered. Only that time, the Abay character was being played by Ismankulov the spook.

Now, Ismankulov's associate drove Pavlyuk to what the journalist thought was the final grant interview. The associate received $1,000 for his troubles. Pavlyuk must have been nervous during the car ride to the nondescript apartment block. A lot of money was at stake, and he needed that money to get his cherished journalistic project off the ground. It is possible that Pavlyuk retained doubts about the unlikely premise for this interview, doubts that must have been reinforced as scenes of swanky downtown Almaty gave way to faceless Soviet-era apartment blocks, where the allegedly rich foundation was headquartered. If Pavlyuk had any doubts, they were not strong enough to prevent him from stepping into the elevator with "Abay" and taking it to the sixth floor. Inside the two-bedroom apartment, rented for this occasion, Ismankulov and two other goons were already waiting. An hour or so later, Pavlyuk was lying in a pool of blood under the apartment's window.[7]

The Kazakh investigators never determined—or at least never said publicly—who exactly ordered Ismankulov into action. But since he was a high-ranking, active-duty employee of the National Security Service at the time of the murder—an organization overseen at the time by the president's older son—few in Kyrgyzstan doubted whose bidding the shadowy Pak-man was doing.

A monument to murdered journalist Gennady Pavlyuk in downtown Bishkek.
(© Philip Shishkin)

When a Kazakh judge sentenced Ismankulov to seventeen years in prison for organizing the assassination, Pak-man's little mouth broke into a smirk. He denied the charges and said he was merely investigating the murder, not planning it. His two logistics associates were sentenced to ten years behind bars. Later, in prison, one of them asserted his innocence in a bizarre videotaped protest: looking into a toy mirror, he picked up a large needle and sewed his lips shut, blood trickling down his chin. The two goons who actually threw Pavlyuk out of the window were never caught.

On a leafy sidewalk in downtown Bishkek, a new statue appeared recently. It is Pavlyuk, shown midstride, his ubiquitous bag flung over his right shoulder, a voice recorder in his left hand. "To those who sowed freedom with their words," the inscription reads.

Meanwhile, on the other side of the globe, a young American lawyer named Scott Lindsay walked into one of the most intriguing investigations of the post-Bakiyev era: the lucrative contracts to deliver fuel to the U.S. military base in Kyrgyzstan. It all began with a leisurely game of doubles tennis.

A baby-faced Seattle native, Lindsay had spent the previous couple of years at a private law firm, where he worked on untangling a Ponzi scheme. A hedge fund called Bayou Group had swindled clients out of nearly half a billion dollars, and Lindsay was helping investors claw some of that money back. After being sentenced to twenty years in prison, Bayou's founder staged his own suicide ("Suicide is painless," he wrote on the windshield of his car) and went into hiding. A month later, bearded and bedraggled, he rode a scooter to a police precinct and gave himself up.

By the time Lindsay arrived for his regular tennis game, he was ready to try something different in his career. A tennis partner mentioned offhand an interesting job opening. The congressional Subcommittee for National Security and Foreign Affairs was looking for a new senior counsel. It sounded like a perfect job. Before his Ponzi-scheme days, Lindsay had worked at the Center for Strategic and International Studies, and he retained an interest in national-security matters. Lindsay applied for the counsel job, got it, and settled into his new gig just in time for the 2010 revolution in Kyrgyzstan.

The ripples from the uprising reached Washington in no time. The interim leaders, from Roza Otunbayeva on down, accused the United States of kowtowing to the Bakiyev regime in order to keep the Manas military base alive. Moreover, the new government alleged, Washington structured its multibillion-dollar contracts to supply jet fuel to the thirsty base in such a way as to funnel money into the pockets of the Bakiyev family, and of the Akayev family before that. It was an explosive allegation, one that had coursed through Kyrgyz politics for years and provided ample grist to those who campaigned against corruption. The allegation reverberated beyond Kyrgyzstan and pointed to a perennial problem for Washington: how should it deal with dictatorial regimes in countries where the United States has broader strategic needs that require help from those dictators? In April of 2010, just days after the revolution, the congressional subcommittee launched an inquiry into the Kyrgyz fuel deals. For Scott Lindsay, the senior counsel who cut his teeth investigating white-collar crime, the inquiry would consume nearly a year of his life and involve stonewalling, intimidation, and travel to Bishkek, Dubai, and London.

The inquiry began with a question that should have been very easy to answer: who owned two obscure-sounding, interlinked firms that over nearly a decade received billions of dollars' worth of U.S. government contracts to deliver jet fuel to the Manas base? When Lindsay asked around, no one seemed to know, or even care. "Our information is sketchy," one Pentagon official wrote to another after the firm won yet another lucrative fuel contract from the U.S. government. Without that fuel, the war in Afghanistan, one of the biggest U.S. foreign entanglements in history, would grind to a halt, and yet neither the Pentagon nor the State Department knew much about the two firms beyond their names: Mina and Red Star. Or, if they knew, they weren't telling Lindsay, which only piqued his curiosity. Clouding it all were persistent whispers that Mina and Red Star were a covert operation run by the Central Intelligence Agency.

Historically speaking, that is not as farfetched as it sounds. In the early 1950s, the agency secretly bought a civilian cargo airline in Asia, gave it a cheerful name, Air America, and used it for nearly two decades to support U.S. covert operations in Vietnam, Laos, and Cambodia. Air America's ownership was hidden behind a facade of straw buyers and holding companies, and its motto was "Anything, Anytime, Anywhere, Professionally." Was it possible that, given the importance of the Afghan war, the CIA had set up a modern-day Air America to keep the sensitive fuel supplies running smoothly in a treacherous landscape of dictators, warlords, and greedy officials? Red Star and Mina operated out of a suite in Bishkek's swanky Hyatt Hotel; they had no websites; they used a Gibraltar mailbox as their corporate address; and "their beneficial ownership is buried deep under layers of shell companies formed in countries whose corporate laws are designed to facilitate secrecy and tax avoidance," Lindsay eventually wrote in his sixty-eight-page report called *Mystery at Manas*.[8] The young lawyer was excited to pursue such an intriguing lead. "I thought, 'Holy shit! The CIA takes money from the Department of Defense'" to run the fuel. "If congressional investigators could win Pulitzer prizes," Lindsay thought, this might be a good candidate.

The investigation got off to a difficult start, giving Lindsay a taste of things to come. An outside counsel for Red Star showed up one day at Lindsay's office to browbeat the young lawyer into dropping the inquiry. The outside counsel wasn't just another gray corporate lawyer, who are a dime a dozen in Washington. The man had served as a deputy White House counsel in the George W. Bush administration, and he had a gold-plated résumé.

"We are not going to cooperate," the big-name lawyer told Lindsay. "And if we are forced to cooperate, we would shut down our operations." In effect, the lawyer was telling Lindsay that Red Star would walk away from a $1 billion contract should the uppity congressional staffer persist with his pesky questioning. Since the fuel-supply infrastructure created by Red Star was so complex and sensitive that replacing it would take time, the implication of that threat was clear: did Lindsay want to be responsible for pulling the plug on the Afghan war just as the Obama administration was doubling down? At this point, it should be noted, all Lindsay wanted to know was who owned the company. Lindsay heard the former Bush lawyer out, called the Pentagon to inform the defense planners of the threat, and proceeded with his inquiry anyway. Red Star, it turned out, was half owned by a Californian man whose previous claim to fame was the ownership of a popular Bishkek bar.

The American, named Douglas Edelman, moved to Bishkek in the mid-1990s, in the first wave of Western expats seeking excitement and riches in a region just opening up to the world after decades under Soviet rule. Edelman dabbled in the trading of commodities, including tobacco, cotton, and fuel. In 1998, he founded the American Pub, a watering hole beckoning expats with chicken wings, fries, and a whiff of Americana. On any given night, the place had guys sitting sentry on bar stools, nursing beers and watching distant ball games courtesy of the Armed Forces Network.

The arrival of the American military base flooded Bishkek with foreigners. Though in most cases the soldiers couldn't venture beyond the wire around the base, the lockdown didn't apply to the many civilian contractors who followed the Pentagon to Kyrgyzstan. Many foreign diplomats, businessmen, students, and drifters also took full advantage of the Wild East flavor of the Kyrgyz capital. These Westerners now roamed Bishkek's budding nightlife scene with mercenary instincts. The American Pub along with a handful of other watering holes became their default stopovers. In a place like Fire and Ice, an average-looking guy of the unkempt type you'd see in the States sneaking a smoke outside a 7–11 would be surrounded by pretty local girls. Maybe they were drawn to the novelty of it, or to the money, or to some imperceptible foreign mystique projected by the cargo-panted individual with a big mixed drink in hand. When one of these men returned from a vacation in the United States, a friend teased him: "So how did it feel to be fat and ugly again?" In the foothills outside Bishkek, a chain-smoking Canadian crane operator working for the Kumtor gold mine raked a barren field of rocks, planted imported grass, and started a popular golf course.

Out of that lively milieu of international contractors, fortune seekers, and party boys rose Edelman. His commercial aspirations were far bigger than selling fellow Americans booze and chicken wings or giving them a manicured lawn to putt around on Sundays. He wanted to sell them jet fuel. Around the same time, Edelman crossed paths with Erkin Bekbolotov, a young Kyrgyz entrepreneur who had spent a year at Pace University in New York and who now worked in petroleum trading. The two began working together, selling fuel for civilian use at the Manas airport.

When the Pentagon set up the military base in Kyrgyzstan, Red Star, jointly owned by the two men, bid on the lucrative fuel-supply contracts. But Edelman and Bekbolotov had no experience in this line of work, so they needed someone who could talk to the U.S. military in a language the military would understand. A chance encounter at the American Pub provided just such a man. Lieutenant Colonel Chuck Squires, a twenty-seven-year-veteran of the U.S. Army, was nearing retirement. A fluent Russian speaker and a self-described "cold warrior," Squires started his army career as an enlisted man and ended it as the defense attaché at the U.S. embassy in Bishkek, a post that gave him a unique inside view into the needs and relationships of the U.S. military across Central Asia. Having met Squires at the American Pub, Edelman later called him out of the blue and offered him a job with Red Star. This trio—Edelman, Bekbolotov, and Squires—would corner the fuel-supply market for the Manas base for nearly a decade. In Afghanistan, they would build a pipeline feeding straight into the major American base at Bagram, giving themselves a natural monopoly on the provision of fuel there too. Squires's intelligence connections—all American defense attachés report to the Pentagon's Defense Intelligence Agency—only reinforced perceptions that Red Star was a front for American spies.

For Scott Lindsay, the congressional investigator, getting any information out of Red Star was like pulling teeth. A breakthrough seemed within reach in late spring of 2010, when after weeks of endless back-and-forth, Red Star principals and their many lawyers and consultants finally agreed to meet the congressional staffer in Dubai. Lindsay flew to the glittering Arab metropolis on the taxpayers' dime. The night before the meeting, he went to grab dinner at an Argentinian place. His phone rang. It was a Red Star lawyer. The meeting was off. Lindsay was beside himself with frustration and anger. Why go through this charade only to cancel at the last minute? The lawyer informed Lindsay that Red Star owners would invoke their Fifth Amendment right against self-incrimination if forced to testify. Empty-handed, Lindsay flew back to Washington. Next, Congress issued subpoenas to force Red Star owners to produce documents and to testify. Red Star lawyers continued to play hardball; they refused to accept service of the subpoenas. Eventually Lindsay negotiated a deal: Squires, the former defense attaché, and Bekbolotov, the Kyrgyz entrepreneur, would speak with congressional investigators on one condition: Congress would have to leave Edelman alone. What was the elusive Californian so afraid of? It was a strange condition, but by then Lindsay was used to the inexplicable secrecy surrounding Red Star.

From interviews and documents that Lindsay was eventually able to obtain, the following picture emerged. Under Akayev, Red Star subcontracted with two firms that held a monopoly on all fuel deliveries to the Manas airport. One firm was owned by the president's son, the other by his son-in-law. Red Star and its paymasters at the Pentagon did funnel business to the Akayev family, but Red Star owners argued they couldn't avoid the arrangement because no fuel would reach the American base otherwise. The Akayev family firms were the gatekeepers. After the Tulip Revolution, the new government pounced on the issue of fuel corruption and swiftly nationalized the Akayev family companies. Kyrgyz prosecutors launched an investigation, and Zamyra Sydykova, the new Kyrgyz ambassador in Washington, raised the issue with U.S. officials.

The FBI eventually produced a classified eight-page report that tied the Akayev-linked airport firms to "transactions with arms traffickers, politically exposed persons, and a myriad of suspicious U.S. shell companies." But the new Bakiyev government in Kyrgyzstan appeared to be losing interest in the matter. "I was made to understand that I shouldn't stick my nose in it anymore," Sydykova told me. "It was a corrupt scheme that was reoriented toward a different group of people." With Akayev firms out of the picture, Red Star had to deal with another set of shadowy subcontractors at the airport, some with links to the new government. Red Star claimed it was eventually able to circumvent their stranglehold on the airport by using a new fuel-offloading depot that was built after a U.S. serviceman shot and killed a Russian truck driver delivering fuel to the base. Base commanders built it to divert truck traffic from security checkpoints and avoid future mishaps. But for Red Star, the new depot presented a chance to get around the government middlemen, the company told congressional investigators. Around that time, Red Star changed its name to Mina, in part to distance itself from the bad publicity of the Akayev era. The extreme secrecy, the company said, was necessary to protect the company from all sorts of sharks circling its business.

There's no question that Mina enjoyed preferential treatment at the hands of the government. When the Pentagon opened the military-fuel contract for a new round of bidding in 2007, the state-owned Manas airport authority sent the Pentagon a confidential letter. The letter advised the Pentagon that the successful bidder would need to meet a detailed list of conditions set out by the airport authority. Without stating so explicitly, these conditions favored Mina so heavily that it seemed impossible for any other firm to win the bid. In fact, the airport authority told the Pentagon the successful bidder would need to obtain a preapproval letter from the airport first. Out of the three companies that applied for the Pentagon contract, only Mina was able to secure this magic letter—and went on to win the contract, according to Lindsay's investigation. All of this raised the question of whether Mina bribed government officials or cut a deal with Maxim Bakiyev to get that kind of treatment.

Mina officials, through highly paid lawyers and PR consultants, denied any bribery or under-the-table deals with Maxim or anyone else. Lindsay too could find no evidence to support the most explosive allegation, that Mina was in bed with Maxim, just like plenty of other businesses operating in Kyrgyzstan. In his final report, Lindsay added a caveat that he "did not conduct a financial audit or interview all relevant witnesses and the investigation identified some circumstances of concern." For one thing, much of the evidence exonerating Mina came from interviews with Mina principals and from documents supplied by Mina itself, more than 250,000 pages in total.

To Mina's many accusers in Kyrgyzstan, the congressional exoneration meant only one thing: that the corruption was so well hidden and devious as to be beyond the reach of Washington investigators. "Don't come looking for concrete evidence of corruption," Edil Baisalov wrote to me one day when I told him I was planning a reporting trip to Kyrgyzstan to look into the fuel story. As chief of staff to President Otunbayeva, Baisalov was among the loudest critics of Mina. "What do you guys want: some videotape where Maxim is seen taking cash from Mina? There is no such thing." Mina itself cast such complaints as an attempt by jealous rivals to muscle it out of the lucrative business. When we met for a coffee shortly before he left his congressional job and moved back to Seattle, Lindsay described his investigation as "fascinating and dramatic in a lot of ways." He acknowledged that "a lot of people were disappointed that we didn't find what we thought we might find."

Lindsay did find one intriguing morsel linking Maxim Bakiyev to Mina. In 2009, President Bakiyev announced his plan to close down the Manas military base. For Mina, this would mean a sudden end to the fuel business. Erkin Bekbolotov, Mina's cofounder and half owner, called Maxim to sound him out on how the base might be saved. Bekbolotov said Maxim was "a social acquaintance" whom he had first met when both were teenagers. On the phone, the two discussed the idea of downgrading the status of the base to a transit center, a largely semantic exercise that, combined with a higher rent, might get the Bakiyev regime to reconsider the eviction threat. Next, Bekbolotov called a Pentagon contracting official and "outlined the agreement he had brokered with Maxim Bakiyev," Lindsay wrote. The Pentagon official had the impression that during the call Bekbolotov "sounded as if he had someone with him who was instructing him on what to say," Lindsay wrote. The official "assumed Bekbolotov was with a member of the Bakiyev family." After lengthy negotiations, President Bakiyev allowed the base to stay in exchange for higher rent. It was officially renamed Manas Transit Center, demilitarizing the title but keeping its essence intact. "While Mina had a huge financial incentive to save the base, it is unknown what motivated Maxim Bakiyev to intervene," Lindsay concluded.

His inquiry also exposed another interesting facet of the fuel trade: Mina's murky dealings with suppliers in Russia. The Manas base is such a voracious consumer of fuel that the only way to meet that demand is to import aviation fuel from Russia, the land of hydrocarbon riches. The irony here is that while Moscow took a well-publicized stand against American military presence in Central Asia, Russia's state-controlled energy giant Gazprom quietly benefited from that presence by peddling fuel to American warplanes. And it was Mina that made those deals possible. There was a small inconvenience to overcome first: Russian export-control regulations restricted the sale of fuel for foreign military purposes.

Mina got around that problem by enlisting high-ranking Kyrgyz officials to issue false certifications to the Russians saying their fuel was intended for civilian use in Kyrgyzstan. When Russian scrutiny of the matter heated up in 2009, Kyrgyzstan's prime minister fired off a letter to Gazprom's chairman thanking him for the continual provision of fuel for the "needs of domestic Kyrgyz aviation." In forwarding the letter to the Pentagon, Bekbolotov noted that "never in the past did we need to involve top official government channels for the support for the flow of fuel. It used to always be handled via private channels only." Chuck Squires, Mina's operational chief, couldn't resist a dig at the Russians when he spoke to Lindsay: "We've got one over on 'em. I am an old cold warrior, I'm proud of it—we beat the Russians, and we did it for four or five years."

It was, of course, a wink-wink exercise. The Russians weren't dumb; they knew exactly where the fuel was headed. The American warplanes at Manas ate up more jet fuel in a single month than the entire Kyrgyz fleet did in a year. The false certifications appeared to provide a bureaucratic cover to keep the fuel flowing. "If they looked at the volumes, they had to know where this was all going," Squires told Lindsay. "But they were making money and they were all happy." The arrangement gave the Russians a powerful strategic weapon: if relations with Washington or Bishkek deteriorated, Moscow could pretend to uncover the ruse, get angry at being "duped," and cut off the flow—or hike prices.

In fact, in the waning days of the Bakiyev regime when Moscow had already grown exasperated with the Kyrgyz president, Russian officials slapped a tariff on all fuel sales to Kyrgyzstan, causing a spike in gasoline prices. That spike, combined with an unrelated wave of price increases for utilities, contributed to the popular anger at the Bakiyev regime in the days before the revolution. The new Russian fuel tariffs were triggered in part by Moscow's "discovery of Kyrgyzstan's re-direction of commercial fuel exports for use by the U.S. military," Lindsay wrote.

After the revolution, Mina joined the rogues' gallery of the associates of the ousted regime and faced unadulterated hatred from senior members of the interim government. President Otunbayeva asked the Obama administration to cut Mina out of the fuel supplies altogether and give the contract to a Kyrgyz state-owned entity instead. Already on thin ice with the new Kyrgyz leadership, American officials agreed, though Mina wasn't entirely out of the picture. The secretive firm retained half of the contract, while the new Kyrgyz company, a joint venture with Russia's Gazprom, got the other half. I once asked Otunbayeva what she thought of Mina's steadfast denials of corruption. "One has to be a complete fool [to believe them]; they keep telling us that they are all white and fuzzy and innocent. They have people everywhere who protect them. They win [fuel contracts] all the time, under any circumstances," Otunbayeva told me and then returned to the issue of Russian surcharges. "Why would Russia all of a sudden raise our fuel tariffs?"

On the ground in Bishkek, Mina launched a campaign to defend itself against the barrage of accusations. "This is a politically and financially motivated attack against the company, multipronged, very coordinated, and never-ending, as far as I can tell," said Dean Peroff, a partner at Amsterdam & Peroff, a legal boutique best known for its involvement in the defense of Mikhail Khodorkovsky, a Russian oil tycoon who crossed President Putin and ended up in jail, his business nationalized. Now, Peroff was sitting in a stuffy conference room of Bishkek's Hyatt Hotel trying to explain how Mina was being "victimized" by the new Kyrgyz leaders, with an eye on muscling it out of the business. It was, Peroff insisted, a massive corporate raid, aided by a disinformation campaign. As hard as it was for Mina to rebrand itself as a victim of corruption, not its perpetrator, Peroff wasn't entirely full of it. For years, one of Mina's biggest rivals was a young and tough local oil trader who eventually became prime minister in the new Kyrgyz government. Peroff and other Mina lobbyists were trying hard to be heard through the din of accusations and portray Mina as a "whipping boy" and a "scapegoat." They failed. In early 2012, Mina lost the Manas business in its entirety. The new Kyrgyz-Russian joint venture took over the Pentagon contract. But Mina's twin sister Red Star still delivers fuel to Bagram in Afghanistan.

And what of Mina's rumored CIA connections? Company owners didn't bother to deny the story too much because it provided a convenient shield against encroachment by greedy officials and business rivals. "Everyone thinks I'm CIA; this image has been very helpful," Erkin Bekbolotov once told an interviewer.[9] But now, he said, it was time to "dispel the myth." Congressman John Tierney, who headed the foreign-affairs subcommittee during the Lindsay investigation, once buttonholed Leon Panetta, the CIA director at the time, and asked him point-blank whether Mina was an agency project. "No, it's not one of ours," Panetta replied, according to Lindsay. With the Manas business taken away from them, Mina's power trio could now relax a bit. Squires was retiring from the company. Bekbolotov, a keen practitioner of yoga, was setting up his own meditation center in India. And Edelman, the man who founded the American Pub followed by the multibillion-dollar fuel business, and then vanished from public view? Well, few people really knew what he was up to.

CHAPTER 7   *Restless Valley*

*T*he policeman should have listened to his wife that evening. Instead, Maktybek Suleimanov brushed off her pleas that he stay home and sit out the commotion on the streets. Suleimanov wanted to be a cop ever since he was a kid growing up in a turbulent corner of Central Asia. He'd ask his mother to pin strips of fabric to his T-shirt so they'd resemble rank insignia. Sometimes he'd go so sleep that way. Now Suleimanov was forty-one years old, had four kids of his own, and wore real epaulets of a police captain. A broad-faced ethnic Kyrgyz with a buzz cut and a thin mustache, Suleimanov was a gregarious man who liked to sing at family gatherings. He was good at it, at least to his wife's ears. He'd been a cop for twenty years.

Now, as Bazar-Korgon, his hometown in southern Kyrgyzstan, stared at civil war between the region's two main ethnic groups, Suleimanov wasn't going to hide at home. "I told him whenever something happens, it's always the police who get caught in the middle," recalled his wife, Chinara Bechelova. "I said, 'Don't go; they'll sort it out without you.'" Suleimanov smiled at this reasoning, shook his head, and had dinner with his family. Then he changed into a fresh set of clothes and headed back to the precinct. Because of the tension on the streets, the cops were pulling all-night duty.

Bechelova had trouble falling asleep that night, and was relieved to get a phone call from her husband. "Please watch the kids," he said amid scratchy cell-phone reception. Before clicking off, he added, "Everything's going to be okay, just go to sleep." Around 8:00 a.m. on June 13, 2010, after a couple of hours of fitful rest, she speed-dialed his cell phone, but it rang and rang without an answer. His charred corpse, with multiple stab wounds, was later found in the weeds by the side of a highway.

In death, Suleimanov became a national hero. But his murder remains a riddle. The most surprising thing about it is the identity of the alleged mastermind, arrested within days of the crime. He's a modest Uzbek artist and grandfather named Azimjan Askarov, well known here for his human-rights work. Could a man with a track record of helping victims of violence have instigated the savage execution of the policeman?

Two months after the fall of the Bakiyev regime, the south of Kyrgyzstan erupted in vicious ethnic fighting between the Kyrgyz and the Uzbeks who constitute a sizable ethnic minority here. The interim government in Bishkek was too weak and incompetent to prevent the outbreak of violence here, and by the time the government realized how bad things had become, it was already too late.

Bazar-Korgon, the hometown of Captain Suleimanov, sits at a jagged meeting point of peoples and histories. The name translates as "fortified market" and refers to its long history as a trading outpost. For centuries, a network of merchant routes now known collectively as the Silk Road traversed these lands. Some things haven't changed much since the days of the caravan. On a recent drive nearby, I saw villagers riding horses and donkeys down a snowy hill and across a frozen stream to watch teams of horsemen toss around a goat carcass, a timeless Central Asian sport.

The Kyrgyz, nomads and mountain dwellers, wandered over here thousands of years ago from the banks of a Siberian river. Just as not all Texans are cowboys, not all modern-day Kyrgyz are nomads, but many of them still raise cattle in mountain villages. Then there are the Uzbeks, descendants of warring Turkic tribes. The Uzbeks tend to live in towns, working as shopkeepers, craftsmen, or laborers. For centuries, the Kyrgyz and the Uzbeks lived side by side in the crowded Ferghana Valley along-side other ethnicities. It was not always an amicable coexistence.

For a historical perspective on the tensions between the two ethnic groups, it's worth turning to Vladimir Nalivkin, a nineteenth-century Russian orientalist with an interesting biography. A decorated officer during the Russian conquest of Central Asia, Nalivkin resigned from the army in protest over harsh treatment of the local population. He served for a time as a senior civilian administrator of the colonies. Nalivkin even-tually went native and settled here with his wife. In one contemporaneous photo, he's shown wearing an ample cleft beard whose two wispy prongs resemble an inverted victory sign.

Nalivkin learned the local languages and became an astute chronicler of Central Asia, often writing in biting, politically incorrect prose that ex-posed the worst tendencies both among the Russian colonial officials and among the local ethnic groups. His magnum opus is called *The Natives Then and Now,* published in 1913.[1] By the time the Communists came to power in Russia, Nalivkin had already retired from government service, but he remained in Tashkent, where his wife soon passed away. In 1918, when he was sixty-six, Nalivkin committed suicide not far from his wife's grave in the Russian cemetery in Tashkent. He's buried there alongside her.

The Natives Then and Now dissects the difficult dynamic between the Kyrgyz and the Uzbeks, whom Nalivkin refers to as Sarts. This was a catchall term to describe the region's settled populations, such as mer-chants, farmers, and professional classes. These Sarts, many of them Uzbeks, were distinct from Central Asia's nomads, most of whom were Kyrgyz. In modern-day parlance, the word *Sart* acquired a deeply nega-tive meaning, as we'll soon see.

One senses that Nalivkin's sympathies lay with the better-educated, wealthier Sarts, and they certainly proved to be more amenable to Rus-sian colonial influence than the nomadic Kyrgyz. Here's what Nalivkin writes about the two ethnic groups. It's an unsparing portrait, but once you scrub away the inevitable colonial condescension of the day, you have a reasonable explanation for the origins of present-day conflict be-tween the two peoples:

The Sart tilled the land, sowed, gathered, milled, planted trees, built houses, forged steel, sharpened knives, stitched, made leather and traded, giving his wife only a minimal set of household chores.

The Kyrgyz, by contrast, assigned to his wife and children the entire burden of his livestock operations, including the saddling and the unsaddling of his horse. Having done that, he ate, drank, sunned himself, sang or listened to songs, particularly songs about folk heroes, visited friends, and from time to time attended to the affairs of his clan. He participated in dispute settlements and vendettas, occasionally raided Sarts, or stole horses from rivals.

During the Kyrgyz raids, the Sart (unless he belonged to a warrior estate) usually hid in the orchards. He viewed the Kyrgyz as godless, desperate goons, whom he had no hope of defeating because the Kyrgyz managed to beat even the khan's own troops despite the fact that the latter had cannons.

But every time the Kyrgyz had to make a peaceful trip to a town bazaar or to a Sart village, he felt lost because he was targeted by absolutely everyone. Sart dogs barked at his furry hat; Sart kids ran after him chanting insulting couplets; and Sart merchants cheated him mercilessly, often laughing at his childlike, confused appearance, his uncouth manners, and his crude, jarring accent.

For all of this, the Kyrgyz sincerely resented the Sart, considering him a coward, a swindler, and a cheat whom you could never trust, but whom you couldn't entirely avoid because you turned to him every time you needed something that couldn't be manufactured by your village women.

In the big Soviet melting pot, these distinctions became blurred, and a relative calm in interethnic relations held sway for decades. Though the Soviets inflicted their fair share of atrocities on the region's populations, they also improved living standards and education. Daniil Kislov, a Russian journalist who grew up near here, has written of his childhood street: "There weren't even two houses next to each other where the nationality of the occupants would be repeated." Kislov's great-grandfather was an imperial engineer sent here to build a railway connecting Central Asia with Russia. Kislov eventually moved to Moscow, where he founded fergananews.com, a kind of *New York Times* of Central Asia. The website's irreverent reporting from the region would eventually earn it a ban in Uzbekistan and Kyrgyzstan.

The region's ethnic tapestry is so rich that just when you think you've encountered all possible ethnic groups and subgroups here, you find someone else. In Jalalabad one evening, my friend Ilya took me to a local nightclub called Erbol, which translates loosely as "Be a man." Ilya is an ethnic Ukrainian but he was born and raised in Jalalabad. Inside the dark, cavernous Erbol, I walked over to the bar, whose centerpiece was a three-foot-tall bottle of vodka called Man's Honor (which in Russian is a euphemism for a man's private parts). I grabbed a couple of beers, and just then the DJ dedicated a song "to our Shanghai brothers." It was a bouncy pop tune with the main refrain "Party like a rock star." The Shanghai brothers, armed with beers, gyrated in the middle of the dance floor, singing along. Shanghai brothers? Turns out they were ethnic Kurds, from a Jalalabad neighborhood called Shanghai.

Soviet dictator Joseph Stalin, who inherited Central Asia from the czarist empire, drew borders that sliced up ethnic groups and made it harder for them to mount any coherent challenge to Soviet rule. If you look at a map of the Ferghana Valley where Bazar-Korgon is located, the feverish lines dividing states zigzag wildly, resembling a cardiogram of a rapidly racing heart.

After the collapse of the Soviet Union, the Kyrgyz and the Uzbeks established their own states infused with a sense of long-suppressed national pride common among new countries. Ethnic clashes over land took place during the messy dissolution of the Soviet Union, foreshadowing the trouble to come.

In the borderlands of the Ferghana Valley, the two ethnic groups could never hope to disentangle themselves from each other, even if they tried. Ties of geography, family, and economy were too strong. And so Bazar-Korgon, a majority-Uzbek town ten miles from the Uzbekistan border, found itself within Kyrgyzstan proper. The police and the local government in Bazar-Korgon are predominantly Kyrgyz, in keeping with the country's long-standing practice of filling government jobs with members of the titular nation. A few dozen Kyrgyz cops watched over a mostly Uzbek town, and that division began to matter a lot when the clashes began.

In the complex political tableau of postrevolution Kyrgyzstan in 2010, Uzbek leaders saw a chance to right a wrong. Despite constituting about 15 percent of the national population (and nearly half in some parts of the south), the Uzbeks felt they lacked political representation and official recognition of their language. Their push for more rights coincided with the rise of Kyrgyz nationalism, the two trends feeding off each other. None of this should have led to slaughter, but these tensions had simmered, unattended, for years. The power vacuum after the 2010 revolution brought forth the provocateurs, opportunists, and criminals looking to stir things up. Within a few hot, smoke-choked, frantic days of June, at least 426 people were killed, according to the official tally. By December, 381 bodies had been identified, and of those 72 percent were Uzbek. Ever since—in keeping with the universal dynamic of civil wars—Kyrgyzstan has been consumed with figuring out who is the true victim of the war and who is the culprit, as if such neat divisions are ever possible.

Bazar-Korgon cops work out of a gray, two-story building, the entrance to which is guarded by a silvery statue of Felix Dzerzhinsky, the founder of the Soviet secret police and Lenin's most brutal henchman. Most of his statues have been torn down across the former Soviet Union. But here the old Iron Felix, with his signature goatee and a trench coat, still stands untouched and sparkly, clenching his fist. Most days, Bazar-Korgon police handle the usual fare of small-town cops: thefts, drunken brawls, traffic tickets.

By the time Suleimanov got to the precinct on the evening of June 12, the south of Kyrgyzstan was already in flames. In the big southern towns of Osh and Jalalabad, the Kyrgyz and the Uzbeks were waging block-by-block warfare. How much longer would it be before Bazar-Korgon was swept up in the civil war? Strange cars with strange men inside were screeching around town, and there were reports of residents quietly arming themselves with guns, makeshift swords, and wooden clubs.

The Uzbeks were afraid the town would be overrun by Kyrgyz militants streaming in on the major highway connecting the Kyrgyz-dominated north with the Uzbek-heavy south of the country. The highway runs along the edge of Bazar-Korgon, where it crosses a bridge over a muddy river. In the Uzbek parts of town, residents built barricades, using carts, trailers, and whatever else they could find. Many Uzbeks decided not to wait for the worst and headed to the nearby border with Uzbekistan, hoping to cross into the safety of refugee camps on the other side.

Just five years earlier, Uzbek president Islam Karimov had sent his own citizens running for cover in the opposite direction, toward Kyrgyzstan, after the bloodbath in the town of Andijan. Fate dealt the Uzbeks a lousy hand. In Uzbekistan, they had a twisted regime, whose abuses and absurdities we'll revisit in this book's final chapter. And in Kyrgyzstan, they were now facing an angry mob, and a fledgling government that, at best, didn't seem to care about them. For the moment, the lesser evil was in Uzbekistan, and the Uzbeks of southern Kyrgyzstan headed toward the border.

Bazar-Korgon's Kyrgyz residents watched the exodus with growing alarm. The Uzbek refugees shuffling past their houses toward Uzbekistan were mostly women and children. So the Kyrgyz assumed the Uzbek men were preparing to start something, but first wanted to send their women and kids out of harm's way. "We heard they asked their blacksmiths to make them weapons," Chinara Bechelova, the widow of the murdered cop, recalled.

It was in this climate of mutual fear that Captain Suleimanov and sixteen colleagues, all Kyrgyz, drove over to the highway bridge early in the morning on June 13. A crowd of nearly a thousand Uzbeks had gathered there overnight, blocking Kyrgyzstan's only major north-south highway. There were rumors that the Uzbeks were planning to blow up the highway bridge and cut off the south. The cops' mission, foolhardy in hindsight, was to reason with the protesters and convince them to disperse. To avoid provoking the crowd, most of the cops had left their weapons in the precinct. Sovetbek Dosov, a traffic policeman who arrived with a gun, was immediately disarmed and knocked down. "Someone yelled, 'Don't touch him, he's a traffic cop'; and then someone else said, 'It doesn't matter, he's a Kyrgyz all the same,'" Dosov told me recently.

We were sitting in his unmarked red car, smoking cigarettes and looking at the desolate stretch of highway where the clashes had taken place. Leaden clouds sailed over sagging power lines, and clumps of grayish snow stretched toward the horizon. Bundled pedestrians moved slowly along the shoulder, leaning into the wind. Dosov recalled that the men on the highway had carried large knives and medieval-looking wooden clubs topped with porcupinelike crests of nails. Dosov thought, "That's it," but then an Uzbek man ran up to him and told others, "Stop, don't beat him up. I know him, he's okay." That bought Dosov just enough time to make a run for it.

Bazar-Korgon's police chief had also arrived on the highway bridge. Seeing him, someone barked an order, "Take the police chief hostage and kill the rest of the cops," whereupon the chief received a blow to the head from behind and crumpled to the ground, according to his later testimony in court. Exactly whom the cops saw on the bridge and what the cops heard that frantic morning would be a matter of controversy during the trial. The police picked up their battered chief and retreated toward their cars. Dosov told me he felt something, probably a rock, hit him in the back, but he kept moving.

Suleimanov wasn't so lucky. He was wrestled down to the ground and dragged off the highway toward a teahouse. There, by a row of gnarly trees, about twenty men set upon the policeman, according to witness testimony. "I ran toward them. When two guys started hitting him on the head with clubs, [Suleimanov] covered his head with both hands and sat on the ground leaning on a tree," a witness later told investigators. "At that time, another guy took out a scythe and stabbed [Suleimanov] in the waist, in the neck, in the back, and in the heel. Then another guy told me, 'Don't interfere, he's just a cop; who cares if just one cop dies?' And he lit up four bottles filled with gasoline and threw them on [Suleimanov]. His right foot caught on fire. I ran up to him, and he kept saying, 'Don't touch me, don't touch me.'"

In the meantime, Suleimanov's colleagues escaped from the crowd and scrambled back to the precinct. There in the courtyard by the Iron

A policeman points to the roadside spot where the mutilated body of Maktybek Suleimanov was found. (© Philip Shishkin)

Felix statue they lit cigarettes, examined their bruises, and took a quick headcount. "Everyone here? Everyone here? Who's missing? Where's Maktybek?" Realizing Suleimanov wasn't among them, the cops drove back to the highway bridge, where the crowd had already thinned out. After some searching, they found Suleimanov right where his attackers had left him: by the trees in the roadside ditch. Pathologists noted twenty-eight stab wounds and significant burn marks. His face was disfigured beyond recognition.

In a civil war where most killings went uninvestigated and unpunished, Suleimanov's murder inquiry was quick and fruitful. On June 15, Azimjan Askarov, the prominent Uzbek human-rights activist, took his camera and went to record the aftermath of the war. By then more than twenty people had been killed (most of them Uzbeks), and about two hundred houses had been burned and destroyed.

A sixty-year-old professional artist, Askarov had become a fixture in

Kyrgyzstan's human-rights circles, helping people tackle government corruption and abuse. On several occasions, Askarov achieved blockbuster results that caused embarrassment for Bazar-Korgon officials. Stumped for a name to give to his advocacy organization, he called it Air, on the theory that people need human rights the same way they need air. Now, on June 15, Air's office in a drab two-story building on Bazar-Korgon's main square was a smoldering wreck.

Askarov and a colleague were taking pictures of the destruction in town, and were about to drive to the morgue to survey the casualties. At that point, a police van pulled over, and Askarov was told to get in. In all his years as a human-rights activist, Askarov had gotten used to dealing with Bazar-Korgon's police. But this encounter would be different. Shortly after arriving at the precinct, Askarov was handed a trash bag and ordered to serve as a human ashtray in the courtyard. "I was forced to walk up to the smokers so they could throw cigarette butts into the bag," Askarov later told a local newspaper. "The policemen were laughing: 'Now you, human-rights defender, will be our servant.' They were taking pictures of me with their cell-phone cameras." Police quizzed Askarov on whether he saw who'd been distributing weapons to Uzbek protesters and asked him to admit that he'd been present on the highway bridge when Suleimanov was killed.

In the meantime, police and prosecutors went to search Askarov's house on a quiet residential street. They banged on the front gate leading into the interior courtyard. When Askarov's wife, Hadidja, couldn't get to it fast enough, they fired at the gate three times, she told me. Scared, Hadidja dashed across the courtyard, fell, and badly injured her leg. The police eventually entered and turned the house upside down, first making sure to lock the family's shaggy dog in the basement. They found things seemingly incongruous with Askarov's work as a human-rights activist and an artist: ten handgun rounds "in a condition suitable for shooting" and a propaganda CD for an extremist Islamic group banned throughout Central Asia, according to court documents. Alongside the evidence, the police hauled away seven large canvas bags of rice, jars of raspberry preserves, and other groceries, Hadidja told me.

Over the next two months, prosecutors placed Askarov squarely at the center of the unrest leading up to Suleimanov's murder. In a rambling village courthouse, Askarov went on trial with seven Uzbek codefendants, including a well-known dentist, a forty-year-old mother of three, and an amateur musician.

In witness testimony, Askarov emerged as a ruthless Uzbek nationalist whose rhetoric inspired others to action. On June 12, for instance, as Uzbek refugees mobbed the border crossing with Uzbekistan hoping to escape, Askarov got into testy exchange with Bazar-Korgon's mayor, according to the testimony of the mayor, a Kyrgyz man named Kubatbek Artykov. Artykov had arrived at the border crossing to urge the Uzbek refugees to return home and stop worrying.

Appealing to Askarov's standing as a figure of authority among the Uzbeks, and using a polite form of address, the mayor asked for Askarov's help, according to his testimony. "Azim-ake, take your people back home, don't agitate them."

"Can you guarantee their safety [if they go home]?" Askarov asked.

"As mayor, I promise that the Kyrgyz population won't harm the Uzbeks," Artykov answered. "But Uzbekistan won't accept the refugees." This was a curious promise to make, considering the civil war was raging just miles away from the border while Kyrgyzstan's fledgling government looked on helplessly.

Askarov grew angry, according to the mayor's testimony: "Uzbekistan will accept us, they'll let us cross the border. And if they don't let us pass, then you'll walk ahead of us, and the border guards will shoot you first."

At this point, Askarov shouted to the Uzbeks around him, "Take the mayor hostage!" Artykov testified. "People started pulling me deep into the crowd." Artykov said he was able to distract his would-be kidnappers by pointing out the car of an even higher-ranking Kyrgyz official: "Here comes the governor, let's talk to him." As the Uzbeks turned to look, Artykov escaped.

Having established Askarov's threatening behavior at the border, the prosecutors next placed him on the highway bridge the following morning, June 13, smack in the middle of a thousand-strong crowd of Uzbeks blocking the north-south road. Throughout the morning, according to witness testimony, Askarov shouted out a medley of quotable sound bites such as "The Kyrgyz are dogs, you gotta kill them!" and "We are going to fight the Kyrgyz and blow up the bridge." As the crowd's belligerence grew, Askarov kept praising "the superior qualities" of the Uzbeks and "insulting the national honor" of the Kyrgyz, witnesses said. And it was Askarov who gave the fateful order: "Take the police chief hostage and kill the rest of the cops," several witnesses told the court. Others acted upon the order and executed Maktybek Suleimanov. Some of them were now in the dock with Askarov.

It seemed like an open-and-shut case. In September, after a brief trial, a judge found Askarov guilty of accessory to murder and sentenced him to life in prison, the harshest penalty under Kyrgyzstan law. All seven of his co-defendants were found guilty of participating either in the murder itself or in the ethnic clashes surrounding it. All got sentences ranging from twenty years to life.

News of Askarov's conviction stunned Kyrgyzstan's tightly knit human-rights community. Valentina Gritsenko, a fellow activist who knows him well, said Askarov recoiled at the very notion of bloodshed. At her request, he once brought her a farm-raised turkey, freshly slaughtered, by the look of it. When Gritsenko inquired if he'd killed it himself, he retorted that he could never do such a thing. "He couldn't even behead a bird."

Of the many interesting things about the case, one detail stands out: the verdict relies heavily on the testimony of a half dozen policemen who had reasons to dislike Askarov even before his alleged participation in the murder of their colleague. In a decade of muckraking, Askarov had accused Bazar-Korgon's police department of torture and abuse of the kind that would make Iron Felix proud. Is it possible that the town's criminal-justice system took revenge on the man who made a career out of needling it?

Askarov's deepest sting came in 2003 when he stumbled upon what initially looked like a boring larceny case. That year, Zulhumor Toktonazarova, an attractive twenty-three-year-old woman born into a poor peasant family, drifted into troublesome company. Apparently short on liquor money, Toktonazarova and her friends stole laundry drying on someone's clothesline, the police said. The loot included an old carpet and some towels worth next to nothing. Toktonazarova denied stealing anything. While the police investigated, the young woman was placed in pretrial detention at the Bazar-Korgon precinct.

Over the next few months, Toktonazarova said, she was repeatedly raped by prison minders and by male inmates to whom she would be sold for a night now and then. "It happened about ten or fifteen times," Toktonazarova told me in the courtyard of her family's modest home in Bazar-Korgon. Her toddler son played on the porch, and she tousled his hair whenever he tugged on her skirt or leaned on her leg.

The jailhouse rapes led to a pregnancy. The abuse stopped only after she started showing, she told me. Still detained without formal charges, Toktonazarova was given drugs to induce a miscarriage, she said. But the fetus survived, and she went into premature labor in the seventh month. When she couldn't stand the pain any longer, the police took her to the hospital. There, handcuffed by one of her wrists to a bedpost, she delivered a boy. "He was alive when he was born," Toktonazarova told me in her courtyard. "But they wouldn't even let me hold him." The baby soon died, and two days later she was taken back to her jail cell. The police, she said, told her not to talk about it too much.

Most likely, the story would have remained hidden if Askarov hadn't gotten wind of it. At the time, the human-rights defender was examining detention conditions in Bazar-Korgon. Aided by a sympathetic law-enforcement official, Askarov gained authorization to visit the detention center and talk to inmates. Toktonazarova's mother had written to Air, his advocacy organization, to complain about her daughter's plight. Askarov visited her in jail several times, "and then at some point in the summer, I noticed her belly was getting bigger," Askarov told me.

At the time, he had no idea how the shy young woman had gotten pregnant, but he said he told the police she should be freed. They ignored the request. After she gave birth, Askarov kept up the pressure, and the police finally let her go. A court would later sentence her to a few months of parole for the laundry theft. Upon her release, Toktonazarova and her mother told Askarov the full story of the pregnancy. The rights defender wrote an article in the local paper, and it soon became a national issue. Fergananews.com carried the story under the headline "If the Police Detain You in Southern Kyrgyzstan, You Can Become Pregnant, Give Birth, Bury Your Child, and Get Tortured."

Askarov made Bazar-Korgon's police department look like a bunch of depraved thugs. Kyrgyzstan's prime minister promised an inquiry, and eventually a handful of local officials were fired. But no one went to jail. The police denied that anyone had raped Toktonazarova in detention, and said she was already pregnant when they arrested her for larceny. Two years later, in 2005, the police arrested the woman again, accusing her of stealing something from a neighbor. Askarov told me he thought the arrest was in revenge for her earlier rape accusations against the police. Toktonazarova also said she had been warned not to run her mouth about anything. "They said they'd pin other thefts on me if I did," she told me.

When she was released three days later, Askarov pounced on the case again and alleged that the police had tortured her by driving needles under her fingernails. In a newspaper column, Askarov wrote the police were so abusive and corrupt as to be beyond redemption. The article was titled "Only the Grave Will Straighten a Hunchback." In Russian, it's an innocuous saying, kind of like "A leopard can't change his spots." The police sued Askarov for slander. The charges were eventually dismissed, but the police and Askarov would remain enemies.

If the cops despised the human-rights defender so much that they framed him for the murder of Suleimanov—as Askarov's supporters have said—could the opposite theory also merit consideration? Is it possible that Askarov held the cops in such a low regard as to think nothing of calling for their murder?

Sovetbek Dosov, the traffic policeman who was on the highway bridge with Suleimanov shortly before his death, told me Askarov had always looked for conflicts with the police. We were sitting in his car looking at the murder scene when Dosov brought up the Toktonazarova case without my prompting. "Nobody touched that woman," Dosov said. Askarov exaggerated the case just to make the police look bad and make a name for himself, he said. "That's the kind of person he is." Referring to Askarov's appearance—he is short, thin, and speaks softly—Dosov countered with a proverb of his own: "Still waters harbor demons" (a punchier Russian version of "Still waters run deep").

The alleged demon resides in a solitary cell in a red-roofed prison on the edge of Bishkek, Kyrgyzstan's pleasant capital. One gray winter afternoon I showed up at the main checkpoint underneath a green watchtower resembling a birdhouse. Concrete walls rose high and ended with coils of razor wire. Inside the entrance shack, a female soldier in a fur hat sat next to a heavy steel door with a menacing array of bars and locks.

My visit wouldn't have been possible without the help of Tolekan Ismailova, the doyenne of Kyrgyzstan's human-rights movement. Over the past decade, Ismailova has led battles on a variety of fronts: the practices of a Canadian gold-mining company, freedom of the press, and government corruption in all its many forms. She had been briefly jailed under the previous regime. After the 2010 revolution, Kyrgyzstan's newly installed president (a longtime friend of Ismailova) appointed her to run the Central Election Commission, a body tasked with organizing ballots—or rigging them, as had often been the case.

Ismailova accepted the job, took one look inside the bureaucratic mess, and quit within forty-eight hours. Since then, she's thrown herself back into human-rights work with renewed gusto, focusing on the civil war and its acrimonious aftermath. That is why Ismailova stood in front of the steel prison door on that winter day. She brought Askarov plastic bags filled with cookies and chocolates, and a reading lamp in a cardboard box.

Behind bars, Askarov became a cause célèbre within Kyrgyzstan's vibrant human-rights community. Ismailova and her fellow activists kept up a steady drumbeat of support that won Askarov some unlikely allies. In March of 2011, around the time his son was going through a famously profane meltdown, actor Martin Sheen appeared in a minute-long video calling for Askarov's release. "Askarov is innocent and needs your help," Sheen said in the clip, recorded by Front Line, a Dublin-based group that defends human-rights defenders in trouble. "Protect one. Empower a thousand," Sheen continued.

Back in Bishkek, the heavy steel door clanged open, and Ismailova and I climbed up a flight of stairs to the spacious office of Colonel Askar Egemberdiyev, the prison's commanding officer. Egemberdiyev was sitting under an embroidered wall hanging featuring the gaunt profile of Iron Felix, the Soviet secret-police chief. What was it with Kyrgyz law enforcement and Iron Felix? Egemberdiyev chuckled and explained the wall hanging was merely a keepsake that had followed him through his military career, not a reflection of his beliefs. Ismailova unloaded her goodies and traded pleasantries with the colonel, whom she knew well from her previous visits. "So, should I call him in?" Egemberdiyev asked, then nodded to a guard.

Minutes later, Askarov entered the room like a soldier reporting for duty. He clicked his heels together, straightened his back, saluted the colonel, and rattled off his full name. With that, Kyrgyzstan's most famous prisoner sat down at a conference table, spreading a notebook in front of him. He wore baggy sweatpants and a gray and black skiing hat that he kept on throughout the interview. Slight of build, Askarov has a face that looks boyish despite his age. His eyebrows shoot outward, forming little triangles that overhang his eyelids. His voice barely rose above a whisper. I asked him to tell me about his life.

After art school in Tashkent, the capital of Uzbekistan, Askarov returned to Kyrgyzstan and started painting impressionistic landscapes that he says received some critical acclaim. Askarov also developed an enduring penchant for self-portraits. For money, Askarov and his wife, also an artist, depended on commercial orders—decorating a restaurant or painting yet another Lenin. By the early 1990s, the Askarovs had a comfortable life, making about seven times the average salary of a collective-farm boss, Askarov told me. That was good money. They had four kids. Their house overflowed with plants, which they both loved. He wrote essays on the history of art for a local newspaper. It is possible that in a calmer time and in a calmer place, Askarov would have stuck to art. But that was not to be.

In the early 1990s, during the messy dissolution of the Soviet Union, Ferghana Valley went through a bout of ethnic clashes over land, foreshadowing, it turns out, the civil war of 2010. Neighbors and acquaintances approached Askarov for advice on how to deal with the officials and the police who seemed to be more sympathetic to the Kyrgyz, Askarov recalled. As an educated man and an artist, Askarov had attained some stature in his hometown's Uzbek community. "So people were coming to me, but I didn't know what to tell them," he said. "I had to get a copy of Kyrgyzstan's constitution, and I began writing letters to prosecutors, to the police."

As years went on, Askarov became absorbed by the work, buying law books and linking up with local human-rights defenders. Art was taking a back seat to advocacy, becoming a hobby. "To be an artist, your head should be wholly devoted to art," Askarov said. "But because of the complex political situation, I couldn't paint decent portraits or landscapes."

In 1993, Askarov homed in on a cop who was shaking down merchants at an outdoor market in Bazar-Korgon. Askarov heard from traders that the policeman harassed them if they refused to pay bribes. This kind of police corruption is an evergreen issue across the former Soviet Union. In most cases, people grumble quietly and pay up. The cops are usually loath to investigate their own, even if someone does complain. It takes a certain kind of person to take on the police. In his hometown, Askarov became that person. He wrote about the shakedown case for the same local newspaper that had earlier published his art essays. Miraculously, the policeman was fired, Askarov told me.

By now a police watchdog with name recognition, Askarov kept sniffing out strange cases. In 2007, in the basement of Bazar-Korgon's Palace of Culture, the police found the disfigured corpse of a woman with multiple stab wounds. She was identified as one Mayram Zahirova. A man and a woman were soon arrested for her murder. The two complained of torture at the hands of the police, and Askarov began to investigate. He looked at the photos of Zahirova's corpse and noticed something strange. Zahirova had been three months' pregnant at the time of her death, and she had an appendicitis scar. But the photos didn't appear to show signs of either condition. Was the body really Zahirova's? Turning on his gumshoe mode, Askarov made inquiries in Bazar-Korgon's seedy underbelly. "I enlisted local prostitutes to help me," he told me. It turned out that Zahirova was indeed alive but reluctant to be found. Askarov convinced her to step forward. In the final flourish, he brought her to the court-room just as her murder trial was about to start. The two suspects were set free. (The other murder is a cold case.) Several prosecutors were later fired for incompetence, according to press reports at the time.

Askarov's advocacy work followed a clear pattern: the victims were regular folks from Bazar-Korgon—and the culprits were law-enforcement officials. The ethnic division flowed naturally from the occupational one: the regular folks here are often Uzbek, and the cops are almost always Kyrgyz. In 2005, Askarov estimated that of some fifteen hundred police in the region, only about ten cops were Uzbeks. In a recent report, Kyrgyzstan's government admitted as much. The number of Uzbeks is "particularly low in the armed forces, in the state security and police services, in the tax and customs service, in the financial police, among prosecutors and judges."

As ethnic tensions grew, Askarov's work took on a heavy ethnic bias in the eyes of Bazar-Korgon's police. "Not even once did he speak up to defend a Kyrgyz," Sovetbek Dosov, the traffic policeman, told me.

The brittle ethnic fabric of southern Kyrgyzstan was ripped apart right after the revolution of April 7, 2010. As spring splashed lush greens on mountainsides, matching the briefly upbeat mood of a nation emerging from misrule, strange things were happening in the town of Jalala-bad, a provincial capital a short drive from Bazar-Korgon. Kurmanbek Bakiyev, the ousted president and of course a Kyrgyz, fled here from Bishkek and holed up in his ancestral village on the edge of town. For a few nervous days, he held court in a massive tent and conferred with his many brothers and hangers-on. He eventually flew onward to Minsk, Belarus, at the invitation of the local strongman. (Bakiyev continues to live there in exile.)

In the meantime, the writ of the interim government that had over-thrown Bakiyev didn't spread far beyond Bishkek, and was particularly tenuous in the south with its clannish loyalties and ethnic complications. What's more, the south sits on a major heroin-smuggling route running from Afghanistan to Europe. Organized crime had long since fused itself with elements of the local law enforcement and power elites. Now the

revolution tore up the old daisy chains of corruption, adding to the insta-
bility. When I hung around Bakiyev's family estate during his brief sojourn there after his ouster, a colleague pointed out a short, stocky man
in the scrum of visitors. It was Black Aybek, one of the most notorious
mobsters of Jalalabad. It was not clear what he was doing there. He drove
off before I could ask. A few days later, Black Aybek was shot dead in
murky circumstances.

By the time of his overthrow, Bakiyev was a thoroughly discredited
figure. But as a Kyrgyz politician with extensive ties of family, clan, and
business, he retained enough support in the south to make things difficult for the interim government. The new leaders in Bishkek needed help
in the south to consolidate their hold on power. And they found an ally in
Kadyrjan Batyrov, a prominent Uzbek businessman and philanthropist
who had a political agenda of his own.

A self-made man born in Jalalabad, Batyrov is one of those entrepreneurs seemingly capable of making money out of anything. In the
Soviet days, he correctly sensed an unmet demand for leather goods,
and started a factory sewing jackets and upholstery for car seats, a hall-
mark of Soviet chic. In the early days of independence, he identified a
market for timber in the largely treeless Central Asian plains, and acquired a chunk of forest in Russia. He imported the timber at a hand-
some profit. Then he dabbled in tobacco, a sure cash cow in smoke-happy
Central Asia. Later, he founded a cargo airline based out of the United
Arab Emirates.

In April of 2010, shortly after the revolution, I went to see him in the
courtyard of the University of Peoples' Friendship, a private college that
Batyrov had built on an empty lot with $4 million of his own money. A
fountain gurgled by the main gate, across a cobblestone path from the
statue of Batyrov's father. Batyrov had also built a kindergarten and a
school. His schools were popular across ethnic lines for the quality of their
education, offered mostly in Russian. "They had very strong teachers; it
was such a great place," Elmira Mavlyanova, a Kyrgyz woman who runs
an NGO in Jalalabad, told me. She sent her son there.

Batyrov's main political project was to gain official recognition of the

Uzbek language alongside Russian. (Kyrgyz is the sole state language.) The linguistic campaign was really a gateway toward redressing a slew of other inequalities related to the Uzbeks' lack of representation at all levels of government. "We were born here, we live in our motherland," Batyrov said of Kyrgyzstan. He spoke right after addressing a rally of Uzbek youths milling about the university's courtyard. It was a jittery time, but Batyrov appeared calm as he leaned back on an ornate couch, clasping his hands on top of his blue shirt. He mentioned, with a snigger, that he'd just gotten word that an Uzbek was appointed to a customs post somewhere, as if that were enough.

What Batyrov really seemed to crave, as wealthy people often do, is for his political stature to match his economic one. The Bakiyev regime, he told me, had "deceived" him in the language quest, and so now he was ready to back the interim government that had overthrown Bakiyev. A hodgepodge of Kyrgyz revolutionary leaders embraced Batyrov, whose power in Jalalabad all but guaranteed them success against remnants of the old guard.

Meanwhile, after much huffing and puffing about his popularity, Bakiyev flew into exile, vacating his ceremonial tent on the edge of Jalalabad. He and his associates and relatives now face criminal prosecution in Kyrgyzstan on charges that include murder and corruption. Hours after Bakiyev escaped, a crowd of protesters set his sprawling family home on fire. Though Batyrov says the place was already burning by the time his men arrived, the prevalent view in Kyrgyzstan is that it was Batyrov's Uzbeks who did it. "I told them, 'Don't touch the house, it belonged to Bakiyev's grandfather, and he's a veteran of World War II,'" Ashukan Saparova, an elderly Kyrgyz woman who lives across the street, told me when I visited.

As word of the bonfire spread, the Kyrgyz grew infuriated. How dared the Uzbeks burn a Kyrgyz home? "They shouldn't have done it. I'm a woman, but if someone burned my father's house, I would also want revenge," Mavlyanova, the Kyrgyz NGO activist who had a son in Batyrov's kindergarten, told me. Though ethnic clashes had taken place even before the arson, they intensified in the following weeks. A Kyrgyz crowd rampaged through Batyrov's Peoples' Friendship University, burn-

During the ethnic clashes in southern Kyrgyzstan, a Kyrgyz mob vandalized the Peoples' Friendship University, owned by a local Uzbek tycoon. (© Philip Shishkin)

ing classrooms, breaking windows, and decapitating the statue of the Uzbek leader's father. It was late May, right around finals.

"Students started running away," recalled Anara Samatova, a professor of literature, who is Kyrgyz. Samatova collected exam papers and followed her students out through the back door. In the next few days, Jalalabad descended into hell. Hiding in her apartment, Samatova peeked out the window and saw a group of armed Kyrgyz men interrogating an Uzbek teenager dressed in a black T-shirt. She knew the kid was Uzbek because his captors called him *sart*, a derogatory term the Kyrgyz use for Uzbeks, the local n-word. Samatova couldn't hear what the gunmen were grilling him about, but she overheard the kid protesting: "But my house was burned too." With that, the men shot him, put his body in a car, and drove off.

Next up in the war's path was Osh, Kyrgyzstan's second-largest city and a bustling hub of the south. Tensions had been brewing there for years, as the Uzbek commercial class dominating the city rubbed up against the influx of poorer rural migrants, most of them Kyrgyz. In fact, an element of class had seeped into the conflict. Many rural Kyrgyz resented the Uzbeks for their perceived wealth. It's a deeply flawed stereotype, but one that proved very resilient.

By June of 2010, scuffles were breaking out on street corners as rival gangs settled scores and responded to slights, real and imagined. One unsubstantiated rumor, for instance, was that Uzbek thugs were raping Kyrgyz women in an Osh college dorm. All of a sudden, the city became a rigidly demarcated matrix of warring blocs.

The city's sole cancer hospital, a collection of whitewashed buildings connected by garden paths, is located deep inside an Uzbek quarter. During the war, the hospital became a triage clinic where the Uzbeks brought their dead and wounded. Kyrgyz cancer patients huddled upstairs, worried about revenge. Angry Uzbek gunmen were milling about the hospital. "Find me just one Kyrgyz," yelled a relative of an Uzbek who'd just died of his wounds, recalled Aijamal Anarbayeva, a Kyrgyz medical resident in charge of the cancer ward. Over the next few hours, Anarbayeva held frantic talks with local Uzbek leaders and Kyrgyz security operatives. She managed to negotiate a safe passage for her Kyrgyz cancer patients out of the hospital.

Wandering around Osh a few weeks before the war, I came across a small Russian Orthodox church. Made of brick and freshly painted turquoise and white, the church sat in a sun-dappled courtyard, serene, quiet, and somewhat out of place in this tortured town. A side door opened, and the courtyard came alive with the cheerful, dissonant patter of kids bounding down the stairs from Sunday school. They looked to be no older than seven. They were all dressed up—white ribbons in the girls' hair; suit jackets hanging loosely on the boys' skinny frames. The boys leaned forward to compensate for the weight of their backpacks, and the effort made them look comically busy and grown-up.

Slender birch trees grew in the courtyard, as if suggesting that nothing Russian can possibly happen without a birch somewhere in the picture. The priest, Father Victor Reymgen, came out to say hello. In his early forties, he had a wispy red beard that fanned out in unruly tufts below his chin. A clingy black robe descended over his stocky frame all the way down to his shoes, rising in a little hump over a paunch upon which, suspended from a neck chain, rested a large silver cross with luminescent red stones.

I told Father Victor that although I was a journalist, this was not a professional visit. I didn't intend to write about the church (which obviously turned out to be untrue). He seemed relieved by that. "Don't worry," he said as we sat down on a wooden bench. "Everything that's worth writing is already written in the book of life." I liked that attitude a lot.

The Osh church, and dozens of others built from the same military blueprints, sprang up to cater to the religious needs of Christian conquerors stationed in these Muslim lands, and later of the civilian settlers who followed them. This one had just celebrated its centennial, but I couldn't tell from talking to Father Victor whether this very eventful century merited so much as a subchapter in the book of life. "One regime, another regime; the Akayevs, the Bakiyevs; the reds and the whites," Father Victor said slowly, almost dismissively. "The church stood then, and it stands now. It's much easier for the church in that sense."

As we spoke, I wondered about his last name. "Reymgen" didn't sound Russian at all. And it wasn't. The Orthodox priest was ethnically German, a descendant of Catholics who once lived in the Ukraine. How a German boy from a Catholic family ended up tending to a dwindling Russian Orthodox parish in a Muslim town populated by the Kyrgyz and Uzbeks is a story worth telling, I thought. Despite my earlier abdication of journalism in front of the priest, I reached for my notebook.

As a lot of Russian stories do, this one starts with Stalin. In his paranoid quest to stifle national consciousness and punish ethnicities he saw as potentially treacherous, the Soviet dictator preemptively exiled the Germans to Central Asia and Siberia. Ordered to leave her native Ukraine, Father Victor's great-grandmother boarded a train to Siberia. With three small children in tow, the great-grandmother flouted her orders and disembarked in Kazakhstan. She ripped out the page from her passport that carried her deportation stamp and started building a new life. It wasn't

Russian Orthodox priest Victor Reymgen in front of his church in Osh, Kyrgyzstan.
(© Philip Shishkin)

easy. Victor's grandparents worked in a lead mine. His father drove a tractor, and at some point converted to Orthodoxy from the family Catholicism. Victor was born in Kazakhstan. He studied science at a Bishkek university, and on weekends began visiting the house of an Orthodox priest whom he'd known back in his hometown in Kazakhstan. The priest was reassigned to Bishkek around the same time Victor arrived there as a student. "He served great dinners, and students tend to be hungry, so I went there often," Victor recalled. At those dinners, he met the priest's daughter. Victor's paths toward marriage and priesthood unfolded together, and neither involved a sudden flash of infatuation. Rather, both were slow, deliberate decisions. "I can't even say I was a strong believer, I was just a regular Soviet student," he said.

Victor got married and became a priest. The couple had two children and were eventually assigned to the Osh parish, where they live in a small house right next to the church. During the Kyrgyz-Uzbek fighting, Father

Victor hosted a dozen refugees who were too scared to remain in their homes. One day, he walked out on his balcony and saw a biblical picture of fires and clouds of black smoke all over the town. "I looked up and it seemed like it was snowing, but it was ash falling down," he recalled. The refugees hiding inside the church were growing worried that gangs would eventually storm this sanctuary. By that time, sour cherries had already ripened on the trees in the church orchard. To distract the refugees, Father Victor suggested they join him in picking the cherries and making jam. Balancing on ladders, they collected four large buckets of cherries. The church had ample supplies of sugar. A few days later, when things quieted down a bit, the priest loaded his jeep with potatoes, cookies, and whatever random groceries he could spare and drove through the devastated town, distributing food to strangers.

Soon after, his wife gave birth to a baby boy. Father Victor was overjoyed—the couple's two older children were already teenagers. But the boy soon died; something was wrong with his lungs. "The doctors told us that the stress from the war took its toll. And we were looking forward to having this baby so much," he said. A few months later, Father Victor decided to take his wife and children on vacation to Egypt. It had been a year from hell, and they could all benefit from a little distraction. His children had never seen the sea, and maybe they could all manage a jaunt to the Holy Land from there. The day before the trip, the tour company cancelled it because of the revolution in Egypt. "I think we are nearing the end of the world," Father Victor told me. I thought it was a figure of speech, but he wasn't kidding.

The mayor of Osh worked from a big administrative building just down the hill from the church. A big statue of Lenin still towered in front of the building. After speaking with the priest, I walked over to meet the mayor, an unabashed Kyrgyz nationalist with wide-ranging business ties. During the fighting, he did little to calm the tensions. Sometime earlier, his office had backed a municipal redevelopment plan that called, in part, for the construction of multistory apartment blocks on the land now occupied by low-slung Uzbek quarters. During the war, some of the violence targeted those very quarters. The mayor, Melis Myrzakmatov, is such a divisive figure that the central government wanted to fire him at one point after the war. When I met him in his spacious office, the burly mayor wore a pinstriped suit, smoked slender cigarettes, and kept glancing at his golden wristwatch. He thumbed his nose at the central government. "No one can fire me," he told me. Local voters had elected him, he said, so only they could get rid of him at the ballot box.

Osh demographics are shifting as Uzbeks with means are leaving the city. Over dinner at California Pizzeria, a cozy joint on a dark Osh street, one Kyrgyz woman told me it was hard to find good hairdressers, a trade traditionally dominated by the Uzbeks.

During the war, the Kyrgyz had the full machinery of the state at their disposal: the police, the security services, and highly sympathetic local officials. The Uzbeks had only themselves.

Facing imminent arrest and quite possibly lynching, Batyrov, the Uzbek philanthropist, fled the country. The Kyrgyz leaders who had only recently courted him now turned away from him and cast him as nothing short of a terrorist.

Such was the state of interethnic relations when Bazar-Korgon's cops dragged Askarov, the Uzbek activist, to their precinct and asked him about the murder of Suleimanov, the Kyrgyz policeman. When Askarov told them he had no idea what they were talking about, the beatings began. "They beat me horribly for three days straight," Askarov told me recently. "When I began to faint, they'd make me sing Kyrgyzstan's national anthem."

Many Kyrgyz were convinced the Uzbeks wanted to break off a chunk of southern Kyrgyzstan and establish an autonomous Uzbek statelet, with Batyrov at the helm. "They even wanted to rename Jalalabad Batyrabad," Bechelova, the widow of the murdered policeman, told me.

By the time Askarov's lawyer arrived in the precinct, the rights defender was so scared he wouldn't tell him about the beatings, the lawyer, Nurbek Toktakunov, said. A policeman was present at the lawyer-client meeting. "You see, when you've been hit in the kidneys for so long, you really don't want to get hit there again," Askarov told me, by way of explaining why he kept quiet. So Toktakunov asked him to lift his shirt instead, which Askarov did, revealing a patchwork of purple and yellow bruises around his kidneys. Toktakunov photographed them.

Officials denied Askarov had been beaten. "A medical examination of Azimjan Askarov didn't detect any injuries. Allegations in the mass media that he had been beaten and tortured by policemen are groundless," Jalalabad's regional prosecutor said in a statement. "In a conversation with prosecutors, Askarov himself denied that he had been beaten and didn't have any complaints against law-enforcement officials."

The interrogation set the tone for the trial. Askarov and his seven co-defendants sat in a metal cage in front of Suleimanov's friends and family, who packed the courtroom and shouted insults throughout the trial. From this cage, Askarov tried to present his version of events. In early June, Askarov was hosting his elderly mother, daughter, and granddaughter, all visiting from Uzbekistan, where they live. On June 12, Askarov, carrying his ubiquitous folder, pen, and camera, went to the border crossing with Uzbekistan to assess the refugee situation. He said hello to Bazar-Korgon's mayor, who was there and whom he knew well. Askarov said he didn't order anyone to kidnap him, as the mayor alleged in his testimony. Instead, Askarov had something else in mind. He wanted to get his family to safety in Uzbekistan.

But his wife Hadidja didn't want to leave her home, so after Askarov drove his mother, daughter, and granddaughter to the border crossing, he returned to Bazar-Korgon. "I couldn't leave without my wife," he told me. That night, Askarov camped out on the central Saidullayev Street, where the Uzbeks were putting up barricades. Askarov took notes and taped the scene with his camcorder. That night, he says, he observed a motorcade of some sixty vehicles, including vans and heavy trucks, arrive from the north and stop somewhere on the outskirts of Bazar-Korgon. Who were those people?

At dawn, Askarov went home and fell asleep. His wife woke him up later that morning, June 13, with an urgent piece of news: a policeman had just been killed. Askarov rushed to the highway bridge. "I told people to stop blocking the highway; everything's going to be peaceful," Askarov recalled. At that point, a shot rang out and "a big guy right in front of me tumbled into the roadside ditch," Askarov told me. The shot appeared to have come from the general direction of a café near which the police were standing, Askarov said. His hands covered in blood, Askarov loaded the wounded man into a car and took him to the hospital, where he was pronounced dead. As the shooting intensified, Askarov went home. Two days later, he was arrested.

In the courtroom, Askarov and his lawyer had a problem: no one was around to corroborate this version of events. "All Uzbek witnesses were threatened—they didn't even dare approach the courtroom," Toktakunov told me. Turdukan Askarova, the artist's sister-in-law, told me a neighbor had seen Askarov in his house on the morning of the murder. "But the neighbor was threatened, and he refused to testify." According to a detailed survey of the trial by independent lawyer Dinara Diykanova, Askarov and his seven co-defendants had a total of two defense witnesses between them. By contrast, the prosecution could call on the testimony of twenty-one witnesses and victims, most of them colleagues of the murdered policeman.

In a tiny victory, Toktakunov got the court to drop the charges of Islamic extremism—the CD found during the search of Askarov's house contained nothing nefarious, just a sermon by a local imam. But the bullets found in the same house search were admitted as a damning piece of evidence against the rights defender. Toktakunov says the bullets were planted during the search.

A forty-year-old Kyrgyz with an easygoing manner, Toktakunov runs a law group in Bishkek focusing on government corruption and transparency. When he showed up for his second meeting with Askarov inside Bazar-Korgon's precinct, the police told him Suleimanov's relatives were looking for him, and that he should hide in the courtyard. Toktakunov didn't make much of the warning—until he was encircled by the relatives. "They tore up my shirt and took my briefcase," Toktakunov told me (the prosecutor's office later intervened to help him retrieve the briefcase, which contained legal papers).

Suleimanov's mother, Karamat Suleimanova, is an elderly woman stricken by grief. She and her husband run a small roadside grocery store on the edge of Bazar-Korgon. When I visited, she didn't hide her contempt

The parents of murdered policeman Maktybek Suleimanov. (© Philip Shishkin)

for Toktakunov, or anyone defending Askarov. "I told [Toktakunov], 'You are Kyrgyz, you have no heart, why are you defending him? You should be ashamed of yourself.'"

The family reserved particular scorn for a defense witness who had evidence purporting to show that Askarov tried to prevent violence, instead of provoking it. In late May, Askarov found out through his extensive network of sources that one night in Bazar-Korgon persons unknown had been unloading firearms. He knew the exact place. He phoned in this tip to Aziza Abdyrasulova, a prominent Kyrgyz rights activist who at the time was involved in monitoring the deteriorating situation in the south. This intelligence preceded the outbreak of full-scale civil war, and may have helped the interim government limit the conflict.

Abdyrasulova deemed the tip important enough to take Askarov straight to General Ismail Isakov. Isakov, a onetime minister of defense who had been jailed under the previous regime, now served as the new government's security chief in the south. In a brief meeting, Askarov briefed the general on the firearms cache, according to Abdyrasulova's sworn affidavit.

Yet, when Askarov's lawyer Toktakunov asked her to testify, she started receiving death threats. "I realized I couldn't guarantee her safety," said Toktakunov, who had been attacked himself by then. "I preferred to overestimate the risk than to underestimate it." Abdyrasulova didn't testify. When I mentioned her name to the murdered policeman's family, the mother deadpanned, "Aziza should be killed."

The family's emotions are understandable, given the brutal murder of Captain Suleimanov. His widow and mother would, of course, take the word of his colleagues and friends over the word of anyone else. They are convinced of Askarov's guilt, and aren't interested in hearing any competing theories. "Why wouldn't I trust my husband's colleagues?" Bechelova, the widow, asked me. When we spoke, her son was a student at the national police academy in Bishkek.

But court officials made no attempt to separate these emotions from the trial. At one point a relative tossed a glass in the courtroom, and it shattered against the cage holding the defendants, one lawyer told me. The relatives kept calling for the death penalty. "The lack of any reprimands against the relatives for disrupting the order in the courtroom, and the feeling of official support they seemed to enjoy, allowed them to behave as they wished," according to the independent survey of the trial.

In between trial sessions, Askarov and his co-defendants were subjected to severe beatings, which remained uninvestigated, Askarov told me when I saw him in prison. After describing one session, he broke down crying. He showed me pencil sketches he drew in his cell: portraits of himself in various stages of gauntness, including one with a heavy chain around his neck, and a portrait of his wife. After a perfunctory review, an appeals court upheld Askarov's guilty verdict and that of his co-defendants.

Though Askarov's case is by far the most controversial, the convictions of some of his alleged co-conspirators also appear to rest on assumptions that were allowed to stand unchallenged in court even as potentially mitigating evidence emerged. On a February morning, I went to Bazar-Korgon to see the defendants' relatives. My taxi skidded down an icy hill and came to a stop against a curbside where a young Uzbek woman in a colorful headscarf was already waiting. Her name was Gulia Tashkenova, and she is the wife of Elmurad Rasulov, an amateur musician sentenced to life in prison alongside Askarov. His alleged crime: tossing a lit gasoline bottle on the dying policeman.

Tashkenova led me up the stairs of a small office building, past a pharmacy kiosk, and into a frigid yellow room. There, crowded around a chipped conference table, were a dozen relatives of Askarov and his co-defendants. A small space heater glowed bright orange and created an island of tropical heat, through which some of us rotated to warm up.

Tashkenova told me Rasulov, herself, and their toddler daughter had already been in a refugee camp in Uzbekistan at the time of the policeman's murder. The family returned to Bazar-Korgon twelve days later, she said. On June 27, like a good citizen, Rasulov went to the local polling station to cast his vote in a hastily convened national referendum on the country's new constitution. The next day, according to his wife, he went to report the theft of his car, which had been stolen during the war. He was arrested, tortured with a plastic bag over his head, and forced to confess that he had set Suleimanov on fire, Tashkenova said. Tatiana Tomina, Rasulov's lawyer, told me she'd obtained a document from the Uzbek refugee camp showing Rasulov's presence there on the day of the policeman's murder. Even though it is possible that Rasulov slipped into Uzbekistan after the policeman was killed, none of this evidence received much consideration during the trial. At one point in the courtroom, someone taunted Rasulov's lawyer about her ethnicity—she is Russian—and threatened to sprinkle sulfuric acid on her, she said.

In our frigid conference room, the assembled relatives laid out folders and notebooks and competed with one another to tell their stories, sometimes speaking all at once. A sister of one defendant—the local dentist—managed to reach him on his cell phone in prison. "You'll be talking about how they electrocuted you, how they wanted to make burger patties out of you," Louisa Mirzalieva told him through tears, then passed the handset to me.

The dentist, Shukurjan Mizaliyev, thirty-nine at the time, was a well-known public figure in Bazar-Korgon, not least because he ran the town's Uzbek cultural center. Many called him simply by his nickname, Shoorik. A father of four, the dentist was sentenced to twenty years for "fomenting mass disorder" and encouraging Uzbeks to build barricades and block the highway. But Shoorik had gotten on the police radar screen even earlier. In the days leading up to the June 13 clashes, Shoorik led a protest in front the precinct inquiring why an Uzbek detainee had died in police custody. The official version: heart attack.

"I was set up, I was set up," Shoorik was now stammering into a cell phone from his prison cell. He told me that after his arrest, he'd been beaten unconscious with a rifle butt.

Amid all the professions of innocence, the relatives have been pushing an alternative theory of Captain Suleimanov's death, one that appears to be rooted solidly in hearsay. He wasn't stabbed and burned, they say, but shot by a mysterious red-haired man, never caught. They'd like Suleimanov's body exhumed and examined again.

For a while, the case of Askarov and his alleged gang was pending in front of Kyrgyzstan's Supreme Court. The court delayed announcing its decision several times. Whichever way it ruled, it was going to make a lot of people unhappy. Kyrgyz nationalism had become a potent force in the country's politics, and the harassment of Uzbeks in the south continued. Many were leaving the country.

There were no signs of reconciliation. In May of 2011, after nearly a year of suspense, an international commission investigating the civil war issued a ninety-page report largely sympathetic to the Uzbeks. The government of Kyrgyzstan reacted angrily and swiftly accused the authors of bias. From Osh came word of a public bonfire in which copies of the report were burned. Kyrgyzstan's Parliament banned the report's principal author—a well-known Finnish politician—from setting foot in Kyrgyzstan ever again. Within the broader national drama, the Askarov case seems stuck between the two competing narratives of the war.

Roza Otunbayeva, who served as Kyrgyzstan's president until 2012, was familiar with the Askarov case. "It's a very controversial story," she told me one day during her presidency. "It's about a murdered policeman, and all the testimony came from his colleagues. There's a sense of solidarity here, absolutely. He was a human-rights defender, he annoyed the policemen, the local authorities. Perhaps there's an element of revenge on their part." She paused to reflect on the broader issue. "Nationalism has grown immensely, particularly in the south. It's hard to work in this situation."

I asked Otunbayeva if her government should have done more to prevent or contain the civil war. "I regret that we couldn't see the problem in all its depth and breadth," she said. We spoke on a flight to Washington where Otunbayeva was going to receive the U.S. State Department's Women of Courage award. But in a sign of just how poisoned the relations between the Kyrgyz and the Uzbeks have become, a prominent Uzbek activist and an earlier recipient of the same prize returned her award in disgust. "Her hands are covered in blood," the Uzbek activist wrote in an open letter.

The Supreme Court eventually rejected Askarov's appeal, and the activist went on a hunger strike. In prison, he had gotten to know another high-profile inmate, Ahmat Bakiyev, the ousted president's younger brother and the only presidential relative to end up behind bars. We met Ahmat briefly earlier in the book, right after the 2010 revolution when he huddled with the ousted president and the rest of his brothers in their family compound in Jalalabad. Back then, Ahmat said he was in a "foul mood." Behind bars, Ahmat and Askarov weren't exactly friends, but they chatted about this and that to while away the time. One day, Ahmat vanished. He had complained of poor health and was allowed a hospital visit. From there he somehow disappeared. Kyrgyz officials pleaded ignorance, but it's inconceivable that such a high-profile inmate could have escaped without official help. Askarov doesn't have those kinds of connections, or money, so he continues to languish behind bars, his health deteriorating.

When I visited Bazar-Korgon one February day eight months after Suleimanov's murder, the whole town appeared to float on a sea of mud, dotted here and there by islands of grayish snow. Gusts of cold wind blew through glassless windows and doorless doorways of the many burned and ruined buildings. There were entire streets filled with these charred ghosts of homes and shops. If there were any municipal efforts to rebuild the town, they were not immediately visible. Askarov's paintings were stacked up haphazardly in a damp basement collecting dust. On a forlorn central avenue, not far from the statue of Lenin, stood the town's most recent sculpture: a gilded bust of Maktybek Suleimanov.

CHAPTER 8 *Our Son of a Bitch?*

*T*ashkent Regional Courthouse is a gray box of a building set off from the sidewalk by a tall metal fence. The courthouse overlooks a busy thoroughfare populated by tiny, locally made cars that look as if their drivers are wearing them like oversized raincoats instead of driving them. On a steamy morning in July of 2010, a group of women in brightly colored traditional clothes waited in front of the court. They fanned themselves with sheaves of papers, whispered to one another, and watched the padlocked gate guarded by a skinny cop in a teal uniform and the kind of cylindrical, short-billed hat once favored by Charles de Gaulle. Whenever the cop turned the key in the lock, the women mobbed the gate, begging to be allowed inside. Somewhere in the bowels of the courthouse were their sons, husbands, and brothers, all defendants in yet another in a long string of dubious trials that have come to define Uzbekistan—Central Asia's strategic linchpin, and once again a key American ally in the Afghanistan war.

In this case, the defendants were accused of following the teachings of Said Nursi, a Turkish Islamic scholar (dead for half a century) who tackled, among other things, Islam's eternal preoccupation of how to reconcile itself with modernity and secular governance. In a lot of places, reading his stuff isn't a problem—a prominent Nursi disciple has lived openly in Pennsylvania for years—but in Uzbekistan such literature runs afoul of an elaborate system of detention and repression in which security forces maintain an iron grip on the frightened population, critical voices are eliminated, and criminal charges are routinely invented— even as the country cultivates closer ties with the West. While the Uzbek regime is particularly vigilant when it comes to observant Muslims, it punishes enemies from all walks of public life: culture, business, journalism, politics.

Back in the courthouse that July morning, things didn't look good for the Nursi defendants awaiting trial. By one estimate, Uzbek courts had handed down more than two hundred Nursi-related convictions in the previous two years alone. And that figure doesn't include many other alleged conspiracies unraveled by Uzbek security forces. Sentences of up to ten years are common. When convicts enter the prison system, bad things tend to happen to them.

"They are being forced to rape one another," Dilorom Mirzayeva, who sells onions at a bazaar outside Tashkent, told me a few days before this latest Nursi trial. Her brother, a taxi driver, was arrested in 2000 for allegedly belonging to another banned Islamic group. A key piece of evidence against him, she said, were two leaflets planted by police on a bookshelf. He got twelve years. Mirzayeva, who visits him in jail every three months, told me that guards often handcuff her brother, string him up on a wall, and beat him until he passes out. In one recent session, his skull was cracked, and for weeks the wound festered with blood and pus.

You don't have to look very hard to find similar stories, usually recounted by women who have written stacks of appeals and complaints over the years. Male relatives of detainees are more reluctant to talk, perhaps out of fear that a similar fate will befall them. In a small Tashkent apartment covered with ornate rugs, Klara Alimova, the mother of another longtime inmate, told me prison enforcers sodomized her son with a baton and electrocuted him. Alimova feared that when his fifteen-year sentence runs out in 2014, authorities would tack on another few years— a common tactic to keep some inmates incarcerated indefinitely, according to local human-rights activists. They call it a "spin-out."

The iron gate in front of the Tashkent Regional Courthouse creaked open, and the relatives of the Nursi defendants scrambled to get in. Although it was an open trial, not everyone was allowed to attend. An Uzbek colleague and I, the only two journalists, were banned. The younger brother of a defendant named Jasur Hassanov was turned away from the gate without explanation. Angry, he fished out a crumpled pack of cigarettes from his breast pocket, lit one up, and said he didn't understand what his brother's crime was. A veteran defense lawyer familiar with the case later told me it was hopeless: "The trial is just a formality. It will follow the prosecutor's script." The case hinged on the fact that all the defendants were observant Muslims and had once attended Turkish-funded schools in Uzbekistan, and some knew each other and bought furniture together. From this, a massive Nursi conspiracy was extrapolated. Within days, Hassanov, thirty-one, would be sentenced to five years in prison.

"The jails are overcrowded, they are bursting at the seams," the lawyer, who pleaded to remain anonymous, continued. "It's painful to watch when innocent people go to jail, but there's nothing I can do to change this."

Uzbekistan has one of the most repressive political systems in the world, but these days the country's strongman, Islam Karimov, is back in Washington's good graces. In the immediate aftermath of 9/11, Karimov became a friend of convenience to America: his country, located on Afghanistan's northern border, was an ideal platform for launching the invasion to oust the Taliban. The Pentagon set up a military base inside Uzbekistan. Yet by 2005, Iraq had edged out Afghanistan from the top of America's foreign-policy priorities, and it became harder for the West to put up with the odious regime in Tashkent. In May of that year, Uzbek security forces killed hundreds of protesters in the town of Andijan. As we saw earlier in the book, the scale of the massacre was such that Washington and the European Union could no longer ignore Karimov's abuses. They demanded an independent investigation. Karimov told them to get lost. The Uzbeks evicted the Americans from the air base. The Europeans slapped Uzbekistan with an arms embargo and a visa ban against key officials.

But now, a few years after Andijan, with Afghanistan returning to the top of America's foreign-policy agenda, Washington reversed course again and began to court Uzbekistan as a major ally. In effect, Washington rehabilitated the wily Uzbek strongman because it needed his country as a warehouse one more time. For much of the fitful, decade-long conflict, American military planners resupplied U.S. troops deployed in Afghanistan by truck convoys running through Pakistani territory. The route was always treacherous, ensnared in the vagaries of the broader U.S.-Pakistani relations. Those relations nosedived in the political fallout over the U.S. killing of Osama bin Laden in his home near Islamabad. They were further battered by American air strikes on Pakistani territory. To retaliate and hit the Americans where it hurt, Pakistani officials occasionally shut down the Afghan resupply route, snarling the complex logistical dance required to keep the war going. To reduce dependency on fickle Pakistan, Washington began ramping up traffic along an alternate network of supply lines running through post-Soviet Central Asia, the so-called Northern Distribution Network. Uzbekistan is an essential node in that network. The northern route will play a big role as the United States begins the massive task of winding down its military presence in Afghanistan. Spotting an opportunity, Karimov took full advantage of this realignment. And suddenly America and Uzbekistan were friends once again, human rights be damned.

It is a remarkable turnaround, considering how broken the relationship was after Andijan. Following the massacre and the onset of a cold war with the West, Karimov resolved to profit from his pariah status. He needed to recalibrate his big-power relationships anyway. The Uzbeks had grown worried about the wave of color revolutions that unseated long-time rulers in Georgia, Ukraine, and even right next door in Kyrgyzstan. Those rulers succumbed to homegrown opposition movements, but Washington's democracy promotion (the rhetoric and funds alike) clearly helped. Karimov needed friends he could do business with without fear of subversion. He found them in Moscow and Beijing, where foreign policy doesn't include democracy promotion. It must be said that Karimov remains deeply suspicious of Russian influence in the former Soviet Union, and enjoys snubbing Moscow and flirting with the Americans from time to time, especially when there's money to be made. To paraphrase the Americans' take on a long-dead Nicaraguan dictator ("He may be a son of a bitch, but he's our son of a bitch"), Karimov is no one's son of a bitch but his own.

During the post-Andijan divorce from the West, Karimov mopped up the meager remnants of a civil society and opposition that managed to survive a decade of purges. In 2005, Sanjar Umarov, a prominent Uzbek businessman who once supplied oil products to the American military base, had the misfortune of launching something called the Sunshine Coalition, a secular opposition group. Here was a wealthy man with connections up and down Uzbekistan who thought he could challenge the regime. Karimov dealt with him the same way Vladimir Putin dealt with Mikhail Khodorkovsky, the politically ambitious oligarch jailed since 2003. Uzbek prosecutors unearthed a litany of alleged violations in Umarov's businesses, including money laundering, and packed him off to prison for fourteen years. "The field has been cleared of dissidents, no one even opens his mouth anymore," says Galima Bukharbayeva, a prominent Uzbek journalist who runs Uznews.net from Berlin (access is blocked in Uzbekistan).

There are some survivors. Surat Ikramov is an energetic man with salt-and-pepper hair whose voice has been polished to a velvety baritone by decades of chain-smoking. One afternoon, I met him in the courtyard of a Tashkent hospital where he'd gone for some injections and a regular checkup. Little pink scars were visible on his neck, marking the spots where doctors grafted new veins after he suffered a stroke. At sixty-five, he's also had two heart attacks, and there are stents propping up veins in his heart. Ikramov sat on a blue bench, his shirt unbuttoned down to his chest, and puffed on a cigarette in defiance of doctors' orders. For nearly a decade, Ikramov has chronicled the regime's abuses, large and small, and he's done so with a stubborn consistency even as many other critics vanished into exile or jail, or simply chose to shut up.

Ikramov is a human-rights defender, a calling that combines legal advocacy, muckraking journalism, psychological counseling, and, perhaps most importantly, a strong sense of moral outrage. He works from a cramped apartment in a Tashkent low-rise. There are thick binders of case files lined up on shelves and an old clunky desktop computer in the corner. That's where he composes his dispatches and e-mails them out to a list of recipients that includes diplomats, journalists, human-rights groups, and even officials in the Uzbek government. Ikramov, who attends trials, reads indictments, and talks to victims, doesn't pull punches. In a dispatch marking the fifth anniversary of the Andijan massacre, he called it "one of the most horrible crimes of the Karimov regime," one that remains "uninvestigated and unpunished." Ikramov went on to write that since then, "the human-rights situation has deteriorated; there are more illegal arrests, indictments, and trials on fabricated charges in religious and political cases. The charges are not proven, and almost every suspect talks in court about being subjected to torture and beatings to force a confession."

This is pretty strong stuff in a country where a typical newspaper front page features a story about a factory that "can produce 5 million pairs of technical gloves a month" (*Pravda of the East*, July 24, 2010).

Ikramov, a Soviet-trained engineer, stumbled into the human-rights field by accident. In the 1990s he launched a small business printing textbooks and visual aids for schools. When a state-owned factory ruined his custom-made mold, he sued, lost, and got angry. The printing business fell apart. He sought help from human-rights defenders and eventually founded his own outfit. Though it bears the grand title Initiative Group of Independent Human-Rights Defenders of Uzbekistan, of which Ikramov is chairman, it is essentially a one-man shop. One associate is a bazaar merchant who once challenged Karimov for presidency, a move that terrified the merchant's wife but achieved no other result. One morning in 2003, while moonlighting as a cab driver, Ikramov was snatched from his car by a group of men, driven out into the sticks, beaten, packed into a burlap sack, and dumped in a ditch, presumably to suffocate. Ikramov survived, declined foreign-asylum offers, and dug in for the long haul. I recently read through an archive of his dispatches and was struck by the range and depth of the abuses he has chronicled. Alongside the grimly repetitive allegations of torture, complete with dates, names, places, and methods, Ikramov has exposed government mistreatment of ordinary people: farmers, businessmen, people utterly removed from politics or religion. It's the kind of work that's usually done by newspapers, but few people do that in Uzbekistan anymore.

One summer morning, I went to Samarkand to check out an Ikramov dispatch. The road to Samarkand, an ancient Silk Road hub and Karimov's birthplace, ran past mounds of watermelons, buckets of apples, and frequent police checkpoints. Cops clung to the highway as if their lives depended on it, and in a way they did. Payoffs from speeding motorists padded their incomes, and they aimed their radars with merciless precision. We got pulled over twice within an hour, and each time my driver followed a prescribed ritual: he reached for a wad of cash in the glove compartment, hopped out of the car, and shook the hand of the approaching cop with vigor. They looked almost happy to see each other, like two old friends reunited by the side of the road. The matter settled, the driver gunned the engine again. Every twenty miles or so, the road narrowed into a single lane of traffic crawling through police checkpoints. Clumps of officers in green uniforms peered at the drivers and their passengers, trying to spot those worthy of a more thorough inspection.

They call Uzbekistan a police state for a reason. Jokes about the multitude of cops on the streets are legion. An Uzbek stand-up comedian captured the issue in a skit on Russian television (such an indignity would never be allowed in Uzbekistan). In the skit, people from different countries wear their national dress, and the Uzbek comedian shows up in a police uniform, dangling a baton. (A brief note on language: in Russian, the word *ment* is derogatory slang for a cop.) When asked by the host where he is from, the comedian answers, "Tash-Ment," mispronouncing the name of Uzbekistan's capital, Tashkent. "And this is our national dress."

With a few hours to spare in Samarkand, I went to see Registan, an imposing medieval ensemble of mosques, minarets, and courtyards arrayed around a plaza. I was there for about five minutes when a cop with a knife approached me. He smiled as he twiddled the knife. A little worried, I noticed intricate engravings on the blade. He asked me where I was from and then whispered a business proposition: for the equivalent of a couple of dollars he'd let me climb one of the tall minarets. "It's a good deal," he said. It did seem a like a decent deal, especially when bro-

Samarkand, Uzbekistan. (© Philip Shishkin)

kered by a cop with a knife. I haggled the price down a little and accepted the offer. I gave him the money. He whipped out a mobile phone and speed-dialed another cop. He told him something in Uzbek. "We found a sucker," I assumed he said. The minaret racket was smooth. I could see this other policeman milling about near the entrance to the minaret about a hundred yards away. He waved at me. I walked over, and he pointed toward a small door behind him. I bent down and went in.

In the courtyard on the other side, a wedding reception was taking place. A local Tajik girl was marrying a Frenchman. There were flutes of champagne. I wasn't supposed to be there, but the access to the minaret also bought me access to the courtyard. One of the guests told me he felt a little odd drinking alcohol in a medieval complex of mosques and religious schools. He offered me a glass of champagne from a large silver tray. I saw no good reason to decline. Upon further reflection, he concluded he'd rather have it this way than the Taliban way.

I climbed my minaret on a spiral stone stairway. Early evening light streamed in through slits in the exterior wall. At the very top of the stairs, I poked my head through an opening under the conical roof that caps the tower, and next thing I knew I had a wraparound view of the city, the mountains in the distance, and a dazzling mosaic of two orange tigers walking across the top of an azure arch of the Registan. The Tash-Ment deal paid off. But I had work to do, so I climbed down reluctantly.

The Ikramov dispatch that brought me to Samarkand began with a typically direct headline: "Arbitrary actions, raiding, and theft of property by government officials." The case concerned a family of Samarkand entrepreneurs who built an outdoor market in a partnership with a local governor. The governor solicited and received a bribe to expedite the necessary approvals, the family said. Once the market started operating, the local governor's office reversed itself and ordered it closed, a decision that coincided with the Uzbek prime minister's visit to the area, Ikramov wrote. Criminal charges against the family of entrepreneurs followed. They included theft, fraud, and—in the case of Abdumalik Sapayev, a key investor—even storage of illegal drugs, a charge based on a pinch of opium planted by police, the family maintained. Sapayev was sentenced to six years in prison. Some bazaar buildings were destroyed, and "ten trucks took the construction materials to another market that the governor was going to build," Ikramov wrote in his dispatch.

At an outdoor café in Samarkand, I talked to Abdumalik Sapayev's son, Farkhad, a stern young man of few words. He gave me a crumpled photocopy of a suicide note written by his uncle, who also invested in the doomed bazaar and faced charges. In the note, the uncle blamed the local governor for what he was about to do and asked his oldest son to take care of the younger siblings; then, three days after his fiftieth birthday, he hanged himself in his bedroom. In response to my queries, the local governor's office said that "all these accusations are groundless" and that the Sapayev family's "guilt was fully proven in court." At the same café, over a massive plate of kebabs, I met the Sapayevs' lawyer, an intense former policeman who said he had quit the force more than a decade ago because he was tired of fabricating cases. He scrutinized every page of my passport and asked me if I was a member of an intelligence service. Then, in hushed tones, pausing every time the waiter swung by with more meat, the lawyer told me he'd handled more than a hundred cases since coming over from the dark side. "There are no acquittals—if they start a criminal case, there will be a conviction," he said.

The bazaar saga is a good illustration of how Uzbek functionaries, from imperious village *hokims* all the way up to officials in the central government, approach private enterprise. For many of them, it's a way to make money or reward their cronies with juicy concessions. The minute a particular company steps out of line or begins to compete with a firm enjoying patronage of a higher caliber or otherwise irks the government, it starts to face all sorts of problems. When government minders wanted to squeeze a British investor out of a lucrative gold-mining venture, they filed espionage charges against one of its employees. When a Russian cell-phone service provider stepped on some toes, regulators yanked its license and left millions of its Uzbek customers with dead mobile phones. Courts are useless in these disputes, as they always side with the government. The Samarkand bazaar battle eventually landed in court, where the former owners promptly lost. In desperation, Farkhad, the son of one of the jailed proprietors, reached out to Ikramov, whose name he found on the Internet.

Ikramov says he picks his cases carefully and gets involved only after he's convinced that the petitioners really have been wronged. Sometimes, he says, his dispatches trigger official inquiries. The mother of one detainee told me her son received better treatment in prison after Ikramov wrote about his case. But mostly, the dispatches seem to channel the collective frustration of a people unable to trust its courts, its government, or its police. Ikramov doesn't charge for his services, having subsisted for years on Western donations, including small grants from the U.S. embassy. A pro-government website accused him of painting a deliberately dark picture of Uzbekistan to keep his "sponsors" happy.

When I last saw him, Ikramov was facing a defamation suit in the case of the strange death of a famous Uzbek singer. According to the official version, she hanged herself. But Ikramov suggested she may have been murdered, and implicated the family of the singer's boyfriend—who just happened to be a brother of the powerful interior minister. Ikramov seemed to be relishing the looming court fight. He likes a good argument.

At the hospital where I went to see him one morning, he'd just managed to pick a fight with the staff who asked patients to repark their cars ahead of a visit by some government commission. Ikramov refused to move his car, a small victory of parking dissidence. There it sat by the side of a lane in the hospital courtyard, proudly alone.

Despite his pesky persistence, the Uzbek government allows him to operate relatively freely, although Ikramov reports frequent surveillance. My guess is the government sees him as harmless in the larger scheme of things, a lone voice whose dispatches may tug at some overly sensitive Western hearts without much effect on the domestic political situation. In the context of the U.S.-Uzbek rapprochement, Ikramov became a useful prop for both sides. When Uzbek leaders caught the ritual flak from the West for eliminating dissent, they could always point to Ikramov and say, "Hey, what about him? He's out there writing nasty dispatches about us, and no one touches him." And visiting American dignitaries could take a break from schmoozing the Uzbek regime and stop by Ikramov's cramped home office for a quick human-rights/civil-society pulse check. None of this is to detract from the importance and quality of Ikramov's solitary campaigns.

Ikramov appeared both frustrated and guardedly hopeful about Karimov's return to the West's embrace. By all accounts, Karimov hadn't changed a single thing since Andijan, but here he was being courted and called an important ally all over again. When I asked Ikramov what he thought of the rapprochement, he said, after a moment's pause, "Karimov won." But then he went on to lay out a more nuanced answer. Although the West's break with Karimov satisfied human-rights advocates, it did little to advance human rights in Uzbekistan. European sanctions proved toothless—enough to be annoying, but not enough to actually hurt. The American military departure mattered even less for the Uzbek regime.

The ensuing rapprochement may not have moved the dial on human rights in general, but it did help at least one actual human. Sanjar Umarov, the jailed founder of the Sunshine Coalition, was freed in 2009, after U.S. officials urged the Uzbeks to let him go on humanitarian grounds. Sick and psychologically shaken, Umarov joined his family in Tennessee.

His release raised hopes that reengagement might prod Karimov to open his jails at least a crack, in the same way that the Soviet Union and China used jailed dissidents as strategic bargaining chips with the West. The Uzbek regime certainly had enough such chips behind bars. "There are so many good people in prison—the best businessmen, writers, journalists, human-rights defenders, religious thinkers," Ikramov told me. "It's important to try to free them. Even if one person comes out of jail, that's already something." Ikramov quoted an Uzbek saying: "It's like digging a well with a needle."

On a particularly hot day in July of 2010, Michael McFaul, a director on the National Security Council and the author of *Advancing Democracy Abroad: Why We Should and How We Can*, stopped by Ikramov's home office to talk human rights. (McFaul is now the U.S. ambassador to Russia.) Within minutes, electricity to the apartment was cut off and air-conditioners whirred to a stop. A retinue of U.S. officials, including the ambassador, sweated profusely in their suits, Ikramov recalled. The timing of the power cut, he says, was "an interesting coincidence."

A few days later, I went to see the father of Erkin Musaev, a former Uzbek military officer who had once served as the Defense Ministry's point man for dealing with the American military contingent in Uzbekistan. In 2006, a few months after the Americans got the boot, Musaev was detained in the Tashkent airport as he was about to board a regional flight. Musaev, who by then worked on a UN counter-narcotics project, was told that sniffer dogs had smelled drugs in his luggage. Customs officials found a computer disk in the outer pocket of his checked suitcase—a disk Musaev said he'd never seen—and booked him for being an American spy. The case ballooned to include outlandish insinuations, Musaev wrote in a detailed account of his detention that he passed on to his family. Investigators threatened to cast him as an American-paid organizer of the Andijan uprising, another dubious, catchall charge that's been used to imprison a lot of people in Uzbekistan.

In the same account, Musaev described several types of torture used against him. In a technique called Northern Lights, Musaev was sat on a stool and repeatedly hit on the head. "At first, you feel a terrible headache, then you see everything in red as if blood is pouring down your eyes, then you see black-and-white stripes. After a while it seems that your entire body has moved into your head, and your head hurts like hell. With that, you feel that your soul wants to break free of your body, and you want to help it [by tearing the body apart], but you don't feel your body." His torturers, Musaev wrote, came from the ranks of seasoned criminals, a setup also described by other detainees subjected to torture in Uzbekistan's jails. (This approach to outsourcing torture was perfected in the Soviet Union's prison camps, where guards often sicced common criminals on dissidents in exchange for prison perks.) Musaev signed a forced confession and was sentenced to fifteen years for treason.

Musaev's father, Haidjan, is a slight man of eighty. When I saw him, he wore a light blue shirt and an Uzbek square black hat with a white embroidered edge. A university professor, Haidjan served apples, cookies, and tea as he pulled paper after paper from his son's long case file. Just that morning, Haidjan had gone to the headquarters of the State Security Service, a regular pilgrimage, to deliver yet another letter, this one comparing Uzbekistan of today to the Soviet Union of 1937, the darkest year of Stalin's purges. Meanwhile, his son kept drifting farther and farther into the archipelago of the Uzbek prison system. In 2011, he was transferred to a remote jail where his mistreatment became so elaborate that he was tortured right in the medical tent as the doctor looked on, he told his family.

Over the years, inmates and their relatives mapped out Uzbekistan's prison archipelago, charting islands known for relative leniency as well as those where survival is unlikely. No place in the system is more dreaded than the Jaslyk prison, located in the harsh steppes of northern Uzbekistan where winter chills reach arctic level, and the summer heat turns the place into a furnace. Prison minders have used the temperature extremes wisely to augment the range of torture possibilities. When inmates die, prison authorities sometimes refuse to hand over their bodies to their families for burial, in an apparent attempt to hide evidence of mutilation.

"His battered hands were cold and had no fingernails. He couldn't even hold a spoon in his hands. He didn't speak a word," wrote the wife of one Jaslyk inmate after visiting him in jail. The note eventually reached Sergey Ignatyev, an artist who grew up in Tashkent and now lives in Miami.

One day, he came across a trove of Uzbek inmates' letters and family testimonials collected by a Central Asian human-rights group. Many of them were scribbled in feverish, barely legible handwriting on scraps of paper folded many times over. Relatives smuggled those messages out of prison, if they were lucky enough to avoid getting caught by overzealous guards. One inmate was denied family visits for ten years but was finally allowed to see his ailing mother, who was by then in her eighties. Since he couldn't rely on her failing memory to carry his words to the rest of the family, the inmate scrawled a brief note right on his mother's bare leg, above the knee. The guards later searched her and found the note. They rubbed it off with a rag. Unable to recall its contents, the mother was crushed. As Ignatyev read the letters and family accounts, he was so shaken up that he distilled all their hopelessness into a series of impressionistic paintings.

The Jaslyk inmate, whose hands, stripped of fingernails, felt so deathly cold to his wife's touch, gave rise to a painting called *Wings*. In it, two raw, reddish hands rest on a woman's back, in what appears to be a farewell embrace. Another inmate wrote this: "Life in a cage is difficult not because you lose your physical freedom but because your body eventually loses all traces of humanity." So Ignatyev painted *Cage*, in which another reddish-raw human frame is stuffed into a birdcage, knees to chin, head downcast, all morphing into a shapeless blob. *Dream* shows an emaciated body rising out of a black hole of a barred window and stretching skyward like a wisp of smoke. One letter that stayed with Ignatyev for a long time contained an inmate's plea to his family to stop praying for him. He wanted to die, he wrote, and those prayers kept him alive.

In the summer of 2012, an Uzbek pop singer made her American debut with a fourteen-track album recorded in English and available on iTunes. Jazzed up with electronic dance beats, the songs sound as if they were assembled by a computer programmed to channel a teenage girl of limited imagination, then Google-translated into English. The unremarkable voice strains to break through the music, and when it succeeds, it delivers the following snippets of wisdom: "Time flies, and you'll just have to chase it"; "I'll take my fate before it's too late"; "I wish I could fly";

A painting called *Dream* by Sergey Ignatyev. (Courtesy of Sergey Ignatyev)

"How dare you be so different?" Lest unsuspecting listeners misjudge the album as something violently mediocre, the artist's promotional materials herald the arrival of a "poet, mezzo soprano, designer and exotic Uzbekistan beauty." The genesis of the lyrics is also explained: "From her desire for self-expression came her poems. From her poems came the music."

And from her father's stranglehold on Uzbekistan came the money to enable this nonsense. The singer in question is Gulnara Karimova, the president's eldest daughter and the lead character in a drama that has convulsed Uzbekistan's elites for years. In her American music debut, Gulnara makes no mention of her pedigree, preferring to call herself by a single stage name, Googoosha, imitating first-name-only stars like

Madonna, Rihanna, and Lady Gaga, to all of whom she compares herself. Googoosha even hired Lady Gaga's DJ to remix one of her tracks. "Love Lady Gaga?" her official Twitter account asked, in a flurry of self-aggrandizing messages. "Follow @realgoogoosha now to check out exotic pop sensation GOOGOOSHA!"

Plenty of presidential offspring indulge in hedonistic pursuits, but Gulnara is not just another entitled airhead, despite Googoosha's best efforts to look and sound like one. She's a tough woman who was once believed to control the most lucrative chunks of the Uzbek economy through a shadowy firm that gobbled up rivals with the same ruthlessness her father showed in politics. Gulnara first attained international notoriety with her 2001 divorce from an Afghan American entrepreneur who controlled a Coca-Cola bottling company in Uzbekistan. Through much of the 1990s, while the couple were married, Coke enjoyed the smoothest of rides in Uzbekistan, easily edging out its archrival Pepsi. Within weeks of the divorce, however, Coke's fortunes changed. "Karimova's response was extreme and vicious," the ex-husband, Mansur Maqsudi, said in a lawsuit.[1]

Uzbek intelligence agents raided the company's offices in Tashkent, seized documents, and harassed employees, he claimed. Then, as he seethed helplessly in New Jersey, Uzbek authorities stripped him of Coke ownership and handed the bottler on a silver platter to a company called Zeromax, a Swiss-registered conglomerate with deep reported ties to Gulnara. He accused her of "kidnapping" the couple's two children from their New Jersey home and fleeing with them to Tashkent. She accused him of bullying and distorting the facts. An American court initially sided with Mansur, which meant Gulnara could be arrested if she set foot on U.S. soil again. A few years later, the estranged couple reached a settlement, with Gulnara retaining custody of the children and Mansur dropping his lawsuit. The deal freed Gulnara to grace America again with the fruits of her creative labors without fear of arrest.

Meanwhile in Uzbekistan, Gulnara controlled a sprawling business empire. Zeromax, the Swiss-registered behemoth, got its start as a pet project of a notorious Uzbek crime boss. According to several lawsuits, interviews with Uzbek businesspeople, and leaked U.S. diplomatic cables,

Gulnara sidelined the crime boss and took over Zeromax. The Harvard-educated Gulnara, who has served as the Uzbek ambassador to Switzerland and Spain, always denied she had anything to do with the firm, but few people took those denials seriously.

In its heyday, Zeromax had its fingers in every pie of Uzbekistan's economy, including gas, oil, cotton, gold, construction, and pretty much anything else that smelled like money. "Zeromax was like a cancer on Uzbekistan's economy," one Uzbek entrepreneur who frequently dealt with the company told me in Tashkent. Negotiating with the company was tough because commercial disputes often led Zeromax managers to invoke a higher power: "Don't you know who we are working with?" The Uzbek entrepreneur continued, "It was an outfit custom-made to feed certain families." Zeromax's business model was beautifully simple: identify a lucrative industry and either take it over entirely or take a cut. Tax agents, the police, and the courts provided crucial backup. For instance, when a British-controlled gold-mining company faced harassment from the government, it sold a fifth of its shares to Zeromax, and its problems disappeared.

Through much of the last decade, Zeromax was pulling in so much cash that it splurged on a soccer team. One evening in Tashkent, I went to see it in action. Down the street from a noisy bazaar, floodlights carved out a green rectangle from the surrounding twilight, and Tashkent's soccer miracle came to life again. Spectators shuffled up to their seats coated in a thick layer of dust. Cigarette smoke settled over the stands in a motionless haze. Music blared from the speakers. Fans chanted the name of the home team—Bunyodkor—and swayed to a drumbeat. Bunyodkor was not just another soccer team. Zeromax brought in Luiz Felipe Scolari, the legendary coach who had taken the Brazilian national squad to the 2002 World Cup victory.

At the stadium, Bunyodkor's players, dressed in blue, ran out to the field through a red sieve in the middle of the stands. Their opponent that evening was Nasaf, a club from a remote desert area near the border with Afghanistan. The audience erupted with applause. Bunyodkor's lineup included two Brazilians and a gangly Serb. Another Brazilian—the 2002 World Cup winner Rivaldo—was sitting out the match because of an injury. A camera picked out his gaunt and aging face on the sidelines—at thirty-eight he was past his soccer prime—and beamed it to a large display, much to the delight of the spectators. In 2008, Rivaldo abruptly broke off his contract with a Greek club after Bunyodkor made him "an extremely tempting contract offer" rumored to be in excess of $10 million. The boards around the field carried the names of the club's sponsors: Zeromax and a clutch of affiliated firms.

Nasaf couldn't match this star power, but got an early chance with a pretty one-timer that hit Bunyodkor's crossbar. A pudgy man to my right gasped and lit another slender cigarette. A graveyard of flattened butts was growing under his seat. I felt like I was chain-smoking with him. Bunyodkor often dominated the Uzbek competition in a lopsided, Zeromax-bankrolled show of force. Nasaf held on for about ten minutes until a slow, long ball somehow slipped past its goaltender. A stocky Brazilian striker named Denilson scored a header minutes later. By half time, it was 2–0.

In the second half, Nasaf got steamrolled. Bunyodkor's Serbian striker scored a hat trick and celebrated by jumping up and down and then stretching out on his back. The fans loved it. Two drunk middle-aged guys were up on their feet behind me, screaming for more goals. It was a dry stadium so they must have gotten tanked before the game. One of them soon lost his voice. The other descended into a jolly stream of profanities centering on the sexual orientation of the players. Two cops led him away. Hundreds of cigarettes had been smoked, gallons of warm Coke drunk, bags of sunflower seeds husked and eaten. It was 5–0 at the end of the game, and Bunyodkor marched on.

In a strange twist in 2010, Zeromax was effectively dismantled, and its mercurial chief, rumored to be Gulnara's moneyman, was briefly detained. One theory behind its demise suggested that Zeromax got too big and corrupt for its own good, and crossed some powerful enemies jostling for influence within Uzbekistan. Another story was that Zeromax accumulated huge debts from its business dealings with Russian companies, and the regime didn't want that kind of liability. A related theory is that Zeromax simply outlived its usefulness to its political backers, who had found other ways of making money. What really happened may never be known—such are the opaque ways of Uzbek politics and business.

Zeromax's demise had an immediate effect on Bunyodkor. First, the golden boys lost Scolari, their star coach. He hightailed it from Uzbekistan six months before his contract was due to expire, diplomatically citing "certain issues" that "have arisen between me and the club." Rivaldo, one of the best-known soccer players in the world, eventually came to regret coming to Uzbekistan. He claimed that Bunyodkor stiffed him out of millions of dollars in salary. "I am sorry it has come to this as I love Uzbekistan and have many close friends there," Rivaldo told a sports website. "I had great plans. But regrettably it amounted to a string of broken promises and I feel incredibly let down."

Once seen as the éminence grise of Uzbek business and a possible candidate to succeed her father as president, Gulnara appears to have distanced herself from the political machinations in Tashkent. Instead, she embraced a jet-setting lifestyle on the international glamour circuit. In addition to Googoosha, she spawned another alter ego, Guli, under which she designs jewelry and clothes with characteristic understatement. Her Guli website says this in broken English: "It is impossible to disregard, the fact, that the founder of these creative collections is a political scientist whose basic education far, at first sight, from design. Having a Harvard Degree (MA) she has received the degree of a doctor of political sciences, professor."

The professor's attempt to infiltrate New York's Fashion Week was derailed when human-rights activists pressured the organizers to cancel her scheduled catwalk show in 2011. Gulnara held the event in a restaurant instead. Whether she calls herself Guli or Googoosha, it's hard for Gulnara to erase her father's big shadow. It's a sore subject for her and her younger sister Lola, another jet-setting philanthropist. When a French website called Lola a "dictator's daughter," Lola sued for defamation in a French court. The court sided with the website. Sometimes, the dictator slurs are even more annoying because they come from people who have no problem taking money from Gulnara. A couple of years ago, Gulnara invited British pop idol Sting to perform in Tashkent. Sting sang, and a British tabloid headlined: "Sting Plays Concert for Daughter of 'Boil-

Your-Enemies' Dictator." In response, Sting conceded that Karimov was "hermetically sealed in his own medieval, tyrannical mindset."

One summer evening in Uzbekistan, Gulnara lashed out at her critics during an outdoor publicity event stacked with admirers. She took a moment to compliment herself on her good looks. "I thank God that he endowed me with my height, my face, my features," she said. "And I thank God that even those who stoop very low in their attacks cannot deprive me of the things that God painted on my face."

In recent years, Uzbek officials hired high-powered lawyers and lobbyists to pretty up the regime's own face in Washington, a job made easier by Washington's willingness to overlook quite a few things for the sake of the Northern Distribution Network.

On a rainy October afternoon in 2010, a typical Washington crowd of men in ill-fitting suits poured into a think-tank conference room to hear out two high-ranking Uzbek officials. The officials were in town to promote Uzbekistan as a beacon of Central Asian stability and to offer advice on securing Afghanistan, the Uzbek regime's big new foreign-policy push. The gathering at the Atlantic Council was sponsored by FMN Logistics, a well-connected American firm that has profited from Washington's decision to open the Uzbek route for Afghanistan supplies. FMN, which says it has delivered more shipments to Afghanistan than any other freight forwarder, has a curious pedigree: it's run by Harry Eustace Jr., whose father helped launch the notorious Zeromax—he was "present at the birth," his LinkedIn bio says. When I reached the younger Eustace in Washington, he told me FMN was in "no way connected to Gulnara." Whatever the case, the firm appears closest to the till when it comes to cashing in on the U.S.-Uzbek rapprochement and the Northern Distribution Network. The looming withdrawal of U.S. troops from Afghanistan, and the massive logistical exercise that will accompany it, will provide a bonanza to companies like FMN.

At the FMN-bankrolled confab in Washington, the Uzbek dignitaries took softball questions from the audience and ignored an occasional query on domestic repression. "The process of forming the civil society in Uzbekistan is going on, and it will be stronger and stronger," said Sodiq Safaev, chairman of the Uzbek Senate's Committee on Foreign

Affairs. A few hours later in Tashkent, a court ordered one of the few remaining members of that civil society—a journalist named Abdumalik Boboyev—to pay a $9,000 fine for spreading lies about Uzbekistan. His crime was writing articles that went a little deeper than *Pravda*'s chronicles of glove production.

Eager to ingratiate themselves with Karimov, American officials have been lapping up the Uzbek propaganda and regurgitating it. For years, President Karimov bristled at what he saw as the West's sanctimonious outbursts on human rights, and he had no problem reminding the Americans of what was at stake. In a 2009 meeting with the U.S. ambassador, the Uzbek strongman, "alternately angry, cajoling, mocking and wise," fumed about the State Department's decision to give a human-rights award to an Uzbek activist despised by the regime. Describing the activist as a "swindler," Karimov talked up Uzbekistan's importance for the Northern Distribution Network and urged America not to jeopardize that relationship. The U.S. envoy got the message: "Pressuring him, especially publicly, could cost us transit [rights for Afghanistan]," the ambassador, Richard Norland, wrote back to headquarters.[2] Months later, Washington resumed military aid to the Uzbek government, which had been suspended after the Andijan massacre.

U.S. officials have given the Uzbek leader a free pass on a lot of things, including his stewardship of the Uzbek economy. At a 2010 business forum held at the stately white-brick Washington mansion that houses the Uzbek embassy, a senior U.S. official said that Uzbekistan "weathered the global economic downturn well and continues to have solid economic growth," an interesting observation to make about a Soviet-style economy where business often succeeds or fails based on its proximity to power—and where farming resembles indentured servitude. In fact, the U.S. official was simply repeating what President Karimov had written in one of his books, which earned an enthusiastic review from the longtime American cheerleader of the Uzbek regime, Harry Eustace of Zeromax fame. "Reading this fine little book can provide valuable insight into Uzbekistan's rock-solid fundamentals and economic policies that will make the country an engine of growth for all of Central Asia," Eustace wrote of the Karimov opus.

On the ground in Uzbekistan, these policies don't always seem so visionary. At the end of a rutted dirt road a three-hour drive from Tashkent one day a couple of years ago, I met Amina Kambarova, a short, stout woman who grew cotton on a small plot of land behind her mud hut. In a typical setup, she leased that land from the state because Uzbekistan restricted private land ownership. There was a catch: each year, Kambarova had to sell the cotton back to the state at a fixed low price. The Uzbek regime then resold the prized commodity on world markets for a lot more. (Zeromax was at one point involved in that trade.) Apparel makers were hungry for cotton, but few of the profits went to the farmers. What's more, the farmers who couldn't meet the state cotton quota had their land confiscated. Not long before we spoke, local authorities had broken off Kambarova's lease, citing her failure to deliver the required amount of cotton. When she protested the quota as artificially high, she was threatened with an eviction to a distant shepherd outpost. Her son was beaten up on the street.

Not far from her plot, I met Nurmamat Yakubov, another farmer who also lost his land for the same reasons. He told me local authorities turned on the water to irrigate his cotton saplings only sporadically, and that better-connected farmers often had a lower quota to meet. Cotton is a notoriously thirsty crop. More alarmingly for scientists, the fecundity of Uzbekistan's soil has been steadily declining because of improper use of fertilizer and intensive cotton farming. The exhausted land yields less cotton, something that is often overlooked in the state quotas. "The soil disagrees with the government plans, and we don't have enough water," Yakubov said.

To avoid the rigid system of Uzbek monopolies, some farmers have taken to smuggling their cotton to neighboring Kazakhstan and Kyrgyzstan, where they can sell it for more. Others survive by planting potatoes, wheat, and other edible crops on the edge of their cotton fields, following the grim logic that even if they don't make any money off the cotton, at least they won't starve.

Kambarova and other dispossessed farmers turned to local human-rights activists for help. "I explained to them that they have to fight back—only then might they win," said Egamnazar Shaimanov, who collected the farmers' complaints. Shaimanov, who also lost his land because he didn't meet the quota, became a conduit for the peasants' grievances, helping them with paperwork and in disputes with local authorities. Under the penname Bitter, Shaimanov also chronicled the farmers' troubles in verse, publishing a collection of poetry called *Why Farmers Drink?* featuring a drawing of a peasant with a hoe in one hand a bottle in the other.

The local courts dismissed the lawsuits of dispossessed farmers, and they took to the narrow, potholed streets of Djizakh under the leadership of Shaimanov, a slight man with gray hair, glasses, and a mustache. Their rally was dispersed, and fights broke out between the landless farmers and assembled young toughs. A few weeks later, several farmers drove to Tashkent and held a small picket here. When they returned, Shaimanov received threats and advice to drop his battle from the local authorities. Several days later, a mob, including strangers and some wealthier farmers, attacked him near his house in front of his wife and children. Bleeding, he fled to Tashkent the same evening. He eventually left the country.

The sudden disappearance of the bruised poet unsettled the dispossessed farmers, who organized another rally, demanding to see their champion and also asking the local authorities to stop the harassment of Kambarova, the farmer who says she was threatened with an eviction. The rally descended into chaos as protesters smashed up the windows in a local government office. Someone set a police car on fire.

The local mayor responsible for the confiscation of land defended his actions, saying he had to follow government regulations on land use. He dismissed the local uprising as the action of a few lazy farmers who couldn't meet quotas, led by that obnoxious rabble-rouser turned poet. "They incurred huge debts," the mayor told me in his office in a decrepit single-story building. "I can show you the papers." He acknowledged there were fights and clashes but denied threatening anyone, encouraging violence, or authorizing evictions.

Kambarova and the others never got their land back. When I talked to her, she kept looking over her shoulder as if expecting more goons to show up. "There's no justice in Uzbekistan," she said.

Uzbekistan's cotton troubles have a long history. In the nineteenth century, Russian imperial planners insisted the Uzbeks ramp up their cotton production to feed the commercial demands of the realm. At the time, Russia was importing a lot of cotton from the United States at a high cost. The newly conquered Central Asian plains, with their arid climate, provided an ideal setting for building a domestic cotton industry. Hundreds of cotton gins sprung up throughout the region. Deeming the local strain of cotton too crude, the Russians introduced an American strain whose longer fibers were better suited to producing fine clothes.

Aided by Russian financial incentives, cotton began to displace traditional food crops grown by local farmers and became the primary cash crop. A senior Russian colonial official "acknowledged bluntly that cotton was 'the central nerve and main point of interest and concern of the local population. At the same time it is also the link connecting Turkestan with Moscow and the rest of Russia.'"[3] Russian engineers built a railway line, in part to facilitate the cotton trade. The Russian push succeeded: in 1860, Central Asia supplied no more than 7 percent of cotton to Russian mills. By 1915, that figure had grown to 70 percent.

The Soviets continued the practice, and the obsession with cotton began to take its toll on the land. "Moscow turned Central Asia into a mega-farm designed to produce ever greater quantities of cotton. To this end irrigation kept being expanded beyond the capacity of Central Asian rivers, the soil exhausted by monoculture kept getting saturated with chemical fertilizers, the crops sprayed by clouds of pesticides and herbicides, and instead of fully mechanizing the production, cheap native labor was routinely used for harvesting the [cotton]," writes Svat Soucek, an eloquent chronicler of Central Asian history.[4] In the waning years of the Soviet Union, fudging cotton-output figures gave rise to a wide-ranging corruption investigation that ensnared high-ranking officials both in Tashkent and in Moscow. The leaders of independent Uzbekistan continued the cursed agricultural model, cracking the whip on farmers like Kambarova to keep producing.

Who might succeed Karimov is a question with no obvious answers. His daughter Gulnara seems to have lost interest and slipped comfortably into an airhead lifestyle abroad. Real power appears to be concentrated in the hands of the country's vast security apparatus. The current extent of the threat militant Islamists pose to Uzbekistan is a matter of some debate. The regime routinely exaggerates that threat to justify its own legitimacy. The government's policy of indiscriminate jailing and torture of alleged Islamists risks turning an extremist threat into a self-fulfilling prophecy. Prisons are incubators of radicalism. Uzbekistan's Islamists may also draw sustenance from another flaw of Uzbekistan's regime: by methodically destroying the secular opposition, the government strengthens the hand of the religious kind. Unlike secular parties, which need leaders, platforms, and some public space to operate, religious groups tend to thrive in decentralized secrecy. There are parallels between Karimov's Uzbekistan and Hosni Mubarak's Egypt, where decades of repressive rule left the Muslim Brotherhood as the single strongest political force in the country.

Unfortunately for the people of Uzbekistan, the story of the Uzbek opposition is one of squabbling, insignificance, and irrelevance—and sometimes of outright farce. Through intimidation, arrests, harassment, and occasional murders, the regime henchmen of course made sure things would be this way—witness the bullying of Sanjar Umarov, the founder of the Sunshine Coalition now living in exile in the United States. More ominously, several antiregime activists have been assassinated abroad in murky circumstances. But some of the opposition's wounds are self-inflicted. They stem from isolation, competing ideologies, and an exaggerated sense of self-worth, all amplified by frustration at being marginalized in Uzbekistan. Karimov must be smiling.

Let's begin with Mohammed Solih, a poet and the godfather of the Uzbek opposition. In the early years of independence, Karimov offered to make him vice president, and then, when the poet refused, had him detained. Solih managed to slip out of the country and has lived in itinerant exile for nearly two decades. He now occupies a small house in the suburban reaches of Istanbul, growing watermelons in his backyard in hopes of replicating the taste of those in Uzbekistan. Chances are Solih isn't going home anytime soon. In 2000, an Uzbek court sentenced him in absentia to fifteen years in prison on charges of terrorism in a trial "reminiscent in all respects of Soviet-era show trials," according to Human Rights Watch.

Solih began a life of wandering abroad, casting himself as the only alternative to Karimov. An international arrest warrant caught up with him on a trip to the Czech Republic, where the fugitive poet was jailed in 2001 while the Czechs studied the Uzbek extradition request. A Czech court soon saw through the charges and set Solih free. Václav Havel, who had once been held in the same prison, met with Solih, two dissident writers trading memories. In a way, Solih foreshadowed his own fate—and that of future Uzbek dissidents—in a 1981 poem called "Tomorrow":

> Tomorrow, we'll definitely be happy
> If today we remain alive.
> Tomorrow, we'll chase down any dream
> If today we succeed in escaping.

This could have been a promising start to a Havel-like dissident career, except Solih's thinking over the years has grown parochial and at times intolerant. Here's one recent gem: "I support a civilized form of isolating gays and other sick people from the society, so they wouldn't contaminate healthy people." Leaning strongly in the Islamist direction, Solih has engaged in a public and increasingly bitter debate with Galima Bukharbayeva, a prominent Uzbek journalist living in exile in Berlin.

Headstrong and outspoken, Bukharbayeva was one of a handful of reporters on the ground in Andijan during the uprising, and she wrote about it in exhaustive, chilling detail. A bullet pierced her backpack during the massacre. Marked by the regime, she left Uzbekistan, settled in Berlin, and founded Uznews.net, an irreverent news portal that made her an influential arbiter of Uzbek public opinion, at least among exiles. As a young, educated woman, Bukharbayeva is a secularist, alarmed by the growing religious sentiment among parts of the opposition. That hasn't endeared her to Solih and his followers.

The simmering animosity boiled over when Solih invited an ethnic Russian human-rights activist from Uzbekistan to visit him in Turkey. In

Istanbul, the activist abruptly converted to Islam, stunning her family and friends back home. When she returned to Tashkent, her family said she acted unhinged, chanting prayers, shouting, "God is great," breaking dishes, and telling her husband not to watch television. She was eventually booked into a psychiatric ward. Having shaken the trance, she suggested she had been drugged into a religious stupor. Solih said he had nothing to do with the activist's temporary insanity. Uznews.net wrote about the bizarre episode at length, accusing Solih of endangering the activist. Anyone meeting with the exiled leader faces extra attention from Uzbek intelligence services.

Meanwhile, the spat between Solih and Bukharbayeva escalated. She accused him of being a threat to democracy and of flirting with Islamism. He responded by accusing her of slander and of "Goebbels-style propaganda against the believers." Bukharbayeva later claimed that a member of Solih's political party e-mailed her images of her face superimposed on pornographic photos.

That two of the most decorated Karimov opponents would be engaging in this kind of rhetoric shows just how successful the regime has been in reducing the opposition to near-total irrelevance. The squabble also captures the general absurdity of Uzbekistan today.

One hot summer afternoon, I went for a walk in downtown Tashkent. There had once been a beautiful park here. The trees, some nearly a hundred years old, had leafy canopies virtually impenetrable to the sun. Old men played chess, mothers pushed strollers down shaded lanes, and young couples lounged on benches. Smack in the middle of the city, the park was a hub, a meeting point, a playground. Several generations of Tashkent residents grew up with it. Then something strange happened. Late in 2009, municipal workers with chainsaws and axes turned up in the park. Within days, they chopped down every single tree. The fallen trees were swiftly replaced by a newly seeded lawn with gnarly saplings poking out of the ground. Tashkent residents were infuriated. Why would you cut down a perfect park to make room for a bad park?

Uzbek authorities didn't bother to explain anything. So rumors proliferated. One was that the regime—paranoid about enemies—was worried that the park provided not only shade for picnickers but also cover to miscreants plotting to attack government officials. Another whispered reason was that the tall, canopied trees obscured the vista toward a newly built palace of a Gulnara-backed foundation, a grandly oppressive structure constructed in the preferred style of official Tashkent architecture: a facade of huge white pillars behind which sit floor-to-ceiling banks of reflective windows. Another, most likely spurious, rumor was that someone wanted to turn all those trees into furniture. Uzbek authorities suggested that the hundred-year-old trees were foreign to the native flora of Uzbekistan and that their sprawling root systems were dangerous.

When I stopped by the park, it was a sorry sight. In the middle of it sat a chubby statue of Amir Timur riding a horse. The government anointed the medieval conqueror as a mythical progenitor of the Uzbek people and worships him with countless monuments, street names, and museums. Newly planted saplings wilted in the summer heat. In the late afternoon, the park was empty except for a group of teenagers sweating on a bench. A few years earlier, I'd played a long, and ultimately unsuccessful, series of chess games against an old man in the ample shade of a century-old tree. Chess junkies used to congregate here the same way they do in New York's Washington Square Park. I went up to the spot where I remembered the chess tables used to be. I touched the paved ground under my feet. You really could fry an egg on it.

Epilogue: Family Connections

One evening in Tashkent, I searched for a tiny apartment hidden inside a maze of squat gray buildings that all looked identical. To confuse matters further, the numbering of the houses bore no relation to any known brand of logic. The numbers seemed to ascend, then descend; then they performed a curious circular dance, retreated, surged forward, and abruptly stopped cold. And just when you thought you'd managed to crack the code, you realized the numbers weren't the whole story. There was a mysterious subset of letters and fractions that rescrambled whatever pattern you thought you'd just divined.

I was looking for Nazilya, my grandmother's older sister who'd been living in Uzbekistan for decades. When I finally managed to locate her place, she looked just as I remembered her from my childhood: a big bun of black hair perched atop her head and a flowing dress reaching down to the floor. An incapacitating smell of fried goodness wafted out of the kitchen. Nazilya wasn't an Uzbek but a Tatar, a member of an ethnic group with an eventful history in Central Asia and beyond.

During the rise of Genghis Khan's Mongol empire, Tatar tribes joined the Golden Horde, the great warrior juggernaut that rolled across much of Eurasia and conquered it. In Russian history books, that period is known as the Tatar-Mongol Yoke, a bleak two and a half centuries when

Russian princes trudged, humiliated and obsequious, to pay tribute to their foreign masters. Victors get to write their own history, and since the Russians eventually prevailed, their historians had little good to say about the Tatars. "An uninvited guest is worse than a Tatar," goes an old Russian saying. Tatars bristle at being portrayed as savages, pointing out that history is made of conquests and that their old empire was not any more evil than its peers. By the fifteenth century, the Golden Horde had splintered and weakened, and the Russians were able to shake off its dominion.

Later, when the Russian empire displaced the Tatar-Mongol state as the dominant force in this part of the world, the Tatars' role underwent a curious transformation. Having ruled the Russians in the Middle Ages, they were now enlisted to help their former subjects colonize Central Asia. By the nineteenth century, the Tatars had become thoroughly integrated into Russian society, although they maintained a distinct identity, practiced Islam, and spoke their own language, which is closely linked to the Turkic dialects of Central Asia. Well educated and often successful in business, they became a perfect colonial vanguard to dispatch to the region. Many Tatars went there to work as teachers, religious leaders, and merchants. In the parlance of the day, theirs was a "civilizing" mission intended to educate the "natives," nudge the nomadic ones toward a more settled lifestyle, and promote organized Islam among them—all seen as stabilizing influences that would aid the cause of Russia's colonial expansion. With their linguistic and religious affinity to the local populations, the Tatars put a friendlier, more familiar face on Russia's march eastward. As years went by, Tatars became woven into the region's ethnic tapestry. The mother of Chingiz Aitmatov, Kyrgyzstan's iconic novelist whom we met in the beginning of the book, was a Tatar.

My own maternal grandmother, Leila, was born in Orenburg, an old frontier town in the Ural Mountains in southern Russia. It long served as a commercial and military gateway to Central Asia. Leila, Nazilya, and their younger sister came from a well-to-do Tatar family that had been stripped of many possessions by the Communist expropriation squads after the 1917 revolution. Their father was killed in World War II. Left to raise three girls alone, their mother, Fatima, made a modest living buying and reselling teakettles—until a neighbor ratted her out to the police. "Speculation" was a serious crime in the Soviet Union, and Fatima spent several years in prison.

Leila eventually moved west, to Saint Petersburg, where she worked as a teacher, speaking Tatar only rarely now. In the 1980s, she went to Tajikistan to teach Russian to barely literate students in a remote mountainous district. The Tatars' educational mission in Central Asia continued, though for Leila the motivation had nothing to do with colonialism. Tajikistan was considered a hardship post, so a stint there would help her qualify for a higher pension once she retired. By the time she got to Tajikistan, my older cousin and I were already toddlers, and Leila, like any proud grandmother, showed our photos to her students. They immediately dismissed my cousin, who has fair hair, as a typical foreign devil. I fared better in their estimation because of my black hair and a darker complexion. "That one's one of ours," they decreed.

Her older sister Nazilya settled permanently in Central Asia. Like Leila, she taught Russian in the mountains of Tajikistan, and worked at a kindergarten in Dushanbe. Like many young Soviet civil servants, she was once sent to the region's cotton fields to help farmers during harvest time. Inexperienced, Nazilya tried to pry open the boll protecting the cotton fibers with her fingernails, and the hard shell sheared off one of her nails. It grew back all crooked, stamping a permanent reminder of the region's obsession with the crop. Incidentally, Uzbekistan still forces many of its citizens, including schoolchildren, onto the cotton plantations every year. Nazilya eventually moved to Tashkent, where for a while she manned an information booth downtown, giving the Uzbeks directions around their own capital. Childless—her husband died early of a heart attack—Nazilya doted on us like her own grandchildren.

My earliest association with Central Asia is the sight of her at the Saint Petersburg airport, coming to see us. She'd wear a dress a bit too bright and colorful for our monochromatically trained northern eyes, and she always arrived with a fragrant wooden crate. Inside were Uzbek melons and lemons, the likes of which we had never tasted. Just as the clothes she wore packed more color than the sartorial grayness that surrounded us, the fruit she brought burst with sweetness and flavor we didn't know existed. And then, after a few weeks, she'd fly back to the impossibly exotic Tashkent, where people wore funny headgear and bright clothes and got to eat tasty things, back to the tiny apartment where she lived with her mother Fatima, the teapot speculator. I last saw Nazilya soon after the Andijan massacre when she and her boyfriend, a nattily dressed Uzbek poet, hosted me for a boisterous dinner. When I returned to Uzbekistan a couple of years later, Nazilya was already gone, buried next to her mother. After visiting their graves, two simple slabs of marble in an overgrown Tashkent cemetery, I sat in my hotel room, eating lemons.

Another thread of my family history took me to a ramshackle wooden cottage at the end of a muddy path on the edge of Bishkek. As I entered the courtyard and walked past the outhouse, feeling my way in the dark toward the front porch, a large dog leapt out of the kennel and lunged at me with a furious, spit-spraying bark. A chain tightened and snapped, yanking the dog back. My heartbeat resumed. The front door creaked open, and yet another great-aunt of mine stepped forward. Inna came from my father's side of the family—Russian Slavs from the endless ochre-colored plains around the Ural Mountains. Inna and her husband moved to Bishkek soon after World War II, and raised three sons. He worked as a crane operator and built resorts on Lake Issyk-Kul. She supervised food safety at a state-owned cafeteria.

They were a typical blue-collar Soviet family living on the edge of the empire, in a town where the Russians felt in charge. It was called Frunze back then, named after a Soviet military commander. Kyrgyz-stan's independence prompted many Russians to leave, but Inna had no desire to go anywhere. She was too old now. And besides, she had lived in Bishkek for most of her adult life, nearly all of it in the same wooden house she and her husband had built with their own hands. The husband was dead now, as was one of her three sons. Another son had moved to Siberia and worked at an airport. Inna rarely heard from him. The third son, Volodya, lived with her, but she worried he didn't have much time left. In 1986, Volodya was drafted into the military and ordered to deploy to Chernobyl to take part in the cleanup of the massive explosion at the nuclear power plant there. Inna pleaded with him not to go, begged him to apply for a deferral based on the recent birth of his daughter. But Volodya went anyway, and drove a truck on the blast's ground zero.

Returning home, he developed a range of ailments, his body ravaged by radiation. His wife and daughter eventually left him and moved to Russia, but Volodya stayed in Bishkek with his mother. It was just the two of them now in the big old house, three if you counted the dog. They lived on her pension and his disability checks. They searched the city's pharmacies for discounted medicine. Volodya didn't like to talk about Chernobyl. He did like to talk about his daughter, whom he didn't get to see much these days, and who now had a son of her own. The only time I saw Volodya produce a big smile was when he reached for a happier past and recalled how his daughter, then still in middle school, fended off a schoolyard bully with a few well-placed kicks she learned in her karate class. Summoned to the principal's office, Volodya nodded gravely to the admonition that he needed to keep his daughter's fighting under control. He was proud of his girl.

The memory dissipated as quickly as it appeared, and Volodya went back to sipping his lukewarm tea in near silence. Bishkek is a small town, and as we sat in the kitchen, Volodya mentioned an old high-school buddy of his: Gennady Pavlyuk, the journalist thrown out of a window and killed for doing his job. For a while, Pavlyuk had lived not far from here and sometimes stopped by to say hello. He was a good guy, Volodya said, it was such a waste. Late in the evening, he walked me back to the neighborhood's main drag so that I could find a taxi. He lit a cigarette, hopped over a ditch, and pondered this strange land that was his only home. "This is such a zoo," he said and wished me a safe trip back. Then he disappeared into the darkness of the alley leading back to his mother's house, the tip of his burning cigarette floating through the air like a firebug.

Over the years, Kyrgyzstan has been called many different things. They include, in no particular order: a display window of democracy in an authoritarian region; a Switzerland of the East; a shining example of kleptocracy by autocrats and their greedy relatives; an anarchy of mob rule; a failing state; a state that has yet to succeed. Kyrgyzstan has been all of those things, struggling to write its own narrative after centuries of having it written by others. The only instant result of a revolution is the downfall of the guy in the palace. Everything else takes time. An old Soviet song glorifying the 1917 Communist takeover has as its refrain the following words: "A revolution has a beginning, a revolution has no end."

November 2012

Notes

Chapter 1. The Tulip Revolution

1. Svat Soucek, *A History of Inner Asia* (Cambridge: Cambridge University Press, 2000), 217.

2. *The Persecution of Solzhenitsyn and Sakharov*, official publications and documents, http://antology.igrunov.ru/after_75/memo/1088679091.html.

3. "Kyrgyz Private Relives Batken Nightmare," February 21, 2005, http://iwpr.net/report-news/kyrgyz-private-relives-batken-nightmare.

4. *On ushel nepokorennim* [He Left Unbowed] (Beyiktik, 2010), 58.

5. Author interviews with Aijan Sadyrkulova and Kanybek Imanaliyev, Bishkek, 2011.

6. "Askar Akayev: 'I Raised Bakiyev Myself,'" *Kommersant,* July 11, 2005, http://www.kommersant.ru/doc/589869.

Chapter 2. On the Heroin Highway

1. Alexander Liakhovsky, *Inside the Soviet Invasion of Afghanistan and the Seizure of Kabul* (Woodrow Wilson International Center for Scholars, 2007), http://wilsoncenter.tv/sites/default/files/WP51_Web_Final.pdf.

Chapter 3. Anatomy of a Massacre

1. Interview with Islam Karimov [in Russian], *Nezavisimaya gazeta,* January 14, 2005.

2. Zahirrudin Babur, *The Baburnama: Memoirs of Babur, Prince and Emperor* (New York: Modern Library Classics, 2002).

3. Council on Foreign Relations, "Documenting Andijan," June 26, 2006, http://www.cfr.org/uzbekistan/documenting-andijan/p10984.

4. Human Rights Watch, "Bullets Were Falling Like Rain, June 7, 2005," http://www.hrw.org/node/11731/section/6.

5. Donald Rumsfeld, *Known and Unknown* (New York: Sentinel, 2011), 635.

6. Author interview with Stephen Young, the U.S. ambassador to Kyrgyzstan at the time, 2010.

Chapter 4. The Dark Years in Kyrgyzstan

1. Ainagul Sadyrkulova court testimony, as quoted in *Delo nomer,* June 28, 2012.

2. Early details of Sadyrkulov's life are drawn from a book of remembrances, *On ushel nepokorennim.*

3. "Azimbek Beknazarov: 'The Family-Clan System Is the Main Enemy of My People,'" June 2, 2008, fergananews.com, http://www.fergananews.com/article.php ?id=5727&print=1.

4. *On ushel nepokorennim,* 6.

5. Usen Sydykov, quoted by Kyrgyznews.com, March 28, 2008, http://www .kyrgyznews.com/news.php?readmore=2335.

6. "Life and Death of Ryspek Akhmatbayev" [in Russian], May 11, 2005, http:// lenta.ru/articles/2006/05/11/ryspek/.

7. Bakiyev's 2010 interview with the Russian edition of *Newsweek,* quoted according to http://www.newsland.ru/news/detail/id/486696/.

8. "These Nephews Are a Whole Different Ballgame," *Delo nomer,* July 7, 2010, http://delo.kg/index.php?option=com_content&task=view&id=1487&Itemid =43.

9. "Complexity of 'Fraud' Boggles the Mind," *Financial Times,* March 6, 2010, http://www.ft.com/cms/s/0/0f2f240c-28bf-11df-b86f-00144feabdc0.html#axzz26 HMqvSvP.

10. "Kyrgyz Elite Fawn over President's Son," June 30, 2009, Wikileaks, http:// wikileaks.org/cable/2009/06/09BISHKEK700.html.

11. Global Witness, *Grave Secrecy,* June 2012, http://www.globalwitness.org/ library/grave-secrecy.

12. *Brief Report on the Results of the Forensic Audit of the Kyrgyz Republic's Development Fund* [in Russian], August 22, 2011, 27, PricewaterhouseCoopers.

13. This account is based on author interviews with Turganbayev and on an article in *Delo nomer,* September 28, 2011.

14. "New Kyrgyz Opposition Asks for Help," February 6, 2009, Wikileaks, http://wikileaks.org/cable/2009/02/09BISHKEK119.html.

15. "Presidential Chief of Staff Sadyrkulov: From Horse Whisperer to Barbarian Handler," March 25, 2008, Wikileaks, http://wikileaks.org/cable/2008/03/ 08BISHKEK279.html.

16. "How to Keep Manas Air Base," January 23, 2009, Wikileaks, http://wiki leaks.org/cable/2009/01/09BISHKEK67.html.

17. "When the Mysteries Are Unraveled," *MSN,* December 2, 2005, http://www .msn.kg/ru/news/12183.

18. "Treasury Imposes Sanctions on Key Members of the Yakuza and Brothers' Circle Criminal Organizations," February 23, 2012, http://www.treasury.gov/press -center/press-releases/Pages/tg1430.aspx.

19. "Head of Secretariat Asserts Sadyrkulov Death an Accident," February 9, 2010, Wikileaks, http://wikileaks.org/cable/2010/02/10BISHKEK98.html#.

Chapter 5. The Land of Perpetual Revolution

1. A survey conducted by the Kyrgyz NGO Citizens against Corruption, e-mailed to author on April 23, 2010.

2. The essay was eventually published as part of a book, *April Events through the Eyes of a Police Cadet* [in Russian] (Bishkek, 2012).

3. "How I Shot at the White House from an Armored Personnel Carrier" [in Russian], http://kloop.kg/blog/2012/11/09/interv-yu-kak-ya-strelyal-iz-btra-po-belomu-domu/.

4. Quoted in Yu Hua, *China in Ten Words* (New York: Pantheon, 2011), 130.

5. The recording of the conversation was widely circulated in Kyrgyzstan, and is available, in Russian, at http://www.youtube.com/watch?v=aFC7Fhbdd3I&feature =related.

6. "The Big Man in Kyrgyzstan: A Canadian's Connections to Gold, Scandals and a Coup in Four Former Soviet Republics," *Financial Times*, February 5, 1994.

7. "How They Auctioned Off the Bakiyevs' Property" [in Russian], *Delo nomer*, October 5, 2011, http://delo.kg/index.php?option=com_content&view=artic le&id=3096:2011–10–06–07–44–03&catid=47:2011–05–19–20–38–52&Itemid=114.

8. *Meskhetian Turks: An Introduction to Their History, Culture and Resettlement Experiences* (Center for Applied Linguistics, September 2006), http://www.cal .org/co/pdffiles/mturks.pdf.

Chapter 6. The Financier Vanishes, and Other Riddles

1. For details, please see *Securities and Exchange Commission v. One or More Unknown Purchasers of Securities of Global Industries, Ltd.*, case 11-CV-6500.

2. The details of Gourevitch's turn as FBI informant are drawn from *Complaint and Affidavit in Support of Arrest Warrant Filed in the case "U.S.A. v. Munir,"* U.S. District Court in the Eastern District of New York, case 1: 2012-mj-00331. (Neither Gourevitch nor Maxim are identified in the complaint by name. They are referred to only as "confidential source" and "co-conspirator #1" respectively. But the document supplies so many key details about both individuals that their identities become obvious.)

3. "The Murder of Sadyrkulov" [in Russian], *Delo nomer*, June 28, 2012, https://delo.kg/index.php?option=com_content&view=article&id=4017:q-q&catid =52:2011–05–19–20–39–42&Itemid=119.

4. Osmonov widow's testimony, in Russian, is quoted according to www.24.kg news agency, http://mirror24.24.kg/community/print:page,1,132401-ajna-sydykova -laquobratanyraquo-poprosili-moego.html.

5. Interview with Anapiayev [in Russian], April 27, 2012, http://www.gezitter .org/interviews/10783_aanapiyaev_razve_janyish_bakiev_stal_byi_uvelichivat _chislo_nenujnyih_svideteley_smerti_sadyirkulova_ispolzuya_prostyih_sports menov.

6. Oksana Malevannaya, "After the Revolution" [in Russian], *Echo of Moscow*, November 18, 2010, http://echo.msk.ru/blog/oksanamalev/727516-echo.html.

7. "Ismankulov Was Going to Investigate the Murder That He Himself Had Planned" [in Russian], *Delo nomer*, April 26, 2012, http://delo.kg/index.php?option =com_content&view=article&id=3143:2011–10–20–08–08–38&catid=52:2011–05 –19–20–39–42&Itemid=119.

8. The full report is available here: http://democrats.oversight.house.gov/images /stories/subcommittees/NS_Subcommittee/Mystery_at_Manas/Mystery_at_Manas .pdf.

9. "Kyrgyz Contracts Fly under the Radar," *Washington Post,* November 1, 2010, http://www.washingtonpost.com/wp-dyn/content/article/2010/10/30/AR2010 103002765.html.

Chapter 7. Restless Valley

1. The Russian text of *The Natives Then and Now* is available at http://news .fergananews.com/archive/nalivkin_tuz.html.

Chapter 8. Our Son of a Bitch?

1. Case 1:06-cv-01040-CKK, *Roz Trading Ltd. v. Zeromax Group, Inc.,* filed in the U.S. District Court for the District of Columbia, June 6, 2006.

2. "At Times Angry Karimov Says Transit Can Continue," March 18, 2009, Wikileaks, http://wikileaks.org/cable/2009/03/09TASHKENT323.html.

3. S. Frederick Starr, ed., *Ferghana Valley: The Heart of Central Asia* (Armonk, NY: M. E. Sharpe, 2011), 81.

4. Soucek, *History of Inner Asia,* 235.

Acknowledgments

This book could not have advanced beyond a vague idea without the help and encouragement of quite a few individuals and institutions. I'm profoundly grateful to all. The Asia Society, a wonderful organization devoted to the study of all things Asian, hosted me as a fellow, a kind offer that gave me the time, and the money, to write this book. At the Asia Society, Jamie Metzl, Mike Kulma, Suzanne DiMaggio, and Hee-Chung Kim saw merit in my Central Asia obsession and allowed me to indulge it. Bernard L. Schwartz, the patron saint of many blue-sky journalistic projects, generously funded my fellowship.

I first began to write about Central Asia in the pages of the *Wall Street Journal*. Mike Miller, the paper's page-one editor at the time, allowed me to explore the region in thousands of words, sparing me the dreaded "Why should we care?" question. His interest helped lay the foundation for this book. Later, Jon Sawyer at the Pulitzer Center for Crisis Reporting sent me back to Central Asia, again with few questions asked, to continue my reporting.

That reporting wouldn't have gotten very far without the help of many people on the ground in the region. In Kyrgyzstan, Ilya Lukash, Leila Saralayeva, Ekaterina Ivaschenko, and Almaz Ismanov shared their contacts and knowledge. Edil Baisalov and Kadyr Toktogulov put up with my frequent visits and questions and always made me feel at home in Bishkek. John Gimbel, an old friend of mine from college, happened to be working at the U.S. embassy in Bishkek when I first got there, and I was lucky to rediscover his friendship and hospitality. I was also very lucky to meet Darryl Salisbury and benefit from his generous spirit. Over the years in Uzbekistan, Abdumalik Boboyev, a fearless journalist, guided me through the maze of the Uzbek dictatorship, often at great personal risk. I would have accomplished nothing in Afghanistan without Qais Azimi. In Moscow, Daniil Kislov created a real treasure: Fergana news.com is the only comprehensive source of analysis on Central Asia. Daniil is as passionate about the region and its history as he's generous with his knowledge and time.

I was fortunate to find a home for this book at Yale University Press, where my editors, Laura Davulis, Margaret Otzel, and Robin DuBlanc, ably guided the manuscript to publication. Ilya Varlamov and Yola Monakhov graciously provided the striking photos they took in Bishkek and Andijan. Philip Willan helped me find key Italian court documents.

My parents, Alexander and Emma, gave me more than any son could ever hope for. And, as always, I'm indebted to my wife, Silvia Spring, without whom nothing at all would be possible.

Index

Page numbers in *italics* refer to illustrations.